PARAMEDIC

PARAMEDIC
On the Front Lines of Medicine

❖ ❖ ❖ ❖ ❖ ❖ ❖ ❖ ❖

PETER CANNING

Fawcett Columbine ❖ New York

A Fawcett Columbine Book
Published by Ballantine Books

Copyright © 1997 by Peter Canning

http://www.randomhouse.com

LIBRARY OF CONGRESS CATALOGING-IN-PUBLICATION DATA

Canning, Peter, 1958–
    Paramedic : on the front lines of medicine / Peter Canning.
      p.   cm.
    ISBN 0-449-91276-0
    1. Canning, Peter, 1958–   .   2. Emergency medical technicians—Connecticut—
Hartford—Biography.
RA645.6.C8C36   1997
610.69'53—dc21
[B]   97-7397
                                                                                CIP

Designed by Fritz Metsch

Manufactured in the United States of America

First Edition: September 1997

10   9   8   7   6   5   4   3   2   1

To all my partners, past, present, and future.

And to my best friends, Barbara Lynne Danley, Ross Wheeler,
and Brad Bailey. Your faith in me means the world.

❖

"Those friends thou hast,
And their adoption tried,
Grapple them to thy soul
With hoops of steel."

—WILLIAM SHAKESPEARE

I would like to thank the following people:

Michelle Gordon for helping me become a paramedic with patience, support, and understanding.

My coworkers—paramedics, EMTs, dispatchers, supervisors, and other personnel—at the Professional Group and at Bloomfield Volunteer Ambulance Association, as well as former coworkers at East Windsor Volunteer Ambulance Association and Eastern Ambulance.

The people who recruited or hired me: Abdullah Rehayem at Eastern Ambulance, Anne Arcari at East Windsor, Al Ullring at Bloomfield, and Harvey Kagan at Professional. Also Jim Paturas, Steve Carden, and Jack Pickering for arranging my internship at Bridgeport Ambulance.

My EMS instructors: Judith Moore, who taught my basic-EMT class at Springfield College, Raffaella A. Coler of Hartford Hospital, who taught my EMT-Intermediate class, Jonathan Hibbard and Conrad Castonguay, who taught my EMT-Paramedic class at the UCONN Health Center.

The physicians, nurses, technicians, and clerical staffs in the Emergency Departments at Saint Francis Hospital, Mount Sinai Hospital, and Hartford Hospital. Special mention to the physicians who gave me medical control, Dr. R. Kent Sargent at Hartford Hospital, Dr. Allison Lane-Reiticker, and Dr. Cliff Wagner at Saint Francis Hospital. Also Debbie Haliscak, who is the EMS Coordinator at Saint Francis.

At the state health department, former commissioner Susan S. Addiss and Deputy Commissioner Yvette Melendez-Theisfield, for their friendship and support for EMS, and the dedicated staff at the Office of Emergency Medical Services (OEMS). Special thanks to Paul Winfield Smith for lending me all those books that make up the great EMS library I have today.

My father for encouraging me to read books.

James Alan McPherson for inspiring me as a writer.

Friends who have encouraged me over the years: Alan Stock, Tom Adkins, Sandy Fowler, Janet Kerr-Tener, Michael Scully, Lisa Davis, Leigh Allison Wilson, Rick Orluk, Tom Dudchik.

Susan Swift for her friendship, conversation, and support.

Jane Dystel, my agent, and Susan Randol, my editor, two special people who believed in me and this book. Thank you.

Contents

Contents   xi

My name is Peter Canning. I am a paramedic who responds to 911 calls in the city of Hartford and surrounding towns in Connecticut. A paramedic is the highest level of emergency medical technician (EMT)—a person capable of performing advanced medical assessment and treatment in the field, including endotracheal intubation, cardiac defibrillation, and the administration of over thirty emergency medications such as morphine and epinephrine. In 1995 at the age of thirty-six I left my job as a speechwriter and a top health department aide to Connecticut Governor Lowell P. Weicker to work as a paramedic on the city streets. The book is about my first year on the job as a paramedic, my struggle to make good, the calls I did, the scenes I witnessed, and how I felt about it all. While there are many drawbacks to being a paramedic—the low pay, the danger, respect rarely given but at an arm's length—it is meaningful work. It challenges you and sometimes rewards you, though often it knocks you down hard. It is about life. The events are true. I've changed only a few details and names to protect patient confidentiality. This is my story about finding my place in the world, and it is the story of the patients I met and the city in which they live.

INTRODUCTION

Paramedic

In November of 1988 when my boss, United States Senator Lowell Weicker, was defeated in his bid for a fourth term in office, I found myself at age thirty suddenly out of work and at a loss about what to do with my life. I had worked for the senator on and off since February of 1976, when I first arrived in his Washington office as a skinny six-feet-six seventeen-year-old with a Beatles haircut, wearing my grandfather's blue blazer, a size too big for me in the shoulders. Twelve years later, my shoulders filled out and two inches taller, I was briefing my boss for debates, writing campaign literature, and traveling with him seven days a week, arriving at his house before breakfast and driving his thirty-seven-foot campaign bus gently home in the night as he dozed in his seat after a long day on the campaign trail. If he had won in 1988, the world would have been mine in a sense. I would have gone from a twenty-five-thousand-dollar speechwriter to a fifty- to sixty-thousand-dollar-a-year staff position in either Washington or Connecticut—my choice—but it didn't happen. We lost by ten thousand votes out of over a million cast.

At the time of the loss, I was living with my girlfriend just north of Connecticut in an apartment on Main Street in Springfield, Massachusetts. In the ensuing weeks I spent hours lying on the couch. Sometimes I'd get up and walk the city streets. I'd usually buy three or four papers and end up sitting in the food court of the Bay State Mall that looked out over the downtown center. I'd have a slice of pepperoni pizza with a sprinkle of garlic powder and hot red pepper on it, and I'd nurse a large Coke as I tried to avoid the "Help Wanted" ads. As I sat there, just passing the time, I often saw ambulances race by on the street, and like anyone I wondered where they were going. One day I read an article about paramedics in the city—the excitement in their lives, the joys and defeats. Every day there were pictures of them in the paper, carrying babies out of buildings, working on patients trapped in cars. These were the same faces I saw picking up the drunk on the corner or sitting in an ambulance, waiting for a call. Real people. One afternoon I saw an ad for an EMT course taught at Springfield College starting in January. Later, at night, I lay in bed listening to the rap music from cars cruising the street and the wail of ambulances racing past. As I debated my future, the sounds called to me: Come have a closer look. Here is a new life, right outside on the street below. Here is a view that you have not seen. You've sat at a desk in Washington, D.C., that looked out over the U.S. Capitol. You've helped write speeches about infant mortality, the war on drugs, and access to health care. Here is your chance to see it up close. Here is your chance to see life as it is without the TV screen protecting you from getting splashed by its grit.

In December I went back to Washington to attend a farewell party for Weicker and to say good-bye to my friends and former coworkers. After the main party broke up, we moved on to the bars on Pennsylvania Avenue, N.E., where I had spent many evenings and late nights cele-brating victories on the Senate floor and on capital softball diamonds or just savoring the greatness of being young and fond of women, beer, and music. That night of the farewell party, under the eyes of the stuffed owl on the wall of the Tune Inn, my favorite Capitol Hill bar, with Conway Twitty and Merle Haggard on the jukebox, we all talked about what we were going to do and where we were going to go. Some spoke of hooking up with another legislator or a lobby firm, going to law school or trying their hand in business. I swallowed hard and announced I had decided to become an EMT. If I could no longer help people with my head, I told them, this would be my chance to at least do so with my hands. There is a scene in *The Quest for the Holy Grail* where Sir Gawain stands up and says he will lead the search for the sacred prize. As soon as the words have been spoken, he is gripped by fear, knowing that the quest will for-ever change his life. But he cannot take the words back. He has said them aloud and made them a true thing. My friends raised their glasses, called me a great, kind, noble crazy man, then drained their beers in my honor. No doubt in the morning they had forgotten my vow, but I hadn't. I was committed. Besides, I had no other ideas about what to do with my sorry self.

In January of 1989 I started the basic EMT course at Springfield Col-lege. Though I already had a college degree (in English), I found the semester-long class demanding. I had little science background and had difficulty memorizing all the bones in the body and understanding the physiology of the human heart. Every night we had workbook assignments that our instructor meticulously checked and graded. Toward the end of the class we had to do ten hours of observation time in the emergency department at Bay State Hospital. As a precaution against vomiting at the first sight of blood, I carried a plastic kitchen bag in my pocket. Though I witnessed the intubation of an eighty-year-old grandmother whose lungs were so filled with phlegm she could no longer adequately breathe on her own, and the trauma-room treatment of a twenty-six-year-old female who had been hit by a car while crossing the street and who had a concussion, shattered leg, and lacerated liver, and who kept crying, "I'm going to the party. I'm just going to the party," I was too fascinated to get sick.

I remember how nervous I was when I had to take the state practical examination, a day-long session of seven stations simulating various scenarios—shock, spinal immobilization, bandaging—in which you had to prove your skills on moulaged patients to impassive examiners. It was a humid summer day. In the unventilated room in the basement of a class building, I stabilized a victim's fractured femur with one hand under the fracture site, and supported the lower leg with the other hand while my partner applied the splint. The examiner, noticing my sweat-soaked work shirt and paling, perspiring complexion, asked if I was all right. "No," I said, "but I am not letting go of the leg."

Three weeks later I received the test result in the mail. Nearly thirteen years before when I was applying to college I had had a similar wait. The question was what size envelope would I receive? A thin envelope like the one that Harvard, the college of my father and grandfather, had sent me two years in a row, denying my application (the last year even sending me an off-centered computer-generated letter)? Or a thick welcoming envelope like the one I eventually received from the University of Virginia that said at least somebody wanted to keep me from being homeless and destitute for the next four years? In my mailbox I found a large brown envelope with a return address from the state Office of Emergency Medical Services (OEMS). Inside were my passing test scores, a Massachusetts EMT patch, and a certificate suitable for framing. I did a Snoopy dance. The unexpected election defeat had shattered my confidence. Becoming an EMT held great meaning for me and lifted my spirits. I had worth again. I called up my instructor, Judy Moore, and thanked her. She had been a tough teacher and I appreciated that. She was glad for me, but reminded me that the best lesson an EMT student can take away from a class is that you don't know anything. The learning begins on the street. The class is only the framework that allows you to learn.

I went to work at $5.50 an hour as an EMT for Eastern Ambulance, a small service that did 911 calls for several Springfield suburbs. At the basic level, the job of an EMT is to stabilize a person's airway or any injuries, give him oxygen if he needs it, and transport rapidly, while taking a medical history to relay via radio to the hospital to help prioritize the patient's care. One of my first patients was an elderly woman having mild chest pain. While everyone was gathered around her trying to make her comfortable, she looked at my sweat-drenched face, and said, "Could someone get this poor dear a towel? Are you all right?"

My first trauma call was a head-on collision on the Boston Road in Wilbraham. We arrived to find a man lying against the front wheel of his car, having difficulty breathing due to what looked like broken ribs. A firefighter was already there attending to him. "He needs his ribs stabilized," the firefighter said to me.

I nodded and did an about-face and went back to the ambulance, where I leaned dizzily against the side door, wondering whether or not I had made a serious mistake and was kidding myself about being an EMT. I looked at the fire engines, ambulances, twisted cars, broken glass, and people shouting. The chaos of the scene belonged on TV, not in front of my eyes. Now that I was actually doing it, I didn't think I could do it. Then I remembered one of the lessons my teacher had taught our class. "If you can't remember what else to do, remember to put your patient on the stretcher and take him to the hospital," which I did. Sound advice.

In time I got better at the job. I learned from each call. I came to like the work more than anything I had ever done before. There is an incredible feeling when you come into a house, and a sick person looks up at you like you are an angel, that is both wonderful and humbling. My teacher had taught us that when you arrive the emergency is over, and even if you are scared, you have to show other people that they needn't worry. A calm word and hand can do more at times than medicine.

Always I wanted to be better at what I did. I wanted to stay with it until I could save a life, until I could say that I had made a difference—that because of me someone walked and breathed and lived and loved who would not have.

In March of 1990, Senator Weicker called me at work and told me to be at the state capitol building in Hartford at 10:00 A.M. that coming

Friday. I knew what it was about. For months, he'd been thinking about making a political comeback. He was going to run for governor.

That Friday I attended his announcement speech in the morning, and in the afternoon was back at work catching dark vomit in an emesis basin from an elderly patient with a gastrointestinal (GI) bleed.

I went to work as Weicker's campaign issues director, but kept a Monday overnight shift at Eastern. I organized issue groups, wrote position papers and editorials, led the debate briefings, and worked with the paid media, who did our advertising. With a week to go and his closest opponent running strong negative commercials—the type of ads Weicker had refused to respond to in his 1988 defeat—we debated what to do. It had been incredibly painful two years before to take the barrage of innuendo cast at him, and not respond. We'd seen a sixteen-point lead evaporate overnight, and crowds that had hailed Weicker in May of 1988 as a returning hero had shunned him in the chill of late October, many crossing the street to avoid him or muttering after shaking his hand that he was a crook who didn't pay his fair share of taxes, hated children, despoiled the wilderness, and never went to work. When he finally fought back, he did so only until he had the lead again; then his pride caused him to go back to positive ads for the last four days of the campaign, a decision that caused euphoria in his opponent's camp. Perhaps the public's guilt at voting out a man who had served them with distinction for twenty years and who was widely praised the day after his defeat by the leading papers as a great man had given him the lead in the three-way race for governor, but now that the attack ads were back on the tube, his slim lead was starting to shrink. His closest opponent in the polls was running an ad that accused him of violating the senate ethics code. We discovered the alleged violation was of a draft code that had never been approved, not the official code. Weicker had a letter from the ethics committee clearing him of any official wrongdoing. "He's exposed—wide open for a blow, and he's doesn't think we're going to hit him back," I said of his opponent. "I say hit him back hard! In the balls!" Which we did—running an ad using newspaper editorial comments accusing him of falsehood and deceit. On election night I walked into a crowded hotel packed with supporters who slapped me on the back and hailed me as they did the others on our staff who worked so hard for redemption. I raised my mug high, enjoying and understanding the transitory nature of victory after having lived and breathed defeat.

After the election, I was appointed to the state health department, which included the administration of the state's EMS system. I had moved back to Connecticut by then and, despite the demands of my new job, began volunteering for my town ambulance in East Windsor, a rural town off I-91 twenty miles north of Hartford. (Connecticut is a state of 169 cities and towns, which prides itself on home rule. Consequently, while in another state, the five-thousand-square-mile area might be covered by five or six county or commercial services, Connecticut has over two hundred ambulance services, seventy percent of them volunteer.) Emergency medical services had gotten in my blood, and I wasn't ready to let it go. In East Windsor, I soon became an EMT-Intermediate, which enabled me to start intravenous (IV) lines. I worked every Thursday night from 6:00 P.M. to 6:00 A.M. I had a portable radio, and when its tones went off, I kissed my sweetheart good-bye, raced out to the car, stuck my green whirly light on the dashboard, plugged it into the cigarette-lighter outlet, and headed off to the rescue. Hi–ho, Silver. While we rarely had more than a call a night and often had none, there were some days when I'd go into my office, shut the door, lay my head on my desk, and try to sleep after a night of doing cardiopulmonary resuscitation (CPR) on the side of the highway, carrying injured passengers on a heavy stretcher to the waiting Life-Star helicopter, or more likely just driving an old lady with an elevated temperature to the hospital.

In 1992, I signed up for a nine-month six-hundred-hour paramedic course, which meant classes two nights a week with Saturdays spent doing hospital clinicals. I wasn't doing enough calls in East Windsor to keep my skills up and I wanted to learn more. I also was frustrated with working in government. The state bureaucracy was a confounding nightmare, and even though I had the power to push it along, I was frustrated that I could not wave a magic wand and say make it be so. Under the state system, it once took me four months to get my answering machine at work fixed when I could have gone to the store that day and bought a new machine for less than it would cost the state to fix mine—except of course that wasn't allowed. Worse, it once took us over a year to pass an emergency regulation to allow firefighters, certified as medical response technicians (MRTs), to use semiautomatic defibrillators—a truly lifesaving matter. The new regulation consisted of a four-word change. There was no opposition to it. Still, it took over a year to move from one bureaucratic step to the next to the next to the next. In Washington, in the legislative branch, it was easy to be for health, education, and the disadvantaged—all you had to do was vote for it, and write laws claiming to help. In Connecticut, in an agency, you had to actually make things work, and that was not easy. In Washington we went from battle to battle on the strength of adrenaline highs, regularly working past midnight. In Connecticut on my first day at the health department I thought I would go home early and take some reading material with me. When I came out of the building at six in the evening, I looked around and wondered if maybe there had been a gas leak and nobody had told me about it. My car was the only one left in the entire parking lot.

While I admired people who were good at government, and I came to know many who were and who worked hard, I didn't feel I was cut out for it. I was too frustrated by the fact that any attempt to change anything meets resistance from one quarter or the other. I was spending a great deal of time organizing a statewide EMS advisory board with committees on every EMS issue from trauma to public information. Not only did I have to argue for EMS among all other competing health interests and problems, I had to argue among EMS groups to get them to agree among themselves—which was difficult given the competing interests between volunteer and commercial and municipal ambulances, regional EMS councils, hospitals, surgeons, emergency physicians, nurses, paramedics, EMTs and police and firefighters. There was an enormous amount of activity, but real progress that translated into change on the street seemed excruciatingly slow. While fire services had long ago learned to approach their elected representatives with a united front, and consequently heard things like, "And how many more fire engines would you like, captain?" EMS groups tended to point fingers at each other and shout and yell and send the legislators running for cover. Stay out of that mess.

I took refuge in the paramedic class and my desire to be back out on the street. The class was fantastic even though I had to put in a great amount of additional work to make sense of everything I was taught. I loved the clinicals—working in emergency departments (ERs) and intensive care units. I also watched autopsies, even getting to hold in my hands a human heart, a pair of lungs, which were like giant Nerf sponges, and a heavy gelatinous brain. I saw three babies come into the world, which to me was as incredible and awesome a sight as seeing giant humpback whales leap out of the ocean. I got to march into an operating room, wearing a sterile mask and gowned in blue hospital scrubs. There with shining stainless-steel laryngoscope in hand, while the entire operating team looked on, I swept the sedated patient's tongue to the side, lifted up on the jaw until I saw the vocal chords, then passed a tube into the trachea

through which the patient would breathe. Then I blew imaginary kisses
to the crowds as I backed out of the operating room, careful not to upend
the tray of sterile instruments, and went on to the next performance. I
rode in ambulances all over the state, and frequently ran into doctors,
nurses, and paramedics whom I dealt with as part of the EMS Advisory
Board. I felt it gave me credibility that, while during the day I was
helping to govern the system, at night I was living it.

I graduated in June 1993, and received a 94 percent score on the state
paramedic exam. The staff of OEMS called me down from my office and
presented me with my card. I was thrilled, but I knew that ability to do
well on a written test didn't count for squat in the street. It was there I
wanted to prove myself, and it was there that I most enjoyed myself
despite the stresses. I was prohibited from working for any commercial
ambulance company in the state while working at the health department, so in order to keep my skills up I volunteered with Bloomfield
Volunteer Ambulance in a Hartford suburb. Unlike East Windsor, Bloomfield was a paramedic-level service. There I was able to use my new skills
while working alongside their paid paramedic. I also arranged to do an
internship with Bridgeport Ambulance, one of the busiest services in the
state.

What I liked about EMS was not just the act of trying to help
someone, but the view of life, of people and society at their best and
worst. In moments of crisis, love, betrayal, grief, and joy are unclothed
before you. When I worked for the senator, I had most enjoyed the personal contact—talking to people and walking the streets of the cities and
towns he represented. And that's what I loved in EMS—the sense that I
was seeing the world as it was, not the view from behind a desk piled with
more memos and reports than I could read. And it gave me stories I
could tell.

On election night 1993 in Bridgeport while doing my internship
there, we were dispatched to a restaurant on the waterfront to do a
standby at the mayor's victory party. In case any of the VIPs or other
attendees got sick we would already be on scene. The parking lot was
filled with luxury vehicles. Men in suits and women in evening gowns
paraded into the restaurant to kiss the ring of the mayor, the man whose
signs we had seen all over the city that day, on billboards, on top of cars,
and held by campaign workers on downtown corners.

The streets were busy that night, and soon we were called away from
the reception—dispatched for a "man choking" in a nearby housing proj-

ect. There, after walking down a dark graffiti-strewn corridor, we entered a dim apartment to find a young man who we learned had tried to kill himself by drinking dishwashing liquid. His false teeth lay on the dirty carpet amid watery vomit.

He sat on the couch and said he was okay and didn't want to go to the hospital. John Pelazza, the paramedic, said someone at the hospital could talk to him to try to help him with his problems, but still he didn't want to go. Before we could leave, we had to ask him a few questions to ascertain his mental competency. You can't take a person to the hospital against his will if he is of sound mind. After asking him where he was— his friend's apartment—and what day of the week it was—Tuesday— John asked, "What's going on in the city today, something that everybody is taking part in?"

He thought for a moment, then said, "People get their city checks."

"Ah . . . yes," John said. "Not the answer I was looking for, but we'll allow it."

We walked out shaking our heads. A tale of two cities.

I could have had a job created for me in the state government, though I might have been rightly laid off by the new administration, just as I had had a hand in laying off holdover appointees from the previous administration when we were ordered to make job cuts at the health department. I had taken nine months' leave in 1994 to help my lifelong best friend, Brad, in his long-shot run for Congress in Massachusetts, and though he lost, I might have been able to parlay contacts into a good job in the Boston area where a suit and a tie and a briefcase of work would have brought in a good paycheck—and Fenway Park and my beloved Boston Red Sox would have been oh-so-close-by. Instead I applied for a job as a paramedic to work the city streets of Hartford.

My reasons? The view of life, the chance to prove myself worthy of other paramedics I respect, and the opportunity to live full days where my heart beats strong and I know that I am alive.

LESSONS

The City

Ihead south on Interstate 91 (I-91) on this January morning. It is a
drive I have made many times over the years, first as a child coming
to the city from the suburbs to visit my father at his office in Constitution Plaza. He'd take me shopping at G. Fox, Korvette's, and Herb's
Sports Shop, and then to dinner at Honess's, where we would eat blue-
fish and steamed clams, or to Valle's for steaks. Later I drove to work
myself, parking on the capitol grounds and entering that grand building
on the hill with the gold dome where I worked for the governor. From
the distance, above the countryside, Hartford's skyline rises as impressive
as the Land of Oz or the metropolis protected by Superman. I used to
think of the city as a symbol of all that was good with America—progress,
jobs. Yet I knew for all the light, there were also shadows. In 1968 when I
was ten, the north end of the city was racked with riots in the wake of the
assassination of Martin Luther King, Jr. One morning our biweekly
cleaning woman who came from Hartford got out of her car, drunk and
shouting that she wouldn't get on her knees "to clean no floors for no
white woman." One year a coworker of my father's had a bullet pierce a
window of his station wagon on his commute to work, forcing my father
and others to start using an alternate route. In later years working for
Senator, then Governor Weicker, I accompanied him into the city's
poorer areas and saw the poverty through the windshield of our escorted
car. And I researched and wrote the speeches, the ones that cited the fact
that Hartford, despite being the capital of one of the wealthiest states in
the union, was one of the country's ten poorest cities, that its infant mortality rate rivaled that of third-world nations, that its schools were segre-
gated and failed miserably to provide their students with equal educational
opportunity.

In recent years, in Shakespeare's words, "sorrows" have come to Hartford, not as "single spies, but in battalions." The city's manufacturing base, which fueled its growth for nearly a century, is gone. The insurance companies and financial institutions that are at the city's heart have undergone mergers, major downsizing, and layoffs. Long-standing stores and restaurants, like some of the ones my father took me to, have closed their doors forever. As the city's tax base has eroded, the number of those needing assistance has risen dramatically. Crime, poverty, unemployment, homelessness, AIDS, and other diseases are at epidemic levels. Today Hartford's population — its lowest since World War I — is predominantly black and Hispanic. The blacks live largely in the north end along North Main Street and Albany Avenue in crumbling private homes and apartment buildings and in notorious public housing projects like Bellevue Square and Stowe Village, centers of a thriving illegal drug trade. The south end, which still houses old Italian families, is increasingly Hispanic. And while there are still mansions in the west end, most of the city's well-to-do residents have fled over the years to the affluent suburbs like West Hartford, Newington, and Simsbury, the town I grew up in. While Hartford was once a bastion of Protestant Yankees, today only 5 percent of its schoolchildren are Caucasian.

Interstate 91 intersects with I-84 on the raised highway east of the city. I follow I-84 west, going through a short aboveground tunnel with its "Welcome to Hartford" message embedded in concrete. The road twists, turns, and rises above the streets. Below are empty factories with broken windows and deserted parking lots with grass sprouting through the cracks in the asphalt. I take the Flatbush Avenue exit and then turn on Newfield just before the railroad tracks. On the left is the Charter Oak public housing project, a collection of small two-story units with rusted bars on the outside windows, a scene of gang warfare, drug trafficking, and several of the city's record fifty-eight homicides in 1994. As in other areas of the city, here a car can be forgiven for not stopping at a red light.

I turn onto New Britain Avenue, passing check-cashing stores, garages, gas stations, doughnut shops. A few blocks away, just across the city line into West Hartford, are the offices and cavernous garage of the Professional Group, the home of Professional, L&M, Maple Hill, and Trinity ambulances. At this hour, young EMTs and paramedics go about checking their ambulances. They stock them with spare oxygen tanks, bandages, IV solutions, and long backboards. Others undo their bullet-proof vests and punch out after a long night of battling disease and violence on the city's streets.

I wish it were not my first morning. I wish that I had been working here for years, and that on walking into the garage and into the supervisor's office, people will hail me by name and think, "It's Peter Canning. He is a grizzled veteran, a great, proven paramedic. I would trust him with my life." Few of them know me. I am a rookie with much to prove.

Checklist

The fundamental idea behind EMS is to commence medical treatment for injured and sick patients as early as possible—to bring the hospital to the patient at the same time the patient is being brought to the hospital. In the old days, the person who responded with the ambulance put the patient in back, got in front, and drove like hell to the hospital. (He often was the same person who drove the hearse the next day.) Today there are two main levels of prehospital care: basic and paramedic. The paramedic, the most highly trained, provides advanced life support—complex assessment and treatment including invasive procedures and the administration of drugs under the direction of an emergency medical physician both through standing orders and direct communication. The worst insult that can be hurled at an EMT or paramedic is to call him an ambulance driver. They are medical professionals, subject to continual education, testing, and medical oversight.

❖

Meg Domina will be my partner on Wednesdays. A nice freckled twenty-five-year-old paramedic, she has been working in the city for five years. With Meg I will function as a basic-level partner to her paramedic, though I will be able to use my paramedic skills if needed. On Thursdays and Fridays, Tom Harper will be my partner and preceptor. After thirty paramedic calls Tom will either recommend me for medical control to work as a paramedic with a basic partner or say I don't make the grade, in which case I will be able to work only as a basic EMT. I do have a little

bit of an inside advantage. When I volunteered as a paramedic in Bloomfield I worked with Michelle Gordon, who precepted Meg years ago, and
had worked with Tom in the city back when he was just a basic EMT
assigned to the city. I go out with her now, so she has put in a good word
for me with them. While I do not like using a crutch such as this, I will
take every advantage I can get. I am rusty, haven't worked for the company before, and have a lot to learn from how to work the radios to how
to be a good paramedic.

Meg gives me a warm good morning, then tells me to check out the
rig, while she gets us radios. The ambulance is a van type, smaller than
the large box ambulances favored by most volunteer corps, who carry
crews of up to four people. The van ambulance is built for twenty-four-
hour, seven-day-a-week abuse. In the back there is room for a stretcher
tight against one wall, and a bench seat against the other with about a
foot of room in between. At the head of the stretcher is another seat
where a rider can sit, facing the patient's head. It is the preferred seat to
manage a patient's breathing. Under the bench seat are two longboards
for spinal immobilization, a metal scoop stretcher that comes apart in the
middle and is used to fit under somebody who needs to be lifted up but
doesn't need spinal immobilization, a traction splint for isolated femur
fractures, a Kendrick Extrication Device (KED) to help stabilize the
spine of someone trapped in a car, a urinal, and a bedpan. By the back
door on the stretcher side is the collapsible stair chair for carrying
patients down from the second, third, and hopefully not much above the
fourth floor, and a wooden short board. The cabinets on the stretcher
wall are filled with linen, cervical collars, IV supplies, trauma dressings,
bandages, oxygen masks, and cannulas (a plastic tube with two prongs
that fit under the patient's nose to give them a richer oxygen to breathe
than what exists in room air). At the head is the oxygen outlet and in-
house suction unit. By the side door is a rack that holds the cardiac
monitor, the pediatric box, and three spare portable oxygen cylinders.
The portable suction is on the inside of the door. It is used to clear
mucus, blood, or vomit from a patient's mouth and throat. The cabinet
between the back and the driver's compartment holds the military anti-
shock trouser (MAST) pants, a spare advanced life support (ALS) supply
box, and run forms, on which we document our treatment of each
patient. The main gear we take into the house in addition to the monitor
includes the blue in-house bag, the airway kit, and the biotech.

The in-house bag has a portable oxygen cylinder, airway supplies,

blood pressure (BP) cuff, obstetrics (OB) kit, burn sheets, trauma dressings, ammonia inhalants, and spare run forms. The airway kit holds the
laryngoscope, and the various sized and shaped metal blades that attach
to the handle. The blades have tiny lightbulbs on the end that illumi-
nate the patient's throat as you search for the vocal chords through which
you will pass a clear plastic endotracheal tube that again comes in various sizes—from a tube for the tiniest baby to the Andre-the-Giant-sized
ten tube. The biotech is a hard black suitcase that holds the emergency
drugs and IV supplies, except for morphine and Valium, which are kept
above the monitor shelf in a lockbox. The heart monitor displays the patient's electrocardiogram (EKG) on a small two-inch screen when attached
•to the patient through three wire leads—the white lead on the upper right
chest, the black lead on the upper left, and the red on the lower left side.
"White is right, smoke over fire," I say to myself to keep the order straight.
The monitor also has detachable paddles, which when applied to the patient's chest and activated can deliver an electric shock of up to 360 joules
(Js) to a patient's fibrillating heart in hopes of stopping it cold, so it can
hopefully restart by itself with its normal rhythm. The newer models have
hands-off pads that can be applied to the chest, one on the right sternum,
the other on the left apex, so the shock can be delivered without having
to be in such close contact with the person.

"Ready?" Meg says, coming back and handing me the company portable
radio as she clips to her belt the portable that connects us to the Hartford
police dispatch and to CMED, an operator who can connect us to local
hospital emergency departments.

"Yeah, I guess."

With my stethoscope around my neck and a pair of trauma shears
sticking out of my back pocket, I climb in the passenger seat.

"Nervous?" Meg says as we head into Hartford.

"Yeah, a little," I say.

"Good, you should be."

I look at her.

"Just kidding," she says. "You'll do fine, I'm sure."

Easy for you to say, I think.

Shootings and Stabbings

We get a call for "shootings and stabbings" at the High Street Liquor store. We have three priorities. Priority one means imminent life-threatening, full lights and sirens, and pedal to the metal. Priority two is possible life or serious health threat, use lights and sirens, and get there expeditiously. Priority three is no lights, no sirens, obey all traffic signals, and if your radio dispatches you while you are in the rest room, go ahead and finish your business. This call—"shootings and stabbings"—is a priority one.

As we race down Albany Avenue, Meg gets on the radio with the Hartford Police Department (HPD). "Is it shootings or stabbings?" she asks.

"I don't know," the dispatcher says. "It came in as shootings and stabbings. We have officers responding to the scene."

I put on my latex gloves. It is not too cool to put on your gloves until you get to a scene, but I want to be prepared for "shootings and stabbings." I have only done one shooting and one stabbing before and never both together. The shooting was in 1993 when I was doing my internship in Bridgeport. There we found a woman in the backyard holding two Dobermans by their choke collars. The dogs had barked and slowly dragged the woman across the yard toward the back porch where the shooting victim was. The cops hadn't arrived. Mike MaGoveny, a former nose-guard who had had NFL tryouts, and I ran into the yard and found a young man leaning against the back door by a set of open basement stairs, shot in the thigh and unable to move.

"The shooter's down the steps!" a neighbor shouted.

We looked down the dark stairway, then at the barking Dobermans who were slavering at the mouth as they dragged their handler closer toward us. It was a Commander McBragg moment. (McBragg was one of my favorite

Saturday-morning cartoon characters who used to say, "There I was, lion in front of me, rhino to the right, a band of savages to the rear . . .") Mike and I picked up the kid, each grabbing a leg and a shoulder, and ran for the gate. We set him down on the stretcher, and lifted him into the back, and slammed the doors. The dogs broke loose and ran at us. The ambulance lurched forward as Mike floored it. When we got out at the hospital, I checked the door handles for Doberman jaws.

The stabbing was in Hartford during my paramedic class ride time. We found a guy who had been slashed vertically up the throat—probably with a razor, exposing but not cutting an artery. "He done fell against the dresser," his girlfriend claimed. The others in the room nodded quickly in agreement. "That's right, he fell against the dresser." Though he bled a great deal, it was not a life-threatening wound. On that hot summer night we carried him down three flights of stairs and out into a crowd on the street that numbered close to two hundred, drawn by the red lights. It was like being in a Hollywood movie with Public Enemy blaring on the soundtrack.

I am sure the scene ahead will be like nothing I have seen. I picture bodies and bloody carnage. Surely a lead story for the six o'clock news, maybe even Dan Rather, the cover of *Newsweek*, an urban massacre that I will be right in the middle of—a horror story to share for years.

Another ambulance arrives simultaneously with us. In front of the store, I see a police officer putting a handcuffed man in the backseat of his cruiser.

"False report," another officer says to us when we get out. "The guy's girlfriend's not feeling well, so he made up a story to get an ambulance here quicker."

I feel both relief and letdown. I want action, but I also fear it.

Just then I notice a tall impassive woman in a soiled light blue snow jacket standing against the side of the building. She is holding her side.

"Are you okay?" I ask.

"My side hurts when I breathe," she says quietly.

I inspect, half expecting a stab wound, but see none.

"I've been sick for a while," she says. "I need to get warm."

Her lungs are junky, and she says she's been coughing up brown phlegm most of the winter.

"You want to go to the hospital?" I ask.

She nods. This will be a priority three.

As we walk to the ambulance, I see her boyfriend press his face against the window of the cruiser. He bangs against the glass. She never once turns to look at him.

For me it is a lesson in the unexpected, the quiet drama of the streets.

Lessons

Tom Harper, my preceptor, is a tall, blond-haired, strongly built young man who works construction, building decks, roofing, and fixing farm equipment on his days off. For the next month, he will be training and evaluating me. If he recommends me for medical control to function as a paramedic on my own, Debbie Haliscak, the EMS coordinator for Saint Francis Hospital, will ride with us for a day, observing me. She will have the final say as to whether her hospital will grant me control. Because a paramedic is an extension of a physician, the hospital is liable for my performance. Granting control is not taken lightly. Not everyone who passes a paramedic course is chosen to precept, and not everyone who precepts makes it. I believe that I will, but inside is the fear I might not. My friends all assure me that I am smart and will be great at it. What they don't understand is that just because I have a college degree doesn't mean I can get an IV in the arm of a trapped dying man while lying under a car in a rainy ditch on a dark night. It doesn't mean I won't puke when I should be suctioning the airway of an eighty-year-old woman who can't breathe because of the pulmonary edema flooding her lungs as her heart is backing up. And it doesn't translate into how well I will be able to deal with a three-hundred-pound man having a massive heart attack on the third floor of a walk-up while his pit bull is growling at me. Many of them think this job, while interesting, is a huge step down for me. They can't imagine that a twenty-two-year-old without a degree can do this better than someone like me. In my time riding on ambulances throughout the state, I have met many paramedics without the educational background I've had, who are crackerjacks, who are artists of this profession.

Tom is a paramedic, respected by doctors and his peers for his knowledge of prehospital medicine, his assessment and practical skills, and his ability to use his head instead of just following a cookbook response to each patient. He's put breathing tubes down the tracheas of young men with gunshot wounds to the head and had them in the trauma room within minutes of their shooting. He's bent forceps pulling obstructions out of the throats of blue infants and breathed pink life back into them. He's used defibrillation, epinephrine, lidocaine, and bretylium to bring people in cardiac arrest back from the dead to return home to their families. He's been spit on and assaulted by patients and bystanders and stuck with contaminated needles. He is twenty-five years old and has only a high school diploma and his paramedic certificate. Though he is more than a decade younger, and at six three, is five inches shorter than I am, I hold him in high regard. His hero is Wyatt Earp, and in my book, he does justice to him.

❖

Tom teaches me to be a blank slate. "Don't assume anything," he tells me. "Just because the call comes in for a diabetic, doesn't mean it's not a stroke victim. If it comes in as not feeling well, it could be a stabbing. It could be anything. You need to do a complete physical assessment; rule out as you go along. Don't assume anything. Don't tunnel. Do your assessments. Don't get caught with your pants down."

He tells me of a paramedic called for a "psych" patient, who had alcohol on his breath, and kept muttering, "They're coming after me, they're coming after me." The paramedic took him into the hospital, where the triage nurse put him in a wheelchair in the waiting room. Ten minutes later the man fell out of his chair, dead. They pulled his jacket back and discovered he had been shot twice. "They" had already come for him.

I know about the need for a thorough assessment, though it never hurts to be reminded. Back when I was first an EMT in Massachusetts I once did a call for a woman with back pain. We arrived at a posh house in Longmeadow where a cocktail party was underway. The hostess, who held a wineglass in her hand, led us into a bedroom where an elderly woman lay on a four-poster writhing in pain. "It's Granny's back," the woman told me. "She just can't bear the pain anymore. Her doctor wants her to be seen in the Emergency Room." We get the medical information from the woman, while other relatives, all holding cocktails, go in and out of the room, lovey-dovey, wishing Granny well. Granny's teeth are clenched and she is muttering as if she would take a chunk out of somebody if only she could bring her teeth apart.

We move her onto our stretcher by rolling her sheet up and lifting her on it. She is making angry sounds like a revving car engine.

"Don't worry, Granny. The doctors will have something to take the edge off it for you," a man says, leaning to give her a kiss. "We'll save you some pie."

"Her poor back," a woman says. "It's always bothered her, but never this much."

En route to the hospital, I am writing my report as I watch Granny moan. I have tried to make her as comfortable as possible, but there is little I can do for her. Right before I call the hospital on the C-Med radio to tell them I am bringing in an old woman with back pain, I ask her, "Just where in your back is the pain located?" I am uncertain if she is even competent to answer.

She looks at me with fire in her eyes, and mutters angrily through clenched teeth.

"What's that?" I say, leaning over so my ear is within inches of her mouth.

"It's not my back; it's my fucking leg!" she says. You moron.

❖

Tom and I are called for a chest pain. The forty-one-year-old man sitting on the couch looks terrible. He is an obese man whose bottom sinks deep into the couch. He is supporting his head with his hand. He has yellow eyes and his skin is warm.

"Are you having chest pain?" I ask.

He nods.

"On a scale of one to ten with ten being the worst pain you've ever had, how bad is it?"

"A ten," he says.

His family says he was treated at Saint Francis yesterday for chest pain, but he is worse today. He has a history of diabetes, hypertension, and congestive heart failure. His blood pressure is okay, 130/80. So is his pulse of 80, but when I put him on the heart monitor, he is in atrial flutter, a rare rhythm that can cause severe symptoms. I put him on an oxygen nonrebreather mask, a face mask with an attached reservoir bag that fills with 100 percent oxygen. A flapper valve on the mask prevents the patient from rebreathing his expired air.

"What does the pain feel like?" I ask. "Is it stabbing?"

He nods.

"Does it go to the left?"

"It goes left," he says.

I look at Tom as if to say I think he is having the big one. Tom looks at me with an amused expression.

We are only a few minutes from the hospital. I try to get an IV en route. I apply a tourniquet to the arm, which slows the return of blood to the heart and causes the veins in the arm to swell and become more visible. I take out a twenty gauge catheter. The needle is inside the plastic catheter. At the end of the needle is a clear chamber that collects the blood flashback to let you know you are in the vein. To do an IV you pick your spot, wipe it with an alcohol prep, then holding the arm with one hand to stabilize the vein and holding the needle between thumb and first two fingers, you make your move. They tell you in the books to go in at a forty-five-degree angle, but when I go in I go in much lower, particularly for hand veins that are right on the surface. Sometimes you feel a pop when hitting the vein. I try to go in quick and firm. I look down at the chamber and hopefully see the blood filling. I advance the catheter over the needle till just the hub is sticking out of the skin, and the one and one-quarter inch of plastic is secure in the vein. I withdraw the needle and hopefully drop it in the sharps box, because with many of the patients we care for an open contaminated needle is now a deadly weapon. A single puncture can give someone AIDS or hepatitis. Sometimes I drop it on the floor and have to remember to find it and pick it up later.

After taking the needle out I press off the vein with my fingers to prevent blood from flowing out of the catheter hub, while I screw on a vacutainer—a yellow plastic device—through which I will draw four small tubes of blood. The tubes have a rubber seal that is punctured by the needle in the vacutainer. Sometimes, if the vein is small, the vein will close down, and I won't be able to get bloods, or if the pressure is low, no blood will flow. I release the tourniquet after the last tube is drawn, then clamp off the vein again and either insert a saline lock, which has a medication port on it, or stick in the IV line, which is also attached to a bag of IV fluid. With the lock, I flush the line with five cubic centimeters of saline in a syringe. With an IV bag, I open up the clamp on the line and watch it run. If the line is blown, it either won't flush or run, or there will be infiltration. A large water mound will start to appear under the skin.

Now I am ready to stick this man with chest pain. I go at a vein in his forearm. I get a flash in the chamber to show I've stuck the vein, but almost instantly I see a purple hematoma growing under the skin. I have gone right through the vein and out the other side causing the vein to bleed into the tissues. I quickly pull out the needle, put a four- by four-inch bandage on the wound and tightly wrap it with tape. I try again on the other arm with the same result. We arrive at the hospital without a line in place. Bad form. And a bad start to my precepting.

I have called ahead to tell them what to expect, but when the three nurses waiting for us see the man, they say, "Oh, it's Marvin," and I can tell they are not too concerned, though they listen to my report politely. "A flutter is his regular rhythm," one says.

"So what do you think?" Tom asks me as we walk back down the hall.

"I think he might have been having a heart attack. He had chest pain of ten. He looked crappy. The pain was stabbing and it went into his left shoulder. What do you think?"

"I think he's a drug addict who is chronically ill and who didn't want to be at home, and his family didn't want him there. Think for a minute about the questions you asked him. 'Do you have chest pain? Is it stabbing? Does it go to the left?' That's like saying to a kid, 'Do you want a piece of candy? How about a Hershey bar? Want a Twinkie?' If that's what he wants, he's not going to say no. He played you for a fool. Think for a minute, how was he acting? What did he really look like, hiding behind his hand there?"

I think for a second, then it comes to me. "He looked like the guys in the car accidents who are faking headaches and back pain."

"Exactly. Don't ask yes or no questions. Don't lead the patient anywhere. Ask: 'What do you feel like?' Say: 'Describe the pain.' Don't give them the answers you are looking for."

❖

We get called for seizures at the Weston Street Jail. En route I find myself trying to remember the protocol. If the person is in status epilepticus, a condition of nonstop full-body seizing without any interval of consciousness, I can give them five milligrams of Valium. But I have to call

Too Young

Tom and I are parked across from the old G. Fox building on Main Street in L&M Ambulance 472. G. Fox was once the leading department store in Hartford, a place where as a boy I did my Christmas shopping on trips into the city, enjoying each floor's treasures and riding the escalators all the way up to the top floor where Santa Claus and his toy shop held reign. For years now, the building has been empty.

We're eating hot dogs we bought from a street vendor and watching people hurry across the street to avoid the winter chill. We've done a couple of calls today, but nothing taxing. I am a little on edge. I haven't had a real call that has forced me to prove myself yet. I wonder if I will ever relax, if I will ever have Tom's ability to sit back in his seat and fall peacefully asleep. I'm tense.

"Four-seven-two," the Hartford EMS dispatch calls over channel nine.

Tom picks up the mike. "Four-seven-two."

"Four-seven-two. Infant unresponsive on Kensington Street. Respond on a one."

"Kensington Street on a one."

Tom hits on the lights and does a U-turn. The address is in Stowe Village, a squalid public housing complex in the north end. Traffic is moderate. Cars pull to the right as we race down the street. Others stop dead in their tracks and force us to maneuver around them. Tom modulates the siren to wail and phaser. We stop briefly at each intersection. At Main and Albany a pickup blows right through the light in front of us.

"Nice move," Tom says.

A moment later, he has to hit the brakes again as two young mothers push strollers across the street in the middle of the block.

"Nobody's got any sense in this city," he says.

As we approach the village, Tom shuts off the siren—a precaution against drawing attention or random gunfire. He takes the portable radio that links us to police dispatch. We take no equipment. "If the baby is not breathing, we'll grab it and beat feet to the ambulance," Tom says.

We enter the building. Amid the graffiti in large red letters is written: "Fuck Everyone!" On the adjoining wall: "Fuck the World!" An expressionless woman on the second-floor landing gestures for us to come up the concrete and iron stairwell. She leads us into an apartment that is dark. It is cold—there is no heat. The apartment reeks of garbage. Water runs slowly from the faucet. The stove, sink, and countertop are piled with black crusted dishes. I can make out two men asleep on decrepit couches.

We turn a corner and there are three people around a bed.

"It's the ambulance," a man says. "They here."

I reach onto the bed and pick up the baby.

"He won't wake up," a young woman says to us.

The baby is cool, but breathing. His eyes are closed. His lungs sound junky even without a stethoscope. I can hear another baby crying.

"Are you the mother?" I ask.

She nods. She is a young girl with buck teeth wearing a snow jacket unzipped and a Snoop Doggy Dogg T-shirt. She doesn't look more than eighteen.

I ask her what hospital she wants to go to. She shrugs and says Hartford.

"Let's go then."

I carry the baby out of the scene. It is too dark in the apartment for a thorough assessment. I want the baby out of the squalor. I ask the girl what happened as we walk. "He just went limp for about twenty minutes, then he wouldn't wake up," she says.

"Has he been sick?"

"He been okay. I haven't been too well. I've got a cold."

In the ambulance, I hold the baby and try to listen to his lungs with a stethoscope. He grabs at it with his hand and tries to move it away. His pulse is 160, his respiratory rate 42—both a little fast for his age. There is crusted snot in his nose. I pry an eyelid open with my finger. He looks away from me. I shine a light into it. His pupils react to the light. We head to Hartford Hospital on a priority three—nonemergency.

When I have finished assessing him, I hand him back to the mother, who gives me her state medical card. On it are the names of five children; only two share the same last name. After I have written down the information, I take the baby back and hold him. His eyes are scrunched closed. I try to bounce him on my knee.

"What time did he go to sleep last night?"

"Two. I think he slept all the way till ten though. Is he going to be all right? Why won't he look at me? Why won't he laugh?"

I hear a burp too late to move and he pukes on me, white milky vomit on my leg and the ambulance floor.

She laughs. "He got his eyes open now."

I look to the front and see Tom laughing at me in the rearview mirror. One of the marks of a good paramedic is to be able to anticipate and get out of the way of puke. I fail this test.

The baby looks at me with cold eyes. He is fourteen months old. He looks like a baby pit bull, staring me down.

"It's okay, little man," I say.

In the ER, I give a report to the triage nurse who sends us back to the pediatric clinic, where the girl and child take a seat in the overcrowded waiting room.

❖

"No kid should live like that," Tom says to me in the cramped EMT room as I sit in a folding chair in front of the small metal desk, writing up my run form. He has a three-year-old at home.

"She gave me a different address as their home," I say.

"Good, she takes her kid with her to score crack," he says.

❖

He is still upset as we drive down Capital Avenue. "They ought to take her kids away from her," he says. "She doesn't know the first thing about being a mother. If you can't be responsible, you shouldn't be allowed to have kids, much less keep them. I'm sorry, Pete, this one just gets me."

I think of all the years I worked for Weicker, in Washington and in Connecticut; how we fought for kids, for prenatal and expanded health care, the school lunch program, Head Start, and other programs that were going to change their world. I remember how excited I was my first days at the health department and how I told the top staff there that things were going to be great now that Weicker was governor, and Susan Addiss was the new commissioner and I was the executive assistant, that health care and kids were going to be a priority and that we would all have an impact. And they all sort of looked at me as if I didn't have a clue. Right now I feel like none of it made any difference—not the legislative victories in Washington, not the programs in Connecticut. I know that's naive and that maybe things would be far worse if nothing at all had been done, but walking through the poverty that these kids live with every day—the cold dark, dirty apartments, the drug abuse and broken dreams of their parents—you can't help but feel failure if you have ever been in a position of power.

We pass the capitol, where they are taking down the grandstands from the inauguration of the new governor.

"What do you think the mother's childhood was like?" I ask.

"Probably just the same," he says.

Maytag Repairman Syndrome

It's a slow day. Most of the calls have been for colds and flu or general "not feeling well." Nothing life and death. At best, I can put some of the patients on the cardiac monitor, give them a little oxygen by nasal cannula, put in an IV, and draw blood. I haven't given any medications in over a week. We sit in the ambulance reading the paper or trying to sleep. I want to do as many "bad" calls as possible while I am still precepting so I will be better prepared when I am on my own, when I am in charge, working with a basic EMT as a partner. I wonder what kind of person I am. I fancy myself a kind, caring, compassionate man of the people, pledged to uphold the public health and do no harm, yet here I am wishing harm on some unspecified person who may at this moment be bouncing a grandchild on his knee, or closing his eyes and puckering to receive a first kiss, but soon will be clutching at his chest in terror or seizing on the ground with a bullet in the head.

Back when I was a basic EMT working for Eastern Ambulance, every Saturday I worked a sixteen-hour shift in Longmeadow, Massachusetts, with my partner David Hanley, another basic EMT. Longmeadow was a sleepy little town. We'd show up at work with rolls of quarters for our

Pac-Man marathons. We knew all the hot babes on "Soul Train" and every line of dialogue on "Cheers." We'd cruise the town, checking out girls. We'd go to Bay Path Junior College hoping to spot bikinied coeds sunning on the lawn, but it was just about always empty because most of the students went home on the weekends.

We'd get to talking about how we'd really like to do a call. Some EMTs would joke about throwing ice water on the back steps of churches in the winter. Driving up behind senior citizens and blasting the air horn. Giving alcohol to minors. Stringing razor wire across the minibike trails. Anything for a call.

You say you don't wish harm on anyone, but if harm is going to come to someone, let it come on my shift. I wonder if presidents ever feel this way: I'm bored, we need a crisis, a good conflict to arouse us, and get our juices and economy flowing. Let me show some leadership and raise my place in history above James Polk and Warren Harding. I want to be a Washington, a Lincoln, a Roosevelt.

I had it get so slow, I used to think about renting myself out to communities as their EMS system. Hire me and you will have no emergencies in your town because I don't get calls anymore. I once worked eight Thursday nights in a row in East Windsor without doing a call.

No one wants to be a novice. You hear other people talking about their calls, about the blood and guts, and the difficult extrications, the helicopter coming in to fly the patients out, and you wish you had been there. Some people say that after all the wishing for trauma, when you get in the middle of it, you wish it hadn't happened. For me, that's true when it is a kid who is hurt, but the honest to God's truth is when it's a faceless adult, I am sort of glad I am there because it is my job to help. Though if something personalizes them, then I feel badly. Once back in East Windsor, when I was working a traumatic arrest (not breathing, no pulse due to trauma inflicted on the body) of a young woman whose car had been hit by a truck late in the night, I saw her driver's license on the seat next to her. In the photo, her eyes were smiling, not bulging and lifeless, and her head didn't spurt blood with each chest compression. She had the stamp of a nightclub on her wrist; her home was just a few miles up the road. I thought about her for days, wondering what she had been like. Would she have turned my head if we passed? What kind of laugh did she have? How devastated must her family feel, awakened in the middle of a rainy night to such flesh-tearing news?

It is easy to forget the link between person and patient.

When I was riding in Bridgeport, I needed to get a field intubation, where you pass a plastic tube through someone's vocal chords into the trachea to secure their airway and better ventilate them. I had done nine in the hospital operating room (OR), but during my paramedic class ride time had never had an attempt in the field. I was going to be taking a leave of absence from the health department to work on my friend's campaign for Congress in Massachusetts and wanted to keep my skills up by working part-time on an ambulance up there. While I was certified in Massachusetts as a basic EMT, I needed to get certified as a paramedic to work as one. In EMS most every state has a different set of requirements. Massachusetts required certain documented field skills, including intubation and defibrillation. (In the end it was impossible for me to complete the required paperwork and additional testing in time.)

We were busy every night I worked in Bridgeport, call after call, all shift long, but no opportunities for a tube. No tube after the first twenty hours. No tube after fifty hours. No tube after eighty hours. I'd work Tuesday, then come back Thursday and they'd tell me I missed one on Wednesday. It got so bad I didn't know if they were busting my balls or if I was just picking the wrong nights to ride. From the disappointment on my face, they even stopped kidding me, stopped telling me I'd missed a bad one the night before.

Everyone in the company knew I needed a tube. Instead of a nod and a hello, people would nod and say, "Get your tube?" Nope. Not yet.

We responded to a woman unresponsive. Airway kit in hand, I charged through the door. The woman was as cold as ice. Her jaw stiffened to her neck. "Sorry, Pete. I don't think we'll be able to work this one," John Pelazza, my paramedic partner, said to me.

I felt bad hoping that somebody would keel over while I was on duty.

Finally, it came. While we were in Bridgeport Hospital Emergency Department (ED), John heard a call for a "man down" not far from the hospital. Though it was dispatched to another unit, he said, "Let's do it."

We arrived just after the other unit.

"Pete's gonna get the tube," John said as we entered.

The other crew stood aside. A man lay on the den floor, dried blood on his nose, his color purple from the shoulders up. Asystole—flat line—on the monitor. I knelt down, went in with the laryngoscope, spread the tongue to the left. I couldn't see anything. I went in again, saw the vocal chords and passed the tube. "I'm in," I said. Mike MaGoveny, an EMT, attached the ambu-bag to the end of the tube, and squeezed the bag, forcing air through the tube into the lungs. I checked breath sounds. Positive. I checked over the stomach for sounds in the belly. None. Bingo. Confirmation that the tube placement was good. Cardiopulmonary resuscitation continued. A round of drugs was given.

"Good job," Mike whispered to me as I ventilated the patient.

The man, though, never really had a chance. He'd been found by a niece. He'd been down awhile and from his color probably had a pulmonary embolus. The ER worked him only about five minutes before they called it.

I was ecstatic about getting the tube. I had been worried that with all the talk about needing a tube, what if I got the chance and didn't get it? But I had done it. I'd passed that sucker right through those chords.

After I'd helped clean the rig, I went back into the ER with a shit-eating grin on my face, so happy I was on the verge of doing a funky break dance. The family was there. Women were sobbing into handkerchiefs. Grown men wept in each other's arms. Children had frightened expressions, clutching to the coats of their elders. I did a quick about-face and went back out into the parking lot and stood in the chill night.

Drug Box

We carry twenty-four different drugs: dextrose and glucagon for hypoglycemia, Narcan for heroin overdoses, epinephrine 1:1000 and Benadryl for allergic reactions, Ventolin for asthma, oxytocin for postpartum bleeding, nitroglycerin (called "nitro" for short) and baby aspirin for chest pain, Lasix for congestive heart failure, dopamine for cardiogenic shock, and adenosine for supraventricular tachydysrhythmias. Our chief drugs for cardiac arrests include atropine, epinephrine 1:10,000, and lidocaine. Our second line cardiac drugs are bretylium, procainamide, and sodium bicarbonate. We also carry Dramamine, magnesium, calcium, isoproterenol, and propanolol. In the lock box above the monitor shelf we keep our narcotics—morphine for chest pain and pulmonary edema and Valium for unceasing seizures. The drugs come in either prefilled syringes or syringe inserts, small glass ampules or single and multisize vials, where the fluid is drawn out with a syringe. Some drugs such as Narcan can be given either through an IV line or intramuscularly (IM). Valium will cause tissue necrosis if given IM, but it can be given rectally if a line is unobtainable and the patient is in serious enough condition to merit going that route. Atropine and lidocaine can be given intravenously or down an endotracheal tube in the case of cardiac arrest. Other drugs such as dopamine are injected into a bag of D5 solution and given by slow IV infusion into the vein to ensure a steady level of the drug in the body.

We have a protocol book that tells us what drugs we can give on standing orders depending on the situation, and when we have to call on the radio for direct verbal orders to give the drugs. For chest pain, our routine care means the patient will get oxygen, cardiac monitoring, and an IV. We have standing orders to give up to three nitroglycerin tablets sublingual (under the tongue) at five-minute intervals provided the blood pressure stays above 100 systolic as well as two baby aspirin, but we must call to get permission to use morphine. For asthma we can give two Ventolin treatments (a mixture of the drug and saline water is put in a small humidifier through which oxygen is run, producing a vapor that is inhaled into the lungs) within twenty minutes, but must call for permission to give epinephrine.

In the case of cardiac arrests we have advanced cardiac life support (ACLS) algorithms that we follow. A person in ventricular fibrillation (v-fib) gets shocked rapidly at 200 J, 300 J, and 360 J provided the rhythm doesn't break after any of the shocks. Then CPR is continued, the person is intubated, and an IV is established. One milligram of epinephrine is administered every three to five minutes through the IV, or down the tube if IV access can't be obtained, followed by a shock at 360 J. After the first epinephrine ("epi" for short), the person gets lidocaine at one point five milligrams per kilogram, again followed by a shock. As long as they stay in v-fib, the algorithm runs through a variety of drugs including bretylium and procainamide. If a pulse returns or the patient converts to another rhythm, there are other algorithms that provide guidance for those situations. There is no need to contact medical control other than to alert them that you are en route to the hospital with a working code (cardiac arrest). All paramedics, as well as emergency doctors and critical care and emergency nurses, are required to pass a biannual two-day ACLS class that teaches the lastest standards for dealing with a variety of significant cardiac events from ventricular fibrillation to hypotension, shock, and acute pulmonary edema. (Some hospitals are offering experimental one-day recertification courses for those full-time paramedics who regularly work cardiac arrests.)

While we sit in the ambulance, I reread the manual.

"What's the dose for Valium in status epilepticus?" Tom asks.

"Five to fifteen milligrams."

"What's the dose for bretylium?"

"In v-fib, it's five milligrams per kilogram IV push, followed by ten milligrams per kilogram if the first dose doesn't convert."

"Wrong," he says. "Think again."

I stutter and fumble. "Damn. Wait, let me think."

"Wrong," he says again. "You were right the first time, but you've got to be more sure of yourself, you have to know it."

He's right. I know it on paper, but can I do it in the heat of the moment, when it's all going down around me? Can I get the job done?

Deportee

I'm jumpy, expecting every call to be the big one.

"Four-seven-two, man down corner of Park and Seymour. Respond on a one."

"We're all over it," Tom says.

We race down Washington Street, full lights and sirens. This is going to be a cardiac arrest, I think, I can feel it. I go over in my head what I will do. Assess responsiveness. If he's not breathing, do a quick look on the monitor and shock him if he's in v-fib. Otherwise, go to the head, ventilate, get out the intubation gear, sweep the tongue to the left and up with the laryngoscope blade, visualize the chords, and bang the tube right between them.

"Eight-forty."

"Go ahead, eight-forty."

"Tell four-seven-two the man's up."

"You got that, four-seven-two?"

"Got it."

We are at the corner now. "It's Jose," Tom says.

A man with a thin mustache and glazed eyes is leaning against a telephone pole, supporting himself with a cane.

We get out.

"You been drinking?" Tom asks.

Jose shakes his head. His face is covered with scabs in various stages of healing.

"I fell," he says.

"Get in," Tom says.

The man walks to the back of the ambulance with an unsteady gait, working hard to swing his left leg ahead and plant his cane.

I notice a fresh hospital bracelet on his wrist.

He tells me he is forty-seven. He has no address other than the mission. I ask him what happened and he says he fell. We are only three blocks from the hospital.

"They are not going to want to see him," Tom says as he brings a wheelchair to the back of the ambulance after we have parked outside the ER.

As I wheel him in, a doctor says, "Isn't that Jose?"

"Jose? We just released him," a nurse says.

"Oh, no," another nurse says. "Get out of here. We just released him. He didn't have time to make it to the liquor store. Who called you?"

"Nine-one-one. He says he fell." I add, "It's cold out."

Jose looks at the floor.

"Oh, brother," she says, grabbing her chart.

She inputs his name in the computer and says to us, "Put him in the waiting room."

❖

"That man gets transported two, three times every day. He costs the state over eight hundred thousand dollars a year just in ambulance and hospital bills," Tom tells me as we leave. "When he gets drunk, he's mean. He whipped his dick out once when I was working with a woman and tried to pee on us. The scars on his face aren't just from falling; they're from other people beating the crap out of him. He's got a foul mouth and an ugly temper. He'll swing at you if you give him space. He is the scum of the earth."

❖

A week later, I am at the hospital when I hear a nurse tell a paramedic that Jose is being deported. They have him in a back room all doped up on Ativan, awaiting the Immigration and Naturalization Service (INS) agent, who will accompany him back to Nicaragua. He is leaving from Bradley Airport in the morning, though no one has told him yet. The hospital has been working with INS for over a month to get the deal done.

❖

I have a dream that night of a small plane landing on an airfield in Nicaragua and a body being thrown out. Jose struggles to get up and balance himself with his cane. He looks around. It is warm; the road is made of hardened mud. To the left is lush jungle; to the right, urban slums where the homeless pick through garbage cans and men yell at each other in the street. Suddenly a dog leaps at Jose, catching him in the jugular vein. Another dog rips into his right arm. A third dog knocks him to the ground and tears at his groin. There is ferocious barking. All you can see are dogs—twenty, thirty of them fighting over the body. When the dust clears, all that is left is a carcass—an empty chest cavity with the backbone showing through like the remains of a postfeast Thanksgiving turkey. There are a few stringy pieces of meat left and lots of dog hair. Jose's cane lies beside the body.

Oh, Mama, I'm glad I'm not a mean, drunk Nicaraguan.

Life and Death

It is three in the afternoon. We get called for a seizure at a factory. A basic unit is closer so they are reassigned the call. We slide over in that direction anyway in case they need us. The traffic is heavy, so Tom says screw it and puts on his lights and sirens. As we arrive, we hear the basic unit call for us.

"Did you hear that, four-seven-two?" the dispatcher says.

"We're out," Tom says.

A woman meets us by a side door and leads us up three flights of long broad stairs. We come out into a large open room. The other crew is by a corner desk. A man is sitting in a chair. He is pale, ashen, diaphoretic, and anxious. He looks like a ghoul—like death is whirling around inside of him. Even to speak seems a great effort for the man, who is fifty-four years old.

"I can't get a pressure," one of the EMTs says.

"Lay him down on the stretcher," Tom says.

He already has an oxygen mask over his face turned up full. He has a weak pulse in his neck. None in his wrist. He has been having pain since nine that morning, which disappeared, then came back at one-thirty. He thought it would pass, but it has gotten worse.

We put him on the monitor. He has a slow rhythm with couplets of ventricular tachycardia (v-tach). I pause. It is a rhythm I studied in class. It is there on the monitor. In real time in real life. Sweat pours from my forehead. We carry him down the stairs on the stretcher. I am at the bottom, and as the EMT pushes the stretcher forward, I trip momentarily and feel myself falling backward. I grab the railing with my left arm and catch myself, relieved not to have me and the stretcher and the patient tumbling down the stairs in speeding somersaults.

We get him in the back of the ambulance. On the monitor he is in full ventricular tachycardia—a lethal rhythm. I go for an IV line in his arm. We need to get medication and fluid into him right away. I find a vein in the crook of his elbow. It's not a big one, but I ought to be able to get it. I go in with an eighteen. I get the flashback in the chamber, but to my horror, I see a hematoma growing around the site. I swear. I'm through the vein. Tom is spiking a one thousand milliliter bag of saline. Rene Barsalou, one of the EMTs and an old partner of Tom's, gets out the airway kit, while the other EMT is preparing to assist the man's ventilations. I spot a thin vein in his hand. I go in with a twenty, a size smaller. I get no flashback, but I feel I am in. Rene looks at it. She has been an IV technician for years and her skills are exceptional. "You're in," she says, "he's just clamping down." We hook up the IV line, run the fluid into the vein. It goes in steadily.

Tom already has the defibrillation pads, one to the right of the sternum, the other lower on the left side. The pads are connected to the monitor by two wires.

I hit the synchronized cardiovert button. "A hundred?" I say to Tom.

He winces. It is the right amount for the protocol, but the man is still responsive, and there is no time to call for orders for Valium to premedicate him. "Fifty," he says, "and tell him it's going to hurt."

I lean over the man. "Sir, you need to keep your hands by your sides and don't grab anything. We're going to apply some electricity to your heart to correct your rhythm. This is really going to hurt."

I set the joules to fifty, hit the charge button, then look to see if everyone is clear. I press the buttons simultaneously. A few seconds later, the charge hits him. His body convulses. His teeth and arms clench. His whole body comes up off the stretcher, then settles back down.

He's still in v-tach.

"We have to do it again. Don't grab out."

I set it for a hundred.

He screams as the electricity hits him.

Still in v-tach.

I set it for two hundred. "Hang in there," I say.

He says through clenched teeth, "You guys are killing me."

We hit him again at two hundred.

The electricity shoots through his writhing soul. We wince.

He is unresponsive. He's in an idioventricular rhythm on the monitor, a flat line with only an occasional beat at a rate of about twenty a minute. He has no pulse.

I screw a one milligram dose of epinephrine into a bristo-jet syringe and plug it into the three-way medication port on the IV line. I push it in quickly.

He goes back into v-tach.

I give him ninety milligrams of lidocaine and defibrillate him at 200 joules.

His whole body seizes. He clenches his teeth. His face swells and turns purple before our eyes. He stops breathing.

"You killed him," Tom says.

I move to the head of the stretcher as Rene hands me the intubation gear.

Laryngoscope in hand, I try to pry his mouth open. His jaw is absolutely locked. I can't tube him. He's clenched.

"Wait a second," Tom says confidently. "He'll loosen up."

His muscles go limp. I put the blade in and sweep the tongue to the side, but I cannot see the vocal chords. I pull out and reventilate with the ambu-bag. I go in again, but still can't see them. Please drop, please drop down into my sight, chords. Let me get the tube. Let me get the job done.

I can't.

Tom and I switch places. I push atropine and epinephrine through the IV line. The EMT is doing CPR. Tom goes in for the tube but can't get it. He switches blades, then passes the tube.

"It's in," he says.

He checks lung sounds to confirm placement, then connects the ambu-bag, and begins ventilating. The man's color improves.

His rhythm is still idioventricular. "Com'on, com'on back," he says, but it's not doing the job for the man. Rene is driving now. I'm doing CPR, and the other EMT is following in the other ambulance. I stop CPR briefly to give another epi and another atropine.

"I want to save this guy," Tom says.

At the hospital, we wheel him straight to the cardiac room, where a team of doctors, nurses, respiratory therapists, and assistants are gathered to take over. We lift him from our stretcher to the bed by pulling him on the sheet. Tom glances at me, then goes ahead and gives the report to the team.

They continue the code, giving him more epinephrine, but they can't bring him back either. He is dead.

❖

We clean the ambulance and write the report. While I am excited by the adrenaline rush of the call and having finally gotten to defibrillate someone (something I never want to do again on a conscious person without sedating them), inside I fight the feeling that I failed badly. I couldn't get the tube, and only got the line on my second try and only got a small hand vein. I don't think I could have handled it on my own without Tom there. Maybe if it had just been him, he might have saved the guy. The death is an anvil in my soul. I step heavily, dragging it behind. Maybe I should have stayed back at my desk, out of harm's way, and my harm out of others' way. I wonder if this playing paramedic hasn't just been a big game to me. Like a soldier going off to war seeking easy glory, only to flinch on encountering real combat. I keep my mouth shut. My mind races.

"Would you do anything different?" Tom asks.

"I don't know, would you?"

"Our treatment was right," he said. "He just didn't make it—he should have, but he didn't. His heart muscle was probably shot. He was having the bad one all day and wouldn't admit it."

He adds, "Did it bother you when I said you killed him?"

"No."

"It seemed to go right past you. I say that sometimes just to see what kind of reaction I can get."

"Sure."

Another crew stops by our open back doors. "Hey, I heard you had a KBP call," one of them says.

"KBP?" I say.

"Killed by paramedic," Tom says. "Alive when you got there, dead when you left him."

"Right," I say.

❖

Later we are back at the office, sitting halfway up a set of stairs, where we can get some privacy as we do our day's evaluation form. There is an entry: "Properly explains procedures to patients." "You did a good job on that," Tom says. "I like the way you told him, 'This is really going to hurt.'"

"Yeah," I said. "This is really going to hurt, but it won't matter because you're going to be dead in ten minutes."

We laugh so hard we nearly roll down the stairs.

"Something is wrong with us," he says.

I say, "It doesn't bother me because I have a cold, cold heart."

❖

That night I keep seeing the man flinch as the electricity hits him. I see his face as he seizes and his complexion turns purple. I wake up gasping for breath.

❖

The next morning Tom reads the obituary page. I have already read the man's entry three times. He had a wife and four children and two grand-children. He was born in Ohio. He'd worked at the same company for twenty-six years. The funeral was to be held in Columbus.

"I don't like it when they die," Tom says.

Waiting

I am worried about how I am coming along. While my IV skills are get-ting better, and Tom has few quarrels with my treatment plans, I feel slow and worry that I will not be able to handle the bad ones on my own. Daniel Tauber, the chief paramedic, asks me about the call where we shocked the guy. "Did you run the call?" he asks. "Tom ran most of it," I say. "I made some of the decisions. He got the tube." Daniel nods. He has been a paramedic for almost ten years, and I find him very intimidating. I want his respect, but know that I am far from it. Tom tells him that we did the call together, that I am coming along fine. I think that another less noble preceptor would tell him that he has doubts about my ability. I know I have doubts about my own. What I know is that I need more calls, more chances to learn, even if it is through mistakes. I'm on line twelve hours a day, waiting for them to call our number. I go to each call, wondering what lies ahead. Will this be the one to give me the boost I need? The chance to stand ten feet tall, to work with godlike speed—to save a life? Or will this one be my undoing? A disaster that will forever shame me?

I wait.

Can I Get a Heartbeat, Please?

Meg and I get a call for a woman with chest pain at the medical clinic of a retirement complex. The woman is lying on the examination table of the doctor's office. She is having, in her words, heart palpitations. She is pale, diaphoretic, and nervous. Her skin is cool and clammy. She developed the pain last night, but didn't want to bother anyone so she waited until this morning to come in. We put her on our cardiac monitor. Her heart rate is 177 with a narrow complex, meaning her atria, the upper chambers of her heart, are firing rapidly, conducting the impulses to the ventricles, the lower chambers, which are responding at the same pace. By firing so quickly, the heart does not have time to fill completely with blood. The volume pushed out with each beat is grossly inadequate. While some people can tolerate this rhythm for quite a length of time, if she's been having the trouble since last night, she is not going to be able to take it much longer.

Fortunately, she has beautiful large veins. Meg spikes a bag of saline and inserts a sixteen gauge IV needle in her left antecubital (AC) vein, which is the big vein in the crook of her arm. I draw up six milligrams of adenosine in one syringe and ten cubic centimeters of saline in another syringe. Meg sticks the adenosine syringe in one port of the three-way stopcock on the IV line, and the saline in the other. She pushes the adenosine, then flips the stopcocks and pushes in the saline. "You'll feel very strange in a moment, but it will pass," she tells the woman. "Watch the monitor," she says to me.

Adenosine shuts down the electrical conduction between the atria and the ventricles at a place called the atrioventricular (AV) node. It has a half-life of only twelve seconds. Unless it is given in the vein close to the circulation center and flushed rapidly, it will lose its effect before it gets to the heart.

Three seconds pass. Suddenly, instead of a mass of beats closely bunched together, the monitor goes flat line. We watch it. It is flat line. It is still flat line. All we see rolling past is a straight flat line. Flat line. Flat line. Flat line.

Meg and I look at each other, then back at the monitor. Our right feet are tapping the floor in nervous time. "Com'on, com'on," she says. I am thinking about what I am going to have to do if the beat doesn't come back. While this is the first time I have seen adenosine used, I have heard stories about it, so I am not in full panic. Still, I am thinking about grabbing the ambu-bag and assisting her ventilations, doing CPR, putting a tube down her throat, and pumping her body with epinephrine and atropine.

"Com'on, com'on," I see Meg's lips motion.

She looks at me and we exchange nervous glances. Sweat is beading on our foreheads.

It is still flat. Still flat. Still flat.

Blip. There is a heartbeat, then more flat line, then, blip, another heartbeat.

The air escaping from our mouths says, "Whew!"

The rate is now 80. We smile at each other. Then in the next second the rate is back up to 178.

I am already drawing up the next dose. This time we will hit her with twelve milligrams.

"We have to try again," Meg says to the woman, brushing the hair back from her forehead.

I push the drug, then switch the stopcock and slam in the saline, shooting the drug up the vein, hurtling it through the venal rapids, through the superior vena cava and swirling into the right atrium, where it again stops the heart dead.

Flat line.

Flat line.

Flat line.

Flat line.

Flat line.

Flat line.

Flat line.

"Com'on, com'on."

Flat line. Flat line.

Flat line.

I look at the woman and she has one of the strangest expressions on her face I have ever seen. It is like she has left her body. I imagine her ghost standing next to us observing the scene.

Flat line.

"Com'on."

Blip. A beat.

Blip. Another.

Then another. Blip. Blip.

Blip. Blip. Blip. Blip.

A beautiful normal sinus rhythm at 80.

"You okay?" Meg asks.

"Yeah," I say.

"Yes," the woman says, "I feel much better."

"Me, too," Meg says.

We transfer her to our stretcher and bundle her up against the cold.

Her rhythm is nice and steady all the way to the hospital.

I think, isn't it great to be a paramedic? Politicians get plaques and awards and get to cut ribbons in front of buildings, but we get this lady's smile. She was sick. We used our skills and our trusty drug box and it worked in front of our eyes. Magic. Paramedicine.

❖

Later, we look at the rhythm strip. Her heart was stopped for six seconds the first time. For ten the next.

I stand there holding the strip. I don't believe it. It was a minute at least. No, two, three, four minutes. Minimum.

Anaphylaxis

The call is for a woman having an asthma attack at the corner of Farmington and Laurel. As we approach we see a woman in a green jacket waving to us from the sidewalk on Farmington. I see two women trying to prop up a third woman who is stricken.

"Four-seven-two on scene," Tom says on the radio.

We get out.

"What's going on?" I ask.

An older woman, wearing an eye patch says, "She's got asthma. She's three months pregnant."

"When did it start?"

"A few minutes ago. She can't get her breath."

The girl, who is seventeen, appears to be crying. She is pale, holding her stomach and breathing rapidly, struggling for a breath. Her skin is hot.

We sit her on the bench in the ambulance. I tell Tom to get a Ventolin treatment set up as I listen to her lungs. There is some wheezing in the upper fields. I look at her face. Her lower lip is swollen out an inch.

"Did you get bitten or eat something strange?"

"I ate a peanut," she cries.

"Does she have hives?" Tom asks.

"I itch all over," she says. "I'm hot. Get my sweater off."

We pull her sweater off. She is wearing just a bra. I can see small raised welts on her stomach. I glance at her face. Hives appear in front of my eyes. She vomits on the floor. I grab an emesis basin and ask her to hold it, but she can't. She is using both her arms to hold herself up. Her every effort is to breathe. She seems like she is about to pass out. Spit drools from her mouth. I throw a towel on her lap and take a quick blood pressure. It is low at 90. Her skin feels cooler. She says her throat itches. Tom hands her the Ventolin breathing treatment—and tells her to breathe in the humidified air, which will help expand her bronchioles, though it will take five minutes to achieve its full effects. We move her across to the stretcher. This is not asthma—it is a full anaphylaxis, a severe allergic reaction.

"What are you going to do?" Tom says.

"I'm thinking about epi and Benadryl."

"Thinking about?"

"That's what I'm going to give her."

"I'll get the IV," Tom says.

She is sweating profusely. Her skin is clammy and cool now. She is crashing in front of us. Her body's reaction to the peanut is releasing histamine, dilating her veins, dropping her pressure, and filling her tissues with fluid. Not forty seconds have elapsed since she stepped into the ambulance. If we don't act right away, she will die. Tom spikes a bag of saline and puts a tourniquet on her arm. I open the med box, take out a one cubic centimeter syringe and break the top of an ampule of epinephrine 1:1000. I draw up .3 milligrams. I swab her right biceps with an alcohol wipe and stick the needle in at an angle and inject the epinephrine. She pukes again. The epi blasts her heart rate up to 140 on the heart monitor. Tom has an IV established in her left arm, and opens up the roller clamp on the bag of saline that allows us to regulate the flow of fluid so it runs wide open, pouring fluid into her veins to try to restore her depleting volume. Her eyes are swollen shut. I draw up 50 milligrams of Benadryl and push it through the IV line, where it will directly enter her veins. The Benadryl will block the release of the body's histamine. The epinephrine will dilate the bronchioles, enabling her to breathe and constrict her veins, increasing her pressure. Without these two drugs, her swelling throat will seal itself shut.

We go lights and sirens. Tom tries to call C-Med for a patch to the hospital, but they don't answer.

In the two minutes it takes to get to the hospital her heart rate comes back down to a hundred on the monitor. Her lungs sound better. Her eyes are still shut, but her breathing is improving. She lies on the stretcher, exhausted.

The C-Med radio operator finally connects us to the hospital as we park in front of the hospital door.

"Seventeen-year-old in anaphylaxis," Tom says. "We're at your door."

"How soon?"

"Look out the window," he says.

When we wheel the girl in, her eyes are open. Though she says her throat still itches, her breathing is unlabored.

The triage nurse looks at us like she doesn't understand what the big deal is. This certainly doesn't look like anaphylaxis. The girl's lip swelling is barely noticeable now. We are just a pair of sparky EMTs all excited over nothing.

Tom explains that we have already given epi and Benadryl. She looks at us like sure you did. And I'm supposed to believe this girl was at death's door. Right. Sparkies. "Room twelve," she says.

We take the girl down the hall and transfer her to a hospital bed.

"Good luck with your baby," Tom says.

"Thank you," she says.

I feel both great and oddly, uncoordinated, like I did something good in spite of myself, like luck and good fortune were on my side.

When we walk back down the hall to our ambulance, Tom says to me, "That was a good job. You saved her life."

"Yeah, I guess, but I was a little slow."

"That's all right. You were right on it."

"I guess. But you were right on it, too."

"You're right, and two seconds earlier than you were." He flashes me a big Wyatt Earp smile as he slaps me on the back. "Pete, you've got to be cocky if you want to be a paramedic."

Kids

W e're a few blocks from Hartford Hospital after dropping off another cold and flu—a mother who met us at the curb with her four-year-old who had a runny nose and a stomachache. Ahead of us I can see the health department where I once had a top-floor office. I think if I were there now I might be at the window looking out on the feast of the snow-covered city, and gazing down longingly at the ambulance approaching, wondering about what great calls and adventures I was missing.

Something thwacks against the side of the ambulance.

"What was that?" Tom says.

I look in the side mirror.

"Are they throwing snowballs at us?" he says, braking suddenly in the middle of the street.

"It's just some kids," I say.

He puts the rig into reverse.

The kids scatter as he stops the ambulance. Three of them pass us, careful not to meet our eyes.

"Roll down the window," Tom orders.

"Hey!" he calls to a fat kid, maybe twelve years old, wearing a New York Giants snow hat.

The kid stops. "I didn't do nothing," he says.

In the mirror I see four other kids have stopped at a safe distance to watch.

"Tell him to wait there, I want to talk to him."

"Tom," I say, but he is already out of the car.

I look at the kid. "He wants to talk to you," I say.

"It wasn't me," the kid says in a high quivering voice. He points down the street. "It was him."

Just then a snowball grazes the kid's shoulder. In the mirror I see the others quickly scoop in the snow to arm themselves. Tom is firing snowballs.

I jump out. I make a snowball as one grazes off my leg. I take a blow to the chest as I fire wildly at the charging tribe.

"Come and get it," Tom shouts, laughing like a wild man.

We are in a pitched battle.

Kids appear out of doorways, from alleys, and around corners. We are overwhelmed. We retreat to the ambulance. Snow thwacks against our side and windshield as we pull away.

"That was fun," I say.

"Ah, winter," Tom says.

I look back up at my old office. The window is empty.

On My Own

"I think you're ready," Tom says. "What do you think?"

"I think so, but I wouldn't mind doing a few more bad calls."

"I think you're ready. You must be sick of me by now."

"Well, I sort of am."

"Get out of here, you are."

❖

On Thursday, Debbie Haliscak, the Saint Francis Hospital prehospital coordinator, rides with us. I know Debbie well from when she was the ALS coordinator for the state office, a part-time job in which she helped ambulance services, mainly volunteer, upgrade from the basic level of service to the intermediate or defibrillation levels. She also helped set me up as a volunteer medic in Bloomfield while I was still at the health department. She is a short, energetic mother of a two-year-old, who is always at her computer in her office, working on policy statements or updating protocols when paramedics stop in to chat. Her undeserved reputation for being more of a paper-pusher coordinator than a street-skilled coordinator will be forever put to rest a few months from now when she and Daniel Tauber will go to a cardiac arrest in West Hartford where a precepting medic will be attempting an endotracheal tube. The precepting medic will fail on two attempts, the medic will fail on two attempts, Daniel will fail on two attempts, then Debbie will step up, and using the laryngoscope blade like an ice pick, will stand over the patient, lift up on the jaw, and looking into the mouth upside down, pass the tube successfully. Daniel, in a rare admission, will tell people that even he learned something new. Debbie will become a legend.

Today is my day to prove myself. The dispatchers are on alert to give us the best calls that come in.

We are sent for a man with chest pain. The fire department is on the scene. We enter the building to find a man in his late fifties with a heart history lying on the floor clutching his chest, diaphoretic, looking like he is wrestling with an invisible superhuman opponent who has him pinned to the carpet, despite his efforts to get up. "Let's put some oxygen on him," I say. "Nonrebreather." Debbie gets it out of the blue bag while I feel for the man's pulse and ask him how he is doing. His pulse is very rapid. The man looks at me through clenched teeth like I am an idiot. I'm fucking dying here, you asshole! he seems to be saying. While Debbie puts the mask on, I take a blood pressure. It is 130/80, but again I am made aware of how fast his pulse is beating. "Let's get him on the monitor," I say. Debbie is right there into it with me, while Tom gets the stretcher. The man is going at 170 on the monitor. "SVT," I say. It's supraventricular tachycardia. "We'll try some adenosine. Let's get a line."

Now comes the hard part. I put on a tourniquet and search for a vein, but see and feel nothing, all the while the guy is looking at me like he wants to beat the crap out of me and will as soon as his mysterious tormentor releases him from his viselike grip. I feel like everyone in the room is watching me, which they are. Debbie helps me look, but we are having no luck. I am cussing under my breath to my guardian paramedic gods. Please, just give me a line on this one. Don't make it so hard, I whine. The longer I look the more I become aware that I am screwing up. My mind starts racing, what do I do, what do I do. I glance at the monitor. Heart rate down to 144. "It's looking more like a sinus tach now," I say. "I probably won't do the adenosine. I'm going to give him a nitro as soon as I get a line."

Debbie nods, and I can see on one hand she is approving how my mind is operating, but on the other I feel like I'm in a game show where everybody else knows the answer and they want me to get it, but I just can't seem to guess it.

Finally, Tom says, "Why don't we get him on the stretcher and get him rolling. We can do what we have to in the ambulance."

Good idea. I undo the tourniquet, and with the aide of the firemen lift the man up and get him on the stretcher. He is still glaring at me like he is going to hunt me down and kick my butt when he gets through this. What's this idea of a numbskull like me taking care of him when The Undertaker is sitting on his chest, squeezing his heart?

In the ambulance, as Tom starts for Saint Francis, I finally find a vein and get the IV, though I have trouble advancing the catheter all the way in. Still, it holds, and permits a small flow of saline into the vein. I give the man a nitro under the tongue. His heart rate falls to 140 and he feels some relief, though the pain is still crushing. I call Saint Francis and tell them we are coming in. I give him another nitro, and again give him some more relief, but he still has chest pain.

At the hospital, I sense his relief as the team of nurses and a doctor gather around him and hook him up to their monitor, give him oxygen, probe him with stethoscopes and blood pressure and pulse monitors, get another IV going, and go to the drug cabinet for morphine.

Tom and Debbie and I stand in the hallway and talk over the call. "He was nervous," Tom says. "He's better than that."

Debbie says she guessed that and what she was most interested in was my thought process for treating the patient, which was on target. She doesn't mention I forgot the most important point of getting the patient moving along to the hospital if I am unable to get treatment initiated right away.

I am glad that they have confidence in me. I do not feel it is warranted. The call has scared me—reminded me that there are calls ahead where I will stumble and won't have someone there to get me back on the right track.

Later we respond for an elderly woman not feeling well, and a woman with throat cancer having trouble breathing. I get all my lines, but am nervous and a bit out of sync on the calls. At three Debbie has to quit for a meeting, and she tells me as far as she is concerned I'm all set. I don't feel I performed that well for her, and am worried that she is cutting me some slack because she knows me. Tom tells me not to worry. "You're ready," he says.

Tom calls the office and tells them I'm cut loose. Though I do not hear it, the dispatcher announces it over the radio. Tom tells me a chorus of voices comes back from other crews saying congratulations.

"They are proud of you," he says.

❖

I call my friend Michelle that night from home and tell her I have been cut loose. She congratulates me and says I will do fine. That is little consolation to me. I am panic-stricken. About to be thrown in the water. I will hit with a big splash and will start to sink. Will I kick and fight and rise up to the sweet air and sunshine and wave to the adoring crowds who hold up "10" signs, or will I keep sinking? The crowds will go home to their lives, and I'll keep dropping down into the darkness so deep they will forget all about me.

I watch the red digital display on my clock all night as it nears the hour of my reckoning.

❖

The next day I am the paramedic and I have a basic EMT for a partner. My first call is for an eighty-five-year-old woman who the visiting nurse says has been having trouble breathing since early morning. She is lying in bed with her hands shaking, which the nurse says is normal. She is alert and oriented. Her skin is warm. There are wheezes in all lung fields. Her abdomen is tender. She complains of pain on inspiration and expiration. It hurts when I press against her chest. She says she has been coughing up white phlegm.

I take her vital signs. Blood pressure: 140/80. Pulse: 106. Respirations: 34. I put her on oxygen by nasal cannula. On the monitor she is in a sinus tachycardia with occasional premature ventricular contractions (PVCs). In the ambulance, I give her a breathing treatment of .5 Ventolin, start an IV line using an eighteen gauge catheter, and hook up a bag of saline at a KVO rate, letting in just enough fluid to keep the vein open to prevent clotting.

She says the treatment is making her breathing a little better. She still has wheezes in all fields. We take her to Saint Francis. There I give the triage nurse my report. Eighty-five-year-old female, not feeling well since this morning. Some shortness of breath, wheezing in all fields, a little feverish, coughing up white phlegm. The nurse gives me a room assignment, and I start to wheel the patient down the hall. Holding the bag of saline in my left hand, pushing the stretcher with my right and with the monitor strapped over my shoulder, I begin to sweat. The sweat starts to pour down my forehead. I feel my hands begin to shake. I understand what is happening. I am a paramedic now. I am on my own.

PARTNERS

Image

Back in the 1970s there was a TV show called "Emergency," about two firefighter/paramedics in Los Angeles, Johnny Gage and Roy DeSoto. They were two sort of "aw, shucks" guys who were always saving lives and delivering babies and burning dinner at the fire station. At the hospital they hung out with sage doctors and Dixie, the beautiful nurse, played by Julie London. I was about twelve years old when it ran. It was my favorite show.

❖

A lot of kids grow up wanting to be a firefighter. I may have briefly wanted to wear a fire hat when I was four, but mainly I wanted to be a baseball player and play right field for the Boston Red Sox like my hero Tony Conigliaro. Then when my Little League career ended with my striking out with one out and nobody on base in the last inning of a heartbreaking two-to-one loss in the state Little League regional finals, I decided I wanted to be a professional tennis player. And that ended when I decided I would rather sit at home drinking lemonade and watching the Red Sox play on TV than play three matches in the hot sun—especially since if I won, I'd have to stay overnight at some stranger's house in some unfamiliar New England town, only to have to play more matches in the hot sun the next day. Then I guess I decided, what the heck, I might as well be president of the United States. In 1976, I went to work as an intern for Weicker in Washington, and showed enough dedication and energy to be hired for a salary of about six thousand dollars to answer constituent mail while I took a year off before college hoping I could get into Harvard on my second try. At age seventeen, I was the youngest Senate aide in Washington. I figured that made me the front-runner for president in 1996.

❖

Back when I was a kid I thought EMTs were nerds. In my town, they wore white uniforms and looked like janitors in mental asylums. When I was in the eighth grade we went on a field trip to Washington, D.C. One of my classmates' father was an EMT, and my classmate often went on ambulance calls with him. We were eating breakfast when an old woman fainted in the breakfast line. He jumped up from the table, leapt over some plants, and knelt by the woman's side. He didn't seem to be doing anything, and the woman was coming around on her own. We all made fun of him for the rest of the week, calling his name for help, grasping our hearts and falling to the ground, kicking our feet for a few moments like the Three Stooges, and emitting gruesome dying groans, before lying still with our dead tongues hanging out the sides of our mouths.

❖

When I was at college, I lived in an apartment complex where the resident manager was this guy with shoulder-length hair and a sweeping black mustache who had the most beautiful tall, blond girlfriend. He was the kind of guy who was nice to everybody and was always suntanned and drinking a beer in the afternoon, but never drunk, and who in a league softball game would hit a line drive in the gap, race around the bases, and slide into home with the winning run, beating the throw by a split second. He always played great music on his stereo. He was also an EMT and had interesting stories about his calls. One day he got a bunch of people together to teach them CPR. I was going to do it but didn't. I had given up the idea of being president by then and was into being a writer, which meant I always had the excuse that I had to go write.

❖

I've done a lot of jobs in my life. I was a cabdriver in Alexandria, Virginia, a job I loved—being on the road, meeting new people, being my own boss. I've been a cook in Iowa, worked in a hardware factory and a meat-packing plant in Minnesota, did telemarketing in California. I've unloaded trucks, done construction, assembled Christmas-tree stands, written for a newspaper, and sold Bibles. I like seeing people and having new experiences. My life has switched back and forth between manual-labor jobs and working in government. My parents always liked it best when I was putting the suit back on, but I always felt I was selling myself out that way. While parts of it I loved—the status and respect—I never felt truly free. I was in someone else's shadow.

❖

When I was taking my EMT class, a paramedic visited us and talked about the life of the street medic. He was an impressive figure—tall, wearing his uniform like a soldier, telling tales from years in New York City. I wanted to be a hero just like him until he started saying derogatory things about minorities.

❖

As an EMT, I always looked at the paramedics with a certain awe. It was hard enough just doing the basic stuff. These people had detailed medical knowledge, they did IVs, pushed drugs, intubated, shocked. They dealt with the bad ones and used their heads and finely developed skills under the worst conditions to save lives.

At East Windsor, we frequently called for paramedic intercepts. We'd load the patients and start to the hospital, and the medic would meet us en route. Our driver would pull over, and a few moments later, the side door would open, and a paramedic would climb aboard, confident, relaxed. He'd listen to my report, then put the patient on the heart monitor, start an IV line, push drugs, while we stood aside. He had the situation under control.

❖

I read once that the paramedic was the second most admired job in the United States, and doctors, lawyers, businessmen, and politicians were rated near the bottom. That may be so, but ask parents who they'd rather have their daughters marry.

During my paramedic intern time, I ran into a doctor I knew from the State Medical Committee. "I've heard you're going to paramedic school," he said. "Given your political skills, why would you want to be a paramedic?" I was a bit taken aback. I muttered something about being tired of sitting behind a desk.

❖

When I started working at Eastern Ambulance, I was getting $5.50 an hour. I could have made more working at Burger King. Today, as a paramedic I make $14.00 an hour, which makes my annual salary about $24,000 a year. I get five vacation days and five sick days after a year of work. At the health department, I made $57,500 with three weeks of paid vacation, three weeks of paid sick time, and twelve paid holidays every year. That for working a thirty-five-hour week.

❖

Every town has a paid police force. Most have paid fire services. Only a few have paid EMS exclusive to that town. In those that do, the EMS is usually part of the fire department. Most towns have volunteer ambulance services and most cities contract out to commercial ambulances. Cops have to wear guns and face down bad guys who may also have guns. Firefighters have to enter burning buildings. Paramedics often enter uncontrolled situations where patients are violent, sometimes armed. Though they are trained not to enter a scene until it is safe, sometimes you learn it is unsafe too late. Also, paramedics have to stick needles into people whose blood could kill the paramedic if he accidently got stuck with the contaminated needle. Cops and firefighters all have lucrative pension deals and other benefits. Few people in EMS stay long enough to collect pensions. Most places don't even have them. The burn out is so high. My employer, Professional Group, has a new plan, where it will contribute a small amount to a 401 (k), but I won't be eligible until I have worked there for a full year.

❖

I go on a call in West Hartford for a young woman having a diabetic problem. It is a rainy night, and the woman lives in a very posh house. "You're tracking mud on the carpet," her mother says as we bring the stretcher into the house. I almost say, "Where do you hide your silver?"

❖

When we go to nursing homes or corporations, they always make us use the rear entrances by the trash bins and loading docks.

❖

In most movies the EMTs stand around at the scene with their hands in their pockets, doing nothing. Once they have the patient loaded into the ambulance they get in the front together to let the patient be alone with the star, who holds his hand as the patient utters his last words.

I get a call to respond as the second ambulance to a motor-vehicle accident on Wethersfield Avenue. It is dark. Ahead we see the lights of another ambulance and two police cars. There are at least three cars involved.

I report to Joe Stephano, who has taken charge of the scene. He points to a car that has run up an embankment. "The woman in the car has neck pain," he says, "The car's unstable. Wait for the fire department before you touch her."

My partner helps the other crew extricate a patient from another car.

My patient is the driver of a green LTD. One of the rear wheels is on the sidewalk, the other is on the first step of some stairs. The front wheels are on grassy embankment. I tell the woman not to move, that the fire department is on the way.

A TV crew shows up and starts filming the scene with a portable shoulder camera that has very bright lights. They are filming the car on the embankment from the other side. I find myself in the camera's glare—standing around with my hands in my pockets. I move my position, only to find the cameraman has also shifted. I think I haven't been on my own a week and here I am hogging all the screen time. I move right, he moves right. I move left, he drifts left. I guess after years of looking he has finally found an EMT of movie-star quality.

Finally, the fire department arrives on scene. A firemen charges up the embankment, opens the car door, and looks in at the woman. The fireman turns and says angrily, "Why doesn't this woman have a cervical collar on?"

"The car's not stable," I say.

He looks down at the front wheel, then at the back wheels, which teeter on the steps. Oops.

"Let's get this car stabilized!" he shouts.

After we extricate the patient on a backboard, we load her into the ambulance, with the camera still on us. With thirty-five-millimeter dreams in my head, I debate climbing in the front with my partner and driving away to a perfect Tinsel Town ending. Instead I get in back to attend my patient. A person has to have his integrity.

❖

I haven't been on my own two weeks when I run into Vinny Cezus of Hartford Hospital. Vinny is a friendly registered nurse (RN) and paramedic, who is Debbie Haliscak's counterpart at Hartford. He helped teach the EMT-Intermediate course I took a few years before and he has served on some of the state committees I helped set up. "So what are you going to do next?" he asks me.

"Huh? I just became a paramedic. I think I'm going to do this for a while."

"You don't want to be a paramedic the rest of your life. You have to look to the future. Maybe go to PA school and become a physician's assistant."

"I'm going to just try to do this for right now. I want to be good at this."

"You don't want to get caught short. You should start planning."

"I just want to be good at this," I say. "Maybe I could be a PA later."

Partners

Your partner is the most important part of your job. A good partner will make going to work fun and he'll save your butt on more than one occasion. A bad partner is worse than sitting in a dentist's chair. Spending twelve hours a day with someone shift after shift is hard. You have to learn to deal with each other.

I was lucky to have a string of great partners when I first got involved in EMS back when I was working for Eastern Ambulance in 1989. Steve Cote, my Thursday partner, was an Amway salesman who mesmerized his patients with his concern and careful attention to their comfort. I saw many patients get so caught up with him they forgot they were in an ambulance en route to the emergency room. David Hanley was my Saturday partner—a nineteen-year-old kid going on forty who could lecture a drunken peer about the stupidness of drunk driving while plugging the gash on the head and deftly catching vomit in the emesis basin. Later, watching a nightclub scene on cable, he would ask innocently how people pay for their drinks in bars. He was a nursing student, and each week he would teach what he had learned in his most recent classes, whether it was about childbirth or geriatrics. My first day at Eastern I rode as a third with Kevin Andrews and Steve Czyprenea. Steve was an intermediate and an EMT instructor in his late forties—he worked sixty hours a week at Eastern and another forty hours a week at the Belchertown State School, in addition to teaching a regular EMT course. He'd been there almost ten years. Kevin was a quiet ex-cop and black-belt karate coach. He'd been there for four years and although still a basic EMT, was one of the most respected EMTs in the city. The two of them had a great time together, with Steve introducing themselves to nurses as "Bert and Ernie." In between calls they made the rounds of the Dairy Marts, refilling their coffee, buying lottery tickets, and joking with the clerks. When they had to respond, they were among the best in the business, both in medical and patient care. Kevin, who became my Monday-night partner when Steve Czyprenea went out with a back injury, was as tough and gentle a friend as you'd ever want. We'd stop in at his neighborhood community center to attend the C.R.A.C.K. watch meeting or at his mother's house, where some of his twenty or thirty siblings and cousins were always gathered, to pick up a sandwich or pass some talk. I never worried when I went on a call with him. He gave me confidence.

The unwritten rule of the street is you protect your partner at all costs. When it's the two of you out there, you have to watch each other's back and know it. Whether it's reminding you to do something you forgot—like put oxygen on the patient—or jumping on someone who just punched you or is about to punch you, you have to know your partner is there behind you. Every now and then you may be called on to reaffirm that trust, and you have to respond. When it comes to violence against your partner, it can range from pulling them away from it, to taking payback, to looking the other way when someone else does.

❖

Now on my own as a paramedic I have been working with a new partner every shift while I wait to be assigned a permanent partner. But whether you've worked with someone one hour or ten years, the same rules of protection must apply. We're called for a violent psych. Ahead there are two police cars, with a third approaching from up the street. On a grass embankment, five people are holding a man facedown. The patient is pinned, arms and legs outstretched.

"Goddamn, motherfucking, honky crackers, get the fuck off me, I'm going to kick your ass. Who are you telling me what I can do? Goddamn motherfuckers," the man says.

"You have a body bag?" a cop asks us.

I shake my head.

"You're going to need one."

"I ain't answering no more of your goddamn questions, honky motherfuckers. Get off me. I'm going to kick your ass."

We call dispatch and they send another ambulance to bring us a bag.

"Every one of your ambulances ought to carry a body bag," the cop says. "There are so many nuts in this city."

"Goddamn motherfuckers. Get off me. I ain't telling what I know. You're not getting answers from me. Honky crackers."

We bring the stretcher over. We can hear the other ambulance approach and see it now coming from downtown.

"Fuck'n goddamn, get off me. I ain't telling what I know. Honky motherfuckers."

The other ambulance parks. The EMT, a strong thin young man in his early twenties, brings the bag up to us. His partner is twenty-two, a pretty soft-spoken girl with black hair, a pink complexion, and still some baby fat in her face. She has a hint of an accent from a childhood in the South.

We put the bag on the stretcher. It is made of thick military green canvas. With the help of the cops, we lift the man and drop him face-down on the stretcher, and try to quickly wrap the bag around him. He fights and squirms. One cop grabs his arm and twists it. The EMT holds him by the hair, pressing his face into the stretcher. It takes all of us to get him subdued.

"Hide the video camera," one cop says.

"I'm going to kick all your asses, honky motherfuckers."

We pull the straps around the bag.

"Motherfucking po-lice brutality. Honky crackers. You're all in the KKK, motherfuckers."

The bag completely holds him, so just his sneakers are out the foot end and his head out the front.

The stretcher is still in the low position. We start to wheel him toward the ambulance. I am at the foot end. The young woman is by the head. He spits in her face. She screams. "You fucking bastard!" She kicks him hard in the ribs. "You fucking bastard!"

"Hey!" Her partner pulls her away.

"He spit on me. He spit in my face." Tears run from her eyes. She tries to kick him again, but her partner holds her off.

"Motherfuckers. Goddamn, leave me the fuck alone, honky crackers," the man shouts.

We lift him into the back and the girl's partner gets in with my partner. The hospital is just around the corner, so he rides with us while she follows in the other ambulance. I hear muffled shouting and thuds in the back. I turn up the music. I don't look in the rearview mirror.

"What Kind of House Do You Go Home To?"

My new permanent partner is Glenn Killion. He is a twenty-three-year-old who has been working in the city for almost two years. He is an EMT-Intermediate, so he can do IVs if I need him to, and he knows the streets well and likes to drive. He is a neat freak, and after every call, I find the ambulance restocked and immaculate. He likes country music and I do, too, so I don't mind if we listen to it all day, though I also love rock and soul. Glenn moved to Connecticut from Pennsylvania coal country, where he had also worked as an EMT. In Connecticut he worked for a while in computers, but didn't like the work and came back to EMS. He is a country boy at heart and doesn't like most of what he sees in the city. At night he frequents a bar called the Cadillac Ranch, where he dons a cowboy hat and takes pride in his country dancing ability.

❖

We get called for an unknown at the Laundromat on Albany Avenue.

"It's a drunk," Glenn says.

The crowd of thirty or so men in their forties make way for us.

"He's in there," a man holding a beer in a paper bag says. "He can barely walk."

"You should have just left him there, let him sleep it off," another man says.

"He done fell down twice. That ain't safe. He needs help."

"All he gonna get is trouble now."

We enter the Laundromat. It is a dim room with just a proprietor standing against a machine watching us. I look around and don't see anyone else. I turn back to the door and see a tall man pressed face first to the wall. I look at his feet and see a puddle forming from the urine flowing down the wall.

"What are you doing pissing in public?" Glenn says. "That's disgusting."

The man turns to face him. We are standing in the doorway.

"Put that away," Glenn says.

The man—who must be six six—has a coy smile on his face. He starts walking out the door, taking his steps real slow. "Take me ho-ome," he says.

"Button yourself up," Glenn says.

"We can't take you home," I say. "It's the hospital or ADRC." ADRC is the Alcohol and Drug Recovery Center, a state facility where we transport many of the drunks we pick up, provided there are still open beds and the person is not on their banned list for poor behavior in the past. Otherwise we take them to one of the hospitals, where they are restrained either in a wheelchair or on a bed until they sober up and can be released.

"Take me home so I can *sleeeep* it off," he says, reaching toward Glenn.

"Put that fucking thing back in your pants, and don't touch me," Glenn says, knocking his hand away.

"You just an ambulance driver. You take me where I say. I want to go home."

"You're going to go to jail if you don't cooperate."

"I don't care. Put me in jail. I can make bail."

"Zip your pants up," I say.

He fiddles with it and finally puts it away.

"Hey, Slim, you left your hat." The proprietor of the Laundromat comes out and hands him a dirty orange baseball hat, which he sets on his head and smiles. He has no front teeth, but big molars, which he grinds together, making a frightful eerie sound.

We lead him to the ambulance.

"You should have just let him sleep it off," a man standing by says to another man in the crowd.

"He done fell down twice. He going to hurt himself. You can't be left like that."

"Take me home, ambulance driver," our patient says to us.

We help him into the back, but instead of sitting on the bench where Glenn has laid a sheet, he falls over on the stretcher. Glenn picks him up and pushes him on the bench.

He smiles at Glenn. "I'll kick your ass."

"Don't make a fist at me," Glenn says.

"What's your name?" I ask.

"Punk," the man says to me.

"Punk," I say, "is that your name?"

He just smiles.

"If you want to go to ADRC, we've got to have your name to see if you're not on their banned list."

"I own a two-hundred-thousand-dollar house," he says. "Take me home so I can sleep it off."

"What's your name?" I say.

He tells me his name. He slurs it, so it takes a few more times asking to get it right. Glenn calls on the radio and we wait to hear if he's clear to go.

"Got a cigarette?" he asks.

"Not for you," Glenn says.

The man tries to lay his head down, but Glenn grabs him and sits him up.

"I'll kick your ass," the man says.

He tries to lie down, but Glenn grabs him by the shirt and sits him up again. "I'm tired of picking up you people."

"You people," the man says. "You people. You calling me nigger? Why, you just a punk ambulance driver."

"I'll sit with him," I say to Glenn.

"I'm fine," Glenn says. "You behave, or we're calling the cops."

"Call. I don't care. I make bail."

"We're calling to see if you can get into ADRC," I say, "so just chill out for a minute."

He smiles at Glenn, who is staring back at him.

The dispatcher tells us it is okay to take him to ADRC.

"I'll be fine," Glenn says to me again.

I go up front to drive.

❖

At ADRC, the security guard comes out and eyes our passenger as I open the back door. They don't like uncooperative or too-drunk patients. "He can't get out on his own, he ain't coming in," the guard says.

"What's for dinner tonight, nigger?" our patient says, sticking his head out and holding his hand out to me to help him down.

"Who you calling nigger?" the security guard says.

"You, nigger." He smiles at the guard.

"He can't walk on his own?" the guard asks.

"He can," I say, holding his arm.

"What's happening, nigger?"

"You gonna have to behave now you going to stay with us."

He just smiles.

"Let's go," Glenn says, grabbing his arm harder and moving him along.

Inside, we sit him in a chair.

In the waiting room, a young man looks at him, then at me, and shakes his head. An older man smiles.

"Hey, who's that spic over there?" our patient asks.

"You can't talk like that," the guard says.

"What's for dinner tonight, nigger? I want something hot."

"You can't eat till we get you checked in. You can't just come in and get something hot. You gotta get checked in. That's the policy."

"I gotta pee," he says.

"You can't pee here."

"I pee whenever I want."

"You better listen to him," Glenn says. "He was peeing right in the Laundromat when we got him."

"Let me help you then," the guard says.

He helps him up and walks him to the bathroom.

"I seen him around plenty," the younger man says to me. "Me, I'm trying to get help, trying to get in a treatment program."

"That's good," I say.

"I just look at myself and see myself headed downhill. Cocaine addiction."

"It's tough stuff."

"You pick him up on Albany Avenue? The Laundromat?"

I nod.

"He probably gets picked up forty, fifty times a year. Me, I'm looking for help."

"Hopefully, they'll be able to help you out."

Glenn is writing up the run report. A woman administrator asks where the patient is. Glenn says he's in the bathroom. She says she needs to look at him before they admit him. She asks us to wait before we leave.

They come out of the bathroom. "He peed right in the middle of the floor," the guard says, shaking his head.

Our patient just smiles and shuffles back to his seat. "What are you looking at, nigger?" he says to the younger man.

"Chill out," the younger man says.

"I kick your ass." The patient smiles and makes a fist.

"Don't be getting into it with me. I know you. We did time together in Morgan Street."

"I ain't been there for five years."

"You wearing jail pants."

He looks at his dark green pants and smiles. "Got a cigarette?"

"Can't smoke in here," the guard says.

"Can I give him one to hold on to for later?" the younger man asks.

"Long as he doesn't smoke it in here."

He gives him a cigarette.

The administrator, hearing that he peed on the floor, tells us to take him to Saint Francis.

"I don't get to eat," he says to the guard.

"You had your chance," Glenn says, putting on a pair of latex gloves. "Now you get me."

"Punk," the man says. "Loser. Ambulance driver." He smiles. "Take me home to my two-hundred-thousand-dollar house so I can sleep it off."

"Behave yourself now," the guard says.

"Take it easy," the younger man says to me.

"Good luck."

He nods.

We take our patient by the arm and lead him out to the ambulance.

I drive. Glenn is sitting on the stretcher. The man is on the bench. I see him take the cigarette out and put it in his mouth. He tries to light a match. Glenn grabs it from him.

"You're not smoking that thing in here."

"Let me know if you need help," I say.

"I'm fine."

The man laughs.

"Don't make a fist at me or you're going to regret it," Glenn says.

I continue through traffic.

There is a commotion in back. Glenn has grabbed the cigarette. The man lunges at him. They wrestle. I stop in the middle of traffic. I open the door to go around to the back to join the fracas.

"Keep going," Glenn shouts. "Call the company, tell them to get the cops at Saint Francis."

"You all right?"

He is on top of the man, holding him down. I can see a cut under Glenn's eye.

I call the company on the radio. We're three blocks from the hospital.

When I pull in to the emergency entrance there are four other EMTs awaiting us.

They open the back door, and a moment later the man is yanked out and thrown into a wheelchair. His orange hat falls to the ground. One EMT holds him by the hair when he tries to get up.

"Punk," the man says, still smiling. "Ambulance driver."

"You all right?" I ask Glenn.

In addition to the cut, he has a shiner growing under his eye. "Fine," he says.

A cop comes out to see what the commotion is about. We tell him the man assaulted Glenn.

"Arrest me, I make bail," the man says.

We take him into the psych room. He is still smiling while restraints are applied to his wrists and feet, and his clothes are cut off.

"Loser," he says to Glenn.

"Loser, you're the fucking one who's tied up," Glenn says.

"I got a two-hundred-thousand-dollar house. I can make bail."

Glenn tightens the restraint on his arm.

"What kind of house you going home to, ambulance driver?" He smiles. "What kind of house you going home to?"

A Smile

We are sent on a priority three for an abdominal pain on Capen Street. We ring the door of the apartment building, and a few moments later a little girl with cornrow hair opens the door for us, then runs up the stairs, pausing at the top to wait for us to get halfway before racing up the next set of stairs. She looks playfully at us.

At the top of the stairs, the girl goes into an open apartment door. The apartment is largely barren. There is a bed on the hard wooden floor. A

"Can you walk?" I ask.

She nods.

"The ambulance is just outside. I'll help you if you feel dizzy at all."

She walks out to the ambulance with us. As she gets in, I have her lie on the stretcher and put her on the heart monitor, then take her arm to give her an IV. I notice Glenn looking at me. He mouths the words, "Is she a man?"

I look at her more closely now. The thought hadn't even occurred to me. Her complexion is clear and smooth, but her features are large for a woman's, too large. Her arm is huge—the arm of a linebacker. I look back at Glenn and nod.

En route, I do my secondary survey, which is required on all patients—a full body assessment. As I listen to her lung sounds I am reminded of the paramedic student we had the day before, who told an attractive female patient he had to unbutton the top buttons of her blouse to listen to her lung sounds. I glance at the woman's breasts. They are well shaped and look hard as rocks. I skip down to palpate her abdomen, which is soft and nontender. I glance at her crotch, but cannot tell what may lie beneath. Again I skip down to her ankles to check distal pulses, which are fine. I buckle the stretcher strap, just beneath her breasts. I fight the urge to brush my hands against her breasts to ascertain their texture.

❖

In the hospital, as I am labeling the blood tubes in her room, the nurse comes in and closes the curtain behind her. "I've got a hospital gown. We're going to have to get you undressed."

I am facing the back wall, and suddenly I feel very uncomfortable. I see my patients naked every day. It's part of the job, and there is no embarrassment about it. But this is different. I don't want to turn around for fear of what I might see. I don't want to turn around because I don't want to be a pervert. And I don't want to turn around because I really want to see what her chest looks like and whether her boobs look as good naked as they do under her blouse. But as I am an ethical man, I avert my eyes as I exit the room.

Cowboy

Glenn likes to drive fast. He is sort of a modern-day cowboy type. When we have female riders, Glenn often turns up his country-music station and sings along to the rodeo songs as if they were written about his life. The ambulance is his horse and he likes to be known as the guy who can handle the fastest ones.

We get a call for a man having chest pain at a nursing home. His first words are "I'm having a heart attack." I am inclined to doubt anyone who tells me he is having a heart attack, but this man does not look well. He is pale, diaphoretic. He has only one leg due to diabetes. He says he had a heart attack two months ago. Today is his first day in the nursing home. I put him on oxygen by a nonrebreather mask and take his vitals. He is tachycardia with a pressure around 110—a little too low for a nitro tab. He has a normal sinus rhythm on the monitor. I get his medical form from the nurse and we move him to our stretcher and take him out to the ambulance. I get in the back and tell Glenn I'll do the line en route. We are on the Bloomfield/Hartford line and are going to Hartford Hospital on the far side of the city. "Take it on an easy two," I say.

The man's left arm is in a sling, so I have to lean over him to put a tourniquet on his right arm. He has a visible AC vein, so I swab it with alcohol and get out an eighteen gauge catheter. I try to time my stick with the bump and jerk of the ambulance. The man screams as I stick him. I have no flashback. I'm off to the side of the vein. I adjust my angle under the skin and press forward. The blood flows into the chamber. I advance the catheter, press off the vein with my finger as I remove the needle, and go to apply the vacutainer to the hub through which I will draw bloods.

Glenn takes a corner like Mario Andretti and I am thrown against the bench. Blood is flowing from the catheter out onto the man's arm and sheet. I quickly lunge forward, clamp off the vein again with pressure from my hand, and insert the vacutainer. My gloves are covered with blood, so I must change them. "Nice corner!" I shout to Glenn, but he can't hear me as he has his country-music station turned up.

I am drawing my third tube of blood, when the ambulance swerves sharp left, then back again right. Again I am thrown. The vacutainer comes loose.

"Slow down!" I shout, moving to stem the blood flow. I need to use a towel to clean things up. Everything I touch with my bloody gloves gets contaminated with blood. I change them again, and finally get the blood drawn and hook up the line of saline. As I go to tape it down I am thrown on top of the patient, who is screaming because I have knocked the monitor on his leg. I try to get up but the g-forces have me pinned. When I finally regain my balance, I see the catheter has nearly slid out of the skin so I have to readvance it delicately into place. Finally, it is secure. I am drenched in sweat. There is a huge blood spot on the man's sheet under his arm.

"Slow down and watch the turns!" I shout to Glenn.

He glances back. "You said an easy two; that's what I'm doing."

I shake my head. Goddamn cowboys.

❖

Occasionally I get testy with Glenn, and he gets frustrated with me just as often. Still he is a decent partner. I trust him. He is a smart kid. I can consult him if I am leaning one way or the other and need a push. And he keeps me calm, simply because I don't want to appear nervous in front of him.

We go to a call for a baby who has fallen down the stairs. "Settle down," he says to me as I fumble with the blue bag taking it out of the side door after we've pulled up.

"I'm calm," I say.

"Yeah, sure you are."

I take an extra breath and then enter the apartment where everyone is shouting and crying. I get the baby in my arms, see it is alert and breathing, and comfort it, as Glenn orders everyone in the room to quiet down and quit screaming.

He has been in the city a year and half and knows all the streets, so I don't have to worry about getting lost on the way to a chest pain or difficulty breathing. I can concentrate on what I'm going to do when I get there. I hate broken bones, so he does all the splinting of isolated fractures, concocting state-prize-winning contraptions that take a while to do, but win praise from the patients for comfort and from the physicians at the hospital for ingenuity. (I consider buying a Polaroid so we can put on a gallery display: "Splinting by Killion.") Every now and then, he teaches me a trick I didn't know.

❖

A man in his twenties is passed out on the steps of a bakery in Hartford's south end. As we approach he is not moving. The proprietor of the bakery, an old man, says, "I find him a few minutes ago and call the police. He don't look to me lika he's breathing." A woman with an apron around her waist stands by him with her hands tensed together.

Glenn and I kneel by the downed man. I feel a pulse and note his breathing. Glenn rubs his sternum, but he does not move.

"Is he dead?" another woman asks. A small crowd has gathered.

Glenn reaches into his pocket and takes out a small green package of ammonia inhalants. He breaks three together in his hand and places them under the man's nose.

The man squirms and moves his hands to push Glenn's hand away, but Glenn keeps it under the man's nose. The man turns and uses his hands to help himself to his feet. His eyes are bleary and I can now smell the alcohol on his breath.

"Are you okay?" I ask.

He mutters and starts staggering off down the street.

Our audience breaks into applause.

"Wow, howa abouta that?" the proprietor says to the woman in the apron. "Thank you. Thank you so much," he says to us.

"Anytime," Glenn says.

The women are smiling.

"That was impressive," I say.

"All in a day's work," he says.

We watch the man stagger down the street. He makes it to the end of the block and turns the corner. We clear ourselves from the call.

❖

Glenn's views and outlook are clearly different from mine, but the combination of the two of us seems to work.

The man is sitting in a chair in a gas station on Albany Avenue. He is in his late thirties. He's about six two with a strong frame. His eyes are bloodshot. He is wearing an army jacket and has a clear trash bag with a small amplifier in it along with some clothes. He is eating saltine crackers. "I called. I'm ready to come in from the elements for a few days."

Glenn puts his "drunk gloves" on. "Okay, buddy. Let's go," he says.

"Hey, man, no need to be throwing an attitude my way."

"You called, so let's go."

"Damn," the man says to me, as I help him with his bag.

"What have you been drinking?" Glenn says.

"Couple fifths. Smoked a few bags of dope. Did some cocaine. I ain't eaten for four days, except these crackers."

"Well, where'd you get the money to buy your drugs?"

"I sold things. I can always get stuff to sell."

"Then why didn't you buy food?"

"Damn, who are you? My mother?"

He wants to go to ADRC, but it's closed. He says to take him to Blue Hills, but we can only take him to one of the city hospitals. He chooses Saint Francis, where he is a regular. I drive. Glenn rides with him in back and fills out the run form.

At the hospital, I get a wheelchair for him and help him with his bag.

"Sit in the chair now," Glenn says.

"Why you giving me the good guy, bad guy routine?"

"Just sit in the chair."

Glenn goes to the triage desk, while I stand by the man who sits in the chair, still eating his crackers.

Glenn says, "Alcohol and drug abuser."

The man looks at me. "He don't have to say it like that. That's cold. Why doesn't he say intoxicated or the man looking for some counseling. Drug abuser—that sounds like I'm a man who'd jump off a bridge or some crap like that."

I nod.

"Hey, you dropped twenty dollars out of your pocket," he says to Glenn.

Glenn looks down at the ground.

"Hah, got you!" the man says.

Glenn looks at him and just shakes his head, then returns to talking to the nurse.

We exchange winks.

A security guard walks by. "What's happening, man?" he says to him.

"Hey, Kenny, how you doing?" the guard says.

"Hanging on, man. Yourself?"

"Getting by."

We take him back to Room 12.

All the way down the hall, he's nodding and saying hello to people.

"Kenny's back," a nurse says.

"He just wants a meal," Glenn tells her. "He says he hasn't eaten for four days."

"He was here last night."

"If I was, I don't remember," he says.

"Spends his money on drugs and liquor. He ought to spend it on food, I told him," Glenn says to her.

I get him set in his room.

"They'll get you something to eat in a little bit," I say.

He nods. He knows the routine.

Glenn comes in to drop off the run form. "I hope you get into Blue Hills," Glenn says.

"Okay, thanks, bad guy," the man says, offering his hand, which Glenn shakes.

"Thanks, good guy," he says to me.

"Good luck."

"You two take care of yourselves now," he says as we leave.

HIV

I learned a great deal from Weicker over the years, most of all the importance of being true to your view of yourself. Weicker was a hero because he believed that was his role, so he did heroic things that other men wouldn't have bothered with because they held no significance for them. I remember picking up a newspaper back in 1984 when I was living in Iowa and reading about Weicker's standing up for more funding for AIDS when most people didn't even know what it was. He would go on to become a leading advocate for AIDS research and treatment, and as governor, support a controversial free needle-exchange program to help prevent the spread of AIDS, none of which was particularly popular as the country turned conservative. He saw AIDS not in terms of politics but in terms of individual lives. He saw people without a voice, who needed a champion.

❖

We get a call to the Charter Oak projects for a woman not feeling well. She meets us at the door, with her jacket already on. She has huge blisters about her mouth.

"What'd you call us for?" I ask.

"I couldn't get a ride. I gotta go to Mount Sinai and see a doctor. I haven't been feeling well."

We open the back door and have her take a seat on the bench. I take a blood pressure and pulse and listen to her lungs, which are junky, then take her name and medical history while my partner drives to the hospital.

"I been getting night sweats and having diarrhea."

"Coughing up anything?" I ask.

"Yeah, brown and black stuff. I'm worried I got the HIV. My brother had it and he died. I've been good. I'm a one-man woman." She has purple welts on her throat and huge blisters on her mouth. Her eyes are sinking into her head. She has a fever.

"How long you been coughing stuff up?"

"Couple months. I've been getting the night sweats real bad this last week."

❖

We go to an apartment building on Oak Street, two blocks from the capitol. A thirty-seven-year-old woman with beautiful cornrowed hair is sitting on the bed, trying to get the energy to put on her shoes. There is a crucifix on the wall and an open Bible on her unmade bed. The police are there, helping her two grandchildren get on their snow jackets and gloves. The woman hasn't been feeling well for the last couple of days. She had pneumonia last month, but it really hasn't gone away. Her skin is hot, her lungs are full of fluid, with decreased sounds in the bases. She says she's been coughing up brown phlegm. We help her down to the ambulance.

I can't take a blood pressure in her right arm because she says she has plastic veins from being shot ten years ago. "Any other medical history?" I ask.

"HIV," she says quietly.

❖

In a bargain jewelry store on Park Street, a forty-seven-year-old man is sitting in a chair, unable to get up. "He did some heroin," the proprietor tells us. "He's got the HIV."

The man is hot. His arms are shaking. It hurts to touch him, he says. He is skinny with sunken eyes and blisters on his mouth. His lungs sound junky even without a stethoscope. He has a fever. His pupils are pinpoint. We help him up and walk him slowly to the ambulance.

"You've got your needle on you?" my partner asks him. "Give it to me now. I don't want to get stuck unexpectedly."

His hands shake as he moves them slowly, almost like a crane, to his pocket, where after half a minute of fumbling, he produces a small syringe, which we deposit in our sharps box.

His hand swings over to the other pocket. He fumbles some more and he removes a stainless-steel spoon with a small amount of burned residue in its bowl.

❖

Weicker used to tell the story of a woman who had come before his sub-committee. She had contracted AIDS from a blood transfusion, and one day after she swam in the town pool, her neighbors had the pool drained. She told his committee, "America is not a very good place if you're sick or different." Weicker would thunder, "It's my job to make America a great place if you are sick or different. Since when in this country does it matter how you got sick? All that should matter is that you are sick, and it is our job to help."

❖

We pick up a young man on Washington Street within sight of the Heath Department. He is shivering, and he has to lean on me to step up into the ambulance. At the hospital, the triage nurse looks to me for the story. "Twenty-seven-year-old male," I say. "Homeless. Not feeling well. Fever. Coughing up brown sputum. Tender abdomen. Diarrhea for a week."

"HIV?" she says.

I nod.

"Put him in the waiting room," she says.

Glenn wheels him into the crowded room. He tucks a thin blanket around him, touches him on the shoulder, and says good luck. Across the room, a woman in a heavy army jacket sits in another wheelchair, looking down, holding her arms together. She has sunken eyes and blisters on her mouth.

The TV plays "All My Children."

The Tube

We pull out onto Albany Avenue behind ambulance 902. It pulls to the side of the road. I grab the monitor and airway kit. Glenn takes the med box. I go in the side door. Glenn goes in the back.

They have a fifty-year-old-male in cardiac arrest. An EMT is doing compressions. A firefighter is doing ventilations with an ambu-bag.

The monitor shows the man is in an agonal rhythm almost flat line.

I get out the laryngoscope and an endotracheal tube. Glenn goes for the IV line.

I sweep the man's tongue to the side and look for the white chords. There is pink sputum in the airway obscuring my view. I am thinking that if I don't get this in, I will never do another call. If I put it in the esophagus, they will take away my medical control, and I am done. I have enjoyed being a paramedic, but this is it. It's over. I got the tube twice before, but I missed in my only attempt in the city, and Tom had to get it for me. This is my first chance on my own. I've got to get it. Got to prove I can do it. I see the chords, pass the tube.

"Something's coming up," the firefighter says. I see pink sputum coming up the tube. I panic, thinking I'm in the stomach. I pull the tube and try again. I can't see the chords, but I'm going to get this sucker. I've got to get it. Com'on. Now wait, there they are. I pass the tube again. I know I'm in.

"I've got the line," Glenn says. "You want epi and atropine."

"Yes," I say.

I attach the ambu-bag and listen for lung sounds. Positive in the right and left sides under the armpits. They are wet. He has edema in his lungs. That's what the stuff was the first time. Nothing in the epigastrium. I start taping the tube down to secure it.

"Let's head in," I say.

We arrive at the hospital moments later. They work the patient five minutes, then call it. It turns out he is in end-stage cardiomyopathy. His heart just gave out.

It is the first code I have done as a cut-loose paramedic. The first code Glenn and I have done together. Glenn shakes my hand. I pat him on the back.

"You got the tube," he says.

"You got the line," I say. "We got it done."

I know I should show more compassion for the departed, but I have a job to do and I need to do it well. That night, I just keep seeing the tube pass the chords. I got the tube. I got the tube. I got the tube. I think someday I'll get the tube and save the patient, too. Someday.

Front Page

Four-seven-two is called for a shooting at a bank on Homestead Avenue. We're in the area, so we ask our dispatcher if they want us to slide over that way.

"Absolutely not," the dispatcher says. "They've got a situation over there. I don't want any other cars in the area. Four-seven-two, be careful, guys."

Two minutes later, HPD dispatches us—451—as a second car for a heart problem at the scene.

We arrive a moment before 472. We're here first, so I want the shooting. There are ten police cars at the curb. As I get out, a woman comes from the crowd, leading another woman and says, "This woman is pregnant and a diabetic. She's not feeling well. Can you look at her?"

"Not right now," I say, grabbing the oxygen bag from the side door.

A man is sitting by the curb; a police officer is holding an oxygen mask to his face.

"He's having chest pain," the officer says.

"Where's the guy who's shot?" I ask.

"Nobody got shot."

"Okay." I sound a little disappointed. I look at the man sitting on the curb. He is wearing a windbreaker and a Boston Red Sox shirt. On the ground a few feet away from him is a stack of one-hundred-dollar bills bound together.

"How are you?" I ask.

"My chest hurts."

"Is he in custody?" I ask the cop. My eyes go back to the money.

"No, he was the hostage."

"Okay." I kneel by him and feel a pulse. His pain is in his chest on both sides. I learn he was Maced when the robbers dropped the money bag and it exploded. My eye catches another stack of one-hundred-dollar bills behind the man.

"They catch the bad guys?" I ask the cop.

"Yeah, it's all under control."

The man is breathing fine. He is not diaphoretic or pale.

Glenn and I help him onto our stretcher. As we are wheeling him to the ambulance, I notice he is holding his head. "Your head hurt?" I ask.

"Yeah, the guy whopped me with his gun."

"Were you knocked out?"

"Yeah for a little while."

"We're going to have to c-spine him," I tell Glenn.

"Wait till we get him inside. The cameras are on us now."

"You have any tingling in your hands or feet?" I ask.

The man says no.

We get him to the ambulance and lift him in.

Once inside, we roll him on his side and slip a longboard under him. I apply a cervical collar. Because he received a blow to the head, we have to guard against a possible injury to his cervical spine.

"We need him for an ID," a cop says, standing by the open door.

Before I can tell the man not to sit up, he is up. "That's him," he says, looking at the young man in handcuffs, who has a stack of bills protruding from his jacket pocket. "That's the dirty bastard who clubbed me."

"Thank you, sir," the cop says, leading the man away.

We get the man back down on the board and secure him with belts, head rolls, and tape. I get a blood pressure, put him on the heart monitor, and give him oxygen via a nasal cannula. His pressure is high, but his rhythm looks good. I suspect his pain is related more to getting Maced and excited than to a cardiac problem, but I go ahead and put in an IV and draw bloods. I need to treat for both potential heart and cervical injury.

"We need him for another ID," the cop says.

"He can't sit up," I say.

"What if we bring him around to the other window?"

"He can't turn his head."

"Screw it," the cop says.

The man says the pain in his chest is gone, but his head hurts much worse now.

Glenn is outside looking at the pregnant diabetic woman, who is fine.

"What a day," the guy says. "You have my jacket? Is my check still in there?"

I find the check.

"I didn't even get to cash my check," he says.

❖

I talk to my friend Michelle that night. "I got sent to a shooting, but it turned out to be nothing again. Just a guy whopped on the head having some chest pain from the Mace." I tell her the story.

"You'll get your share of shootings, believe me." She worked in the city for five years before shipping out to the suburbs.

"It's just that I want to have done a good one so I won't be frightened at the prospect of the unknown."

"You'll get one."

❖

That night on the eleven o'clock news, I watch the story about the holdup and see the police putting the two suspects in squad cars. I see the shot of Glenn and me wheeling the man on the stretcher and lifting him into the ambulance. I see the shots of the stacks of money lying scattered on the ground. I pat my pocket. Empty.

In the morning I pick up the paper. There we are in color on the front page, wheeling the guy to the ambulance while he holds his head. In the photo spread they identify the arresting officers, the bank robbers, and the victim by name. They don't use our names, just list us as ambulance personnel. While I am sort of thrilled to be on the front page, all I can think of is the photo being shown to every EMT class in the state that day, with the teacher asking what's wrong with this picture? The article says nothing about the man's chest pain, only that he got whopped on the head and knocked out. And there we are wheeling him along without having his spine immobilized. I think, why couldn't they have a photo of us wheeling him to the ER, c-spined, IV in place, bloods drawn.

I wait for someone to say something about his c-spine, but no one does. Michelle says I am overreacting. It's just that I want to be respected and thought of as a good paramedic.

Circles

It is a beautiful day, temperature around seventy-two, the sky clear blue. We're playing basketball in Sigourney Park, up ten to two against another crew—Darren Barsalou and Matt Rynaski. My height has led to our dominance, as I have swatted balls left and right and easily tossed rebounds back through the iron rim. Then just as Darren drives by me, faking me out of my size thirteen boots, and Matt taps the rebound in for a basket, the radio calls their number—a transfer from Saint Francis going back to a nursing home in South Windsor. They shake their heads and start away slowly.

"We'll get you next time," Darren says.

"Have fun, boys," Glenn says.

I am wearing the HPD radio on my belt. Just then I hear it crackle, and in a dramatic gesture, bring it up to my ear. I feel a call coming. "Hartford EMS to . . ." the radio crackles.

"Four-five-one," I say hopefully.

"Four-five-one. Respond on a one to a shooting on Main."

Glenn and I shout, and we break into a run for the ambulance.

"Four-five-one responding," I say.

We pass our disgusted opponents. "See ya, boys," Glenn says.

I strap in tightly. We race east, swinging the corner hard onto Main Street heading north. Ahead we see five or six squad cars. When we arrive we see several cops on different corners all looking about. We can't see any patient.

"Four-five-one's out and looking," Glenn says into the radio.

A cop says he thinks the guy might have left in a private car.

I ask a tall girl sitting on a rock in an abandoned lot what happened. "They stabbed him and took off. Then he got in a car and his friends drove him to the hospital."

The cops aren't having any luck finding anyone, so we get back in the ambulance and clear ourselves on the radio.

"Four-five-one, you take the motor-vehicle accident at Wooster and Pavilion, you're right on it."

We look quickly at the map. Glenn hits on the lights. We lurch forward. We take our first right. Wooster is the next right. We come around the corner and see Pavilion is the next right. Before we know it, we are right back where we were.

The cops and the girl on the rock are all looking at us.

"Did you see a car accident?" I ask.

The girl shakes her head.

"Somebody get hit by a car?" a cop asks.

"No, they stabbed him," the girl says. "He's probably already at the hospital by now."

"Busy neighborhood," the cop says.

Intercept

Most of the suburban and rural communities outside Hartford have their own volunteer ambulance services who respond to all 911 calls within the town's borders. If the volunteers decide the patient needs a paramedic, they can either call the Life-Star helicopter, which they do in cases of severe trauma, or call for a paramedic intercept. They package the patient and start toward Hartford, while the paramedic unit starts out toward them. They communicate via the C-Med radio and agree on an intercept point, where they both pull over. The paramedic jumps out with his equipment, gets on board their ambulance, and they continue toward the hospital.

Simsbury Ambulance calls for an intercept for a man having chest pain. We meet on Route 185 on top of Talcott Mountain. I get in the back. The man is pale, diaphoretic, having pain at the level of four on a one-to-ten scale, with ten being the worst pain he has ever felt. The oxygen has made him feel better. His pressure is okay and he has a normal sinus rhythm on the monitor. My plan is to give him some baby aspirin, which will thin his blood and help prevent further formation of any clots in his heart that can keep oxygen from the heart muscle, put in a line of saline, and start giving nitro to see if that takes the pain away. The nitro will dilate his vessels, again opening up more oxygen to the heart, decreasing the heart's workload. The problem is, he is allergic to baby aspirin, and I can't give him the nitro until I get the line and I can't get the line. My first shot blows. He has flabby arms and nothing is visible. I try again for one in the hand but get nothing. I sit back and wipe the sweat from my brow. If I give him nitro without a line in place, his blood pressure could bottom out, and I'd have no way to pump it back up with fluids. I look at the Simsbury EMT and shrug. Sorry. We continue on to the hospital. So much for the paramedic saving the day. I feel like a complete waste.

Wrestlemania

It's Sunday morning. I've switched shifts with Scott Hanson—his Sunday for my Wednesday so he can go to South Carolina. I'm working with Sean Brown. It's quiet. We've just done one call—a seizure at a nursing home. We're covering the downtown area, parked in a lot just off the street where they hold the farmers' markets during the week.

I'm reading the sports section. Wrestlemania is in town. I have already told Sean about all my favorite wrestlers of past and present—George "The Animal" Steele, Professor Toro Tanaka from Hiroshima, Japan, and King Kong Bundy, who once committed the ultimate act of villainy by body slamming a midget in Wrestlemania IV at the Pontiac Silver Dome before eighty thousand screaming fans and a worldwide Pay-Per-View audience.

I am telling Sean about the time I saw El Olympico, a masked wrestler and the master of the flying dropkick, get knocked unconscious and carried from the ring on a stretcher. When I left the arena, I saw a man in a business suit carrying a briefcase exit from a side door and get into a Cadillac. It was El Olympico—still wearing his mask.

"Four-seven-two. Respond to the Civic Center. Man fell off the scaffolding on a one."

"This could be a good one," Sean says.

Within two minutes we are driving down the service entrance of the Civic Center. An automatic door opens for us, and we are waved through. We park, grab the stretcher, backboard, collar, and oxygen bag. We wheel the stretcher into the arena, where work is proceeding at a feverish pace for the night's big event. A lighting trestle has fallen into the ring. One half is attached to a structure twenty feet up, the other half lies like a grounded seesaw in the ring, where several people hover over a downed man. I toss my oxygen bag into the ring and crawl in under the bottom rope. The floor is firm but soft and springy almost like a trampoline. I imagine flying off the top rope to flatten a helpless opponent before a capacity crowd. I kneel by the man, who is alert but in obvious pain. "What happened?" I ask.

A bystander tells me the trestle broke and he rode it down to the ring, landing hard with his legs around the beam. He did not strike his head.

"What hurts?" I ask

"My pelvic area."

I press against his hips. "Does this hurt?"

I press against his abdomen. "Does this hurt?"

"No, no, man, it's my pelvic area."

I inspect. He is in great pain for understandable reasons, falling twenty feet with legs straddled around a metal trestle and coming to a fairly sudden stop despite the soft, springy surface. His pulse is good, and I see no signs of hemorrhage.

We put him on a backboard and carry him to the side of the ring. I hand my end of the backboard to a stagehand, then bound spryly out of the ring. They pass the boarded patient to me through the ropes, and I get him set on the stretcher. En route to the hospital, I bang in an IV line with a sixteen gauge needle in the massive vein on his left forearm and attach a bag of saline, ready to run if his pressure, which is good right now, starts to crash. He is crying, "Oh, Lord."

At the hospital, they triage us to the trauma room, given the mechanism of injury. The patient has also begun complaining of tingling in his right thigh. I hear one of the doctors giving a report over the phone to another doctor. "He has right thigh pain," she says.

"Excuse me," I say. "His main complaint is pain in the pelvic region."

She looks at me blankly.

"His balls are killing him," I say.

"Testicular pain," she says.

"Right."

She speaks back into the phone. "He has great testicular pain," she says.

❖

I walk into the EMT room to do my paperwork. I see Sean and say, "Yes, we were there! In the ring at Wrestlemania!"

❖

It's Tuesday. Glenn and I are sitting outside Saint Francis. "Did I tell you I was in the ring at Wrestlemania on Sunday?"

"Several times," he says.

"The place was packed," I say. "Thirty thousand screaming fans. I leap spryly into the ring. Over the top rope, of course. The popular champion is lying there holding his nuts. What do I—the ambulance driver from hell—do?"

"You climb the corner post."

"I climb the corner post. I leap into the air and slam down on him. The place goes wild! I lift him up and, wrapping my arms and legs around him, pound him into the ground with the pile driver. The crowd is appalled at the villainy. I bounce off the ropes and catch him in the face with the flying dropkick. I lift him up, twirl him around, and body slam him. Then it's one, two, three pin! And the World Wrestling Federation has a new world champion! I lift the golden championship belt high to the boos of the multitudes."

"You could lose your cert for that."

"But I'd be somebody. I'd be famous."

Glenn grabs a portable radio. "I'm going to take a leak," he says.

"The villainy, the villainy," I say, hearing the beautiful boos of the Pay-Per-View audience as far away as Jakarta and Bora Bora.

A Little Touchy

We're parked in front of Saint Francis when the Hartford dispatcher gives a call for an unresponsive person on Vine Street to a basic unit.

"This is getting ridiculous," Glenn says.

The dispatching system is screwed up. Paramedic units are sent to cold and flu calls and the basic units that lack advanced life support equipment and training get the difficulty breathing and unresponsive calls. We're getting nothing good. Where's the glory? I ask. All I'm getting is BS.

"Four-five-one." We're called on the company radio. I am sure the company will reassign us the call.

"Four-five-one. We have a transfer coming out of Saint Francis. Bring your monitor and oxygen, going to the Cancer Center."

We look at each other and shake our heads. It is our third transfer of the day. The only 911 call we've done has been for a drunk.

Upstairs in the intensive care unit (ICU), the nurse, a young heavyset girl with thick glasses, says, "We'd about given up on you."

We say nothing.

"I just need to give the patient her medication. I'm sure you won't mind waiting."

The patient is a sixty-seven-year-old woman with brain cancer. She has a feeding tube in her nose. We hook her up to our oxygen and heart monitor. As we go to transfer her by rolling up her sheets and lifting her across onto our stretcher, I see that she has diarrhea in her bed. I don't say anything.

As we walk down the hall, the nurse walks ahead of us carrying the patient's chart; I notice a streak of shit on the back of her white sweatpants at calf level.

The new Cancer Center is just across the street. When the new addition to the hospital is finished an ambulance won't be necessary. They will be able to wheel patients over by the skywalk. But for now we have to transport them and wait with the patients while they get their radiation, then transport them back.

Outside, we lift her into the back of the ambulance. The nurse climbs in, then I get in. The nurse says to me, "It's so close, yesterday I asked the ambulance driver if I could drive."

"Do me a favor," I say. "Don't call us ambulance drivers. It's like calling you a bedpan changer. I'm sure you understand."

She looks very taken aback. "Oh, what should I call you?" she says.

"Paramedic would be good." I am tempted to tell her how well trained we are. How I run codes by myself, perform intubation, needle decompression, intraosseous lines, cricothyrotomy, and can administer over thirty emergency drugs, but I don't.

❖

When we bring the patient back to her bed, I go to disconnect her from our monitor by pulling off the three wires from the electrodes on her chest. I pull off the red wire and the black wire. My hand is on the white wire and I am about to tug, when I realize I am holding the thin white feeding tube that is running into the woman's nose. I let go gently and pull off the proper wire.

Close to being an asshole.

The Park

It's lunchtime. We get together with another crew at Bushnell Park and throw a Frisbee. State workers buy hot dogs and taco salads from the lunch trucks lined up along the street and sit on the park benches or walk to the downtown for some quick shopping or a meal at one of the lunchtime restaurants.

I see a woman I knew from the health department and she does a double take on seeing me. "I thought you went to Washington," she says.

"No, I quit when the administrations changed. I'm a paramedic now. I work three days a week, twelve-hour shifts. I like it. I have the rest of the week to myself to read, write, and take it easy." I am tempted to say, "You mean you didn't see me on the front page of the *Hartford Courant?* Above the fold? In color?"

"You look tired," she says.

"I get plenty of rest on the weekends."

"Well, if that's what you like doing."

"I do like it. Every day's different."

She pauses, and I sense she feels an awkwardness toward me. We chat a little bit more about nothing in particular, then she says, "Well, nice seeing you."

"Good seeing you, too."

I watch her walk off through the park. I don't think I convinced her how much I really do like what I do. I'm not stuck in that drab building with the stale air and dirty carpets and mountains of unfiled paper. Still, her reaction depresses me.

Now in the park I wonder how others on their lunch hour see us — four EMTs in boots and uniforms with radios on their belts. We are somewhat of a motley crew. Alex is barely five feet tall and stocky as a fireplug. He works seven days a week for two different ambulance companies. Ray is a young man with a wild past, who through EMS has gotten his life back together. Glenn is just a country boy come to the city looking for work. He wants to be a cop. For now, he's an EMT by day and a bartender/bouncer by night. I'm six foot seven or eight depending on my mood, my hair's a little shaggy, and I have trouble keeping my shirt tucked in because my long-tailed shirts are still on order.

Of the four of us, only Glenn throws a Frisbee well.

EMT SPORTS
PAGES

❖   ❖   ❖   ❖   ❖   ❖   ❖   ❖   ❖

Trauma

Many people in EMS are trauma junkies. All the medicals, transfers, and drunks are just fillers, as they wait for the big bad one—the shooting or the head-on crash at eighty miles per hour. The call where, heart pounding, you race the clock to get the patient, lights and sirens wailing, to the trauma room, and, surrounded by gowned doctors and surgeons, give your report as they descend on the patient. It is the call that leaves you exhausted and your ambulance a mess, but afterward, sweaty and bloody, you shake hands with your partner or crew and say good job. It's the call you'll talk about for days, and other people will ask you about when they hear you were on it. You'll see yourself on the news and read about it in the paper. Even though trauma—particularly broken bones—gives me the creeps, I'd rather be telling the story than hearing it from someone else.

❖

We're at Hartford Hospital when the call comes in. "Eight-forty, respond to Charlotte Street on a one for a shooting."

We sit up straight, haul our shoulder belts on. Charlotte is all the way across town in the deep north end. Glenn hits on the lights and sirens and we lurch forward.

"Eight-forty, an update for you—shooting to the chest."

We have a rider with us, a young female paramedic student from New Hampshire named Vicki. "This is the big one," Glenn calls back to her. She is buckled into the captain's chair. All day long we have been doing drunks and homeless people—giving her a view of city life but nothing medically challenging.

I put on a pair of large latex gloves.

Glenn speeds across town.

"Let's get him on a board and in the back of the ambulance as soon as we can," I say.

Another ambulance has cleared Mount Sinai and is sent to assist us. As we hit Charlotte Street, they swing in right behind us.

The police department is on scene. A cop stands on the sidewalk and directs us to the curb.

I grab the green bag, which has the oxygen, airway, and bandaging supplies.

The cop directs us to the backyard, where another cop points me toward the back door. Glass is on the porch. The window of the door has been shattered. I enter the house and go through the kitchen, through the living room, and into another room, where a forty-one-year-old man lies on his back. His eyes are open and he is breathing. His color is poor and he is sweating. I set my bag down and kneel over him. He has a rapid radial pulse. I pull up his shirt and see a round bullet hole, smaller than a quarter but bigger than a nickel. There is no air sucking out of the wound.

Jeff Quinn, another paramedic, hands me a stethoscope. I listen to lung sounds, which are clear.

"Let's cut his shirt off," Jeff says.

I slice the front of his shirt open with a seat-belt cutter, a small plastic device with a razor blade in a slit. Jeff cuts his right sleeve and Vicki the left sleeve.

"Let's get him on a board and get him out of here," I say.

Glenn hands me the board as we roll the patient on his side.

"Exit wound under the scapula," Jeff says. Glenn drops a trauma dressing under it as we set him back on the board. Vicki puts an oxygen mask on him. Glenn hands me the oxygen tank, which I put between his legs. Jeff's partner, Chris Bates, and I strap him to the board. Vicki tries to take a blood pressure, but Jeff says, "Later."

Chris and I lift him on the board and backtrack out of the house.

Glenn has the stretcher set up in the backyard. We lay the patient down and wheel him around to the ambulance. Glenn and Jeff are in the back setting up IV bags. We lift the patient into the back.

"Drive," I say to Glenn. "Drive!"

Vicki holds his head stable. Jeff puts an IV dressing over the bullet wound. He takes a blood pressure of 140. I am going for an IV line. We are hurtling down the street. Glenn patches to Saint Francis, telling them we are four minutes out with a shooting victim. Chris is following us in the other ambulance.

The man has no veins visible or palpable in his AC joint. I take an eighteen gauge needle and go in blind. Nothing. I try again. I fish around. Nothing. Jeff is trying for an IV in the other arm. He's not getting anything either.

The man's lung sounds are decreased now on the right side. His chest cavity is filling with blood. He is still with us. He is sinus tachycardia on the monitor at 120. His respiratory rate is 26.

We're at Saint Francis now. The back door opens and another crew pulls the stretcher out. A doctor gowned in green is standing by. With Chris, Glenn, Jeff, and Vicki, they race the stretcher through the ER doors, down the hallway, and into the trauma room, where eight or nine nurses, doctors, and assistants, all in green and wearing paper masks over their noses and mouths, wait. The board is lifted from our stretcher onto the bed. Jeff, who is only twenty-one, known as "Doogie" after Doogie Howser, the boy MD of TV fame, rifles out a crisp verbal report when I hesitate.

The trauma team descends on the patient.

Standing back against the wall is Dr. Morgan, the head of trauma at Saint Francis Hospital. As a member of the health department I sat in his office and he in mine to discuss regulations to implement a statewide trauma network. But here and now I am just a paramedic and he is a legend to paramedics in the street. A former gang member, who was once knifed and another time jailed, he has risen to become one of the top trauma surgeons in his field. He is an extraordinary man whose approval I desire. The paramedics who work the city's streets love the man because he takes time to educate us. He treats us like professionals and demands our best. He drills it into us—trauma patients need a surgeon. Get to a scene, get the patient on a spinal board, intubate if indicated, get a line en route if you can, get to a trauma center, and get there fast.

He watches the team work. The man's pressure is down to 90. "Let's go, people," he says. "You're moving in slow motion."

They start two central lines, do a chest tube to drain blood from the chest cavity, then rush the patient off to surgery.

"You drove like the wind," I say to Glenn.

"Way to be quick on the scene," Chris says to me.

"You guys were great," I say.

We call dispatch for our times. Response: four minutes. On scene: seven. Transport: five. Total call: sixteen minutes.

We slap high fives.

Skip

Those who have been in EMS the longest are the ones who no longer wish for trauma. I remember once returning from a fatal accident in East Windsor with Skip Woodward, a man not yet fifty who'd been responding to calls in that town for over twenty years and had the small-town volunteer's burden of knowing many of the victims. A truck driver had fallen asleep at the wheel and drifted across Route 5 on a curve, slamming into a car driven by a young girl headed home from a night out. It was pouring rain. Half her body lay out of the car, her leg trapped by the crumbled steel. She'd been killed instantly, but still we worked her, pumping on her chest as the rain hurtled down and her lifeless eyes bulged almost out of their sockets, and the fire department worked to free her with the jaws of life.

Driving back, still pitch-black out but the rain lighter, Skip said, "I don't care for it (trauma)." A few weeks later, I was on I-91, headed home. I had my portable radio on when I heard Skip clear from an accident scene at the intersection of Routes 5 and 140, where one patient had been declared dead and another helicoptered out in critical condition. I swung by the ambulance bay and saw him. He looked whipped. He said nothing to me. He just shook his head. He looked old.

Do Not Resuscitate

We're sent for a person not breathing in West Hartford. The police are on scene doing CPR. The woman is cold. She is flat line on the monitor. Her arms are still limber, but her neck is too rigid to intubate. Her husband returned home to find her on the floor. The last time he saw her alive was four hours ago. He is distraught. Meg Domina, who is on scene with me, makes the decision to keep working the code. Cardiopulmonary resuscitation had already been initiated, and it seems like the right thing to do for the husband's sake—to give him the feeling that everything possible is being done.

When we arrive at the hospital, the doctor looks at the patient and calls her dead right on the stretcher. The next day Meg brings in another code to the same hospital. "At least you brought us a warm one this time," a nurse cracks. Meg has too much class to tell him to get bent.

❖

The job of EMS personnel is to respond and to save lives. There are three rules for not initiating lifesaving care for a person without pulse and breath. Death may be presumed in the following instances: advanced decomposition; injury incompatible with life, meaning decapitation, body transection (cut in half), or body consumed by fire; and rigor mortis with dependent lividity, which means the body must be stiff with a purple hue where it is touching the ground from blood pooling in the skin. Any other person found not breathing and without a pulse must be subjected to resuscitation efforts. While there is a good reason for this—evidence the occasional news stories about people waking up on the coroner's table—the decision to work or not to work a cardiac arrest is one of the toughest situations an EMT can face, particularly when the patient's death was expected and the family either panicked or didn't know better and called 911, initiating an EMS response.

I have had other EMTs tell me about arriving at the scene of a departed cancer patient and finding themselves in the midst of a family fight. Half the family is yelling at them to stop resuscitation efforts, while the other half is yelling to continue. They have no choice in those situations but to work the call. A worse case is when the entire family is demanding that you cease efforts. It is not as simple as just yielding to their wishes. Who is to say that maybe the patient wasn't about to rewrite his will, leaving everything to his youngest daughter, who has gone to the grocery store, prompting the rest of the family to apply a pillow over the dying man's face? An option an EMT has is to call their medical control, detail the situation, and get orders to cease their efforts, but not all doctors will take responsibility for terminating efforts based on a phone call, particularly if the EMT is not well known to them.

The state of Connecticut has instituted a program where patients with terminal illness can wear an orange Do Not Resuscitate (DNR) bracelet, which must be signed by their physician and is valid for six months. If an EMS responder finds a person wearing a valid bracelet, they can withhold efforts. The program has not yet met with widespread acceptance and there has been some foolish controversy as to whether the bracelets are demeaning to the patients. I encountered a young man—a terminal leukemia patient—who wore a bracelet. His family, who had last talked to him at eleven-thirty the night before, found him in the morning no longer breathing. They called 911. When I got there he had rigor mortis in his neck, but the rest of his body was warm, even sweating due to the heat in the house. While the family wailed around me, urging me to do something, I put him on my heart monitor, confirmed a flat line in all three leads, then called the hospital, reported my findings to a physician, and asked for permission not to work the code, which was granted. "He is dead," I told them. "Departed." If he had had any activity at all on the monitor, I know the weeping family would have fought me to the death had I done nothing. As long as people call 911 when their loved ones breathe their last breath, there will be tough choices.

❖

Back in 1992 when I was working my weekly Thursday night 6:00 P.M. to 6:00 A.M. shift in East Windsor, I spent the night sleeping on the couch at the ambulance bay. I was tired because we'd gone out at three-thirty for an old woman vomiting. I was awakened at seven-thirty by the tones going off. This was one of the days East Windsor did not have a scheduled crew and relied on a commercial service two towns away if it could not raise a crew with the "all call." While my shift had ended, since I was at the bay I felt I had no choice but to respond.

The call was to view a body and presume it dead. I was told not to go lights and sirens. En route I picked up Colleen Woodward, a nineteen-year-old EMT and the daughter of Skip Woodward. The address was an old farmhouse on the outskirts of town. Two police cars were there. We walked in and found the officers talking with an old woman. She was saying, "He went so peacefully. He called me at four o'clock this morning and said, 'Flo, bring me a cool glass of water.' I brought it to him, then he said, 'Take me off this contraption.' The sound of the oxygen machine and the tubing in his nose bothered him. He took a drink of the water, then laid the glass down and said, 'Now I can rest.' When I found him this morning, he was gone."

I nodded respectfully. The police officer pointed to a room off the living room. "In there," he said.

We went in. A bony old man lay on his back, with covers up to his chest. His mouth was open, his skin an opaque white. He was not breathing. He was as still as stone. It was clear his spirit had left him.

In the other room, I could hear his wife saying, "He lived a good life. This last week in the hospital was hard on him. They resuscitated him once. He was in such pain. At least he made it home to die."

I felt the carotid artery in his neck for a pulse. For a moment I thought I felt one, but knew it was just the throbbing from my own fingers. "He's got a pulse," I said to Colleen.

She hit me. "He does not," she whispered.

His skin was cool but not cold. I felt his fingers. They were stiff, but I'd seen hands with arthritis that were stiffer. His arm was on the way there, but it wasn't completely "rigored." You turn over some rigid bodies and they pop you with stiff left hooks that you're not expecting.

I listened with my stethoscope. Nothing. I checked for lividity. There was none yet. I looked at Colleen. She knew what I was thinking. Our gear was out in the ambulance. If we went and came charging back in, threw him on the stretcher, started IV lines, and performed CPR on his frail old chest, we would have a major situation. The woman would be traumatized. The man would still be dead, but he would have his ribs broken. We'd have to call paramedics, who would stick a tube down his throat and pump him full of drugs. The family would get a bill for several hundred dollars. The cops would hate us for the rest of our lives in town. We personally would feel like shit.

"Go get some ice packs," I whispered.

She hit me again.

One of the cops, a new member of the force, came back. He was a good guy to have on calls because he knew his medicine and wasn't afraid to get his hands dirty. He nudged Colleen. "Boo," he whispered suddenly.

She hit him.

He knew just what was up. We all looked at each other.

"He's dead," I said. "He is dead."

They nodded as if we were in conspiracy. Together we walked back to the living room and nodded to the other officer and the woman.

The family doctor had been called. While EMTs can presume death, only a physician can pronounce it. He was expected in half an hour. I was already late for my day job, but I decided to stay around until he came. Although I knew the man was dead, I did not want to spend the day at work imagining the physician arriving, going into the room as the woman again told her story about how peacefully her husband had died, and pressing his stethoscope to the man's heart only to hear a beat. "My God! He's still alive," the man would declare in a voice the whole county could hear. I imagined the dead man rising and doing a jig on the wooden floor, then whirling his stunned wife around with a little do-si-do.

The officer coughed. I saw Colleen jump and look toward the bedroom. The cop smiled at her. She glared.

The man was dead, but we were going to wait until it was official. The older cop left, the younger one stayed with us.

The woman told us stories and showed us pictures of all the fifty-nine foster children they had raised on their farm, how healthy and strong her husband had been up until the last few years when he'd become an invalid, and how it pained her to see him confined to his bed. "He had a good life," she said.

"It sounds like the two of you had good lives," I said.

"We did," she said, "we did."

The doctor was late, but I didn't mind. More time for the body to get cold.

Nursing Homes

I hate going to nursing homes. The places depress me. There is the procession of bodies in wheelchairs lining the corridors as you pass. Some are happily simpleminded. Others have in their eyes the horror of souls trapped in bodies, living in hell on earth. Always there are a few with their walkers, moving an inch a minute. We need to maneuver around them or else help them to the side. I try not to breathe in the smell of age and death, the combination of feces and baby powder that wafts in the air.

Our company has contracts with most of the nursing homes in the area. If they need an ambulance for a routine transfer to a hospital, a basic ambulance is sent. If the call is for a heart or breathing problem or other serious medical emergency, a paramedic unit responds. Most of the emergency calls are for sepsis, stroke, or difficulty breathing. The bottom line on most of them is that the person is old and his systems are slowly failing and he is going to die soon no matter what you do.

❖

We get called for an allergic reaction and find a man unresponsive with a rash on his face and legs. Yesterday the nursing-home staff thought he had pneumonia, so they put him on IV antibiotics, which they have just discontinued. But I am not worried about the rash. The man is septic with a temperature of 103. He has recently spit up blood, and I hear the distinct gurgling sound of aspiration in his upper lungs. They have a tiny twenty-two needle in his wrist and have him on oxygen by cannula at two liters per minute. There are multiple Band-Aids on his arms from where they have tried to stick him. At least they have tried to care for him. Often, we are called for unresponsive patients and have to hunt through the halls trying to find a nurse who can give us any information. Some of them say just to have the hospital call them directly, or they seal up the medical papers and get pissy when we open them up. Excuse me, they say, that's confidential. I say, this is now my patient, and I not only need to know this, but I am responsible for the patient, who is going to die unless we get him some fluids, oxygen, and medications, and get him to the hospital as close to five hours ago as possible, the time when it appears his condition first became acute.

I put the man on an oxygen nonrebreather at fifteen liters per minute, and en route to the hospital, I put a large bore needle in an arm vein, run some fluid, and give fifty milligrams of Benadryl, which clears up the rash. I suction blood from his airway.

❖

We get called to a nursing home for a person with no blood pressure. Fortunately, instead of just saying Room 206 and pointing us down the hall, the nurse accompanies us to the room and says the patient is the one in the bed by the door. As I go around to the side of the bed to evaluate the patient and help lift him across to our stretcher, I notice the old man on the other bed is awfully gray and still. Our patient looks crappier as he struggles to get his breath. I get a pressure of 70, a pulse of 112. His lungs are full of fluid.

"What a morning this has been," the nurse says to me. "He can't breathe, and this one over here died a half an hour ago."

I look over at the other man. He is a corpse.

❖

The woman is in third-degree heart block, but for the most part she is asymptomatic. Her pulse is just thirty-four. The nurses can't tell me much about her other than that she is bedridden and her normal state is one of confusion. They don't think she's had any heart problems in the past. I need to get an IV so I can give her atropine if her pressure starts to plummet. Glenn tries for a line in her right arm, while I put her on oxygen. She fights the cannula, but I whisper gently that she needs it, and it will be good for her. She relents. Glenn gets the line, but it blows when he tries to draw bloods from it. I put a tourniquet on her left arm and go quickly for a thin hand vein. I get a flash that tells me I'm in, but she jerks her hand and the catheter flies out. "Jesus Christ!" I say angrily.

"I know what you're doing," she says. "You're bad men."

I hold a cotton two by four on her hand, which by now has a golf-ball-sized hematoma on it. I am angry at losing the line and a little frustrated at myself for yelling. "I'm sorry, ma'am," I say. "I didn't mean to yell." I should have prepared her for the stick, but for a moment, I'd stopped thinking about her as a person, just as an old object I had to deal with.

Glenn drives, and I manage to get a line en route. At the hospital, when we transfer her to the bed, she reaches for my throat and tries to strangle me. I ease her hands away. When the nurse comes in, I tell her that even though she doesn't look it, she can be combative. The nurse looks at me sternly. I think it shows in my face that I yelled at the poor woman.

❖

Sometimes when I'm transporting an elderly male, I look down at him on the stretcher and imagine myself there in another forty years looking up into the eyes of a faceless EMT. Neither of us speaks.

❖

Most of my family has ended up in nursing homes. My mother died from multiple sclerosis in one. Though they took good care of her, I didn't like visiting. My father, even though he was divorced from her, visited almost every day. His visits let the staff know she was cared about and kept them attentive to her. Many of my great-aunts and -uncles died in nursing homes. Both my grandfathers, too sick to care for themselves, were put in nursing homes, and both died within two weeks, broken men. My great-grandmother on my mother's side went into a nursing home at death's door and lived there for fourteen years, loving it. She was the queen of the place, proudly showing off her bracelet with the lockets bearing the names of her nine great-grandchildren. She died at ninety-four after being manhandled by an attendant who was supposed to be gentle with frail old patients when bathing them.

When I was at the health department I went with an investigator to follow up on complaints against a certain home in Hartford. The department had a deserved reputation as ball busters for any violation, which I came to believe was a good thing. Old people need someone looking out for them. After reviewing records and interviewing random patients, we met with the president of the home, who got upset with us. "Old people get bruised," he said. "I get bruised. I don't need some muckety-muck"— he looked right at me; I had been introduced as the commissioner's executive assistant—"telling me how to run my business." I stared at him then gave him a mysterious smile. I was thinking what his reaction would be if I were to suddenly shout, "You murdered my great-grandmother, you bastard!" as I leapt up and choked him, knocking him clean over backward until three big orderlies pulled me off. He looked at me twice, grumbled, but said nothing more, and just nodded sullenly when the investigator said he'd be receiving a written report in the mail.

The Age of Love

Austin Jones is a fifty-one-year-old man with lung cancer, on oxygen and a morphine drip to help him cope with the pain. We're taking him from the Veterans Administration (VA) hospital in Newington to New Britain General for radiation treatments. This is the second day we've drawn him. Not that he's a bad guy, but we'd rather be in the city doing 911 calls than running a transfer.

He's doing worse today. They had to give him an IM injection of four milligrams of morphine before we left. The student nurse stuck him three times before she could get the needle to work. He says he's feeling better, but he is very diaphoretic, and I have to break open a cotton four by four to wipe his brow. Yesterday when we were coming into New Britain, he saw a Ferris wheel out of the back window and asked if there was a carnival in town. I said it looked like there was a traveling show setting up in the supermarket parking lot. He said he wanted to take his grandson to one. His grandson was the one who kept him going, he said. The truth is, I don't think he'll make it out of the hospital before what is eating up his insides does him in.

Austin Jones. He told us he wasn't from Texas. He is an Alabama native, named after an uncle who drove a truck and got killed in Texas before he was born. He got the name Austin to remember the man by.

Now, over the radio, we hear a car dispatched to a shooting on Weston Street.

I hear Glenn swear in the driver's seat.

A second car is dispatched.

"We've got a one hundred," a voice crackles. A one hundred is a full cardiac arrest. "We need a medic."

"Isn't eight-six-six on scene?"

"Eight-six-six, we're down the street. We're working another one hundred, and we have two other patients."

"You hear that?" Glenn calls back to me.

"Yeah," I say.

"The city's going wild," I say to Austin. "It sounds like they've got four people shot."

"Where?" he asks.

"I think Weston Street."

"Oh."

I know he lives on Edgewood Street. I dab more sweat off his face. "How are you feeling?"

"I'll get by."

I listen to the radio. Two ambulances head to the hospital, one to Hartford, one to Saint Francis, both priority one.

"Where were you in the service?" I ask.

"Germany."

"Yeah, how was that?"

"Nice," he says. "Nice."

"How were the German women?"

He grins. "German women, Belgian women, Danish women, Swedish women. They were all fine. Treat you like a man there. It was like one giant shopping trip. Like nothing I'd ever seen before or since. Copenhagen, Denmark. That was the place we'd go." He pauses at the memory and smiles. "It was the age of love."

"How long were you there?"

"Eighteen months, nearly two years."

"That's great."

"I would have stayed longer if that shit hadn't broken out."

"Vietnam?"

He nods and looks hard into my eyes like I don't want to know about it. "Rough. Rough," he says.

"You were in the field?"

He nods then looks down at his chest. I watch his lips move. He mutters.

I look away.

A moment later, I feel his hand on my arm. "My anger is not toward you," he says.

"I understand."

"It was just a lot of shit. I left friends there and I got friends who are sick now like me." He shakes his head.

A few minutes go by. It's quiet. I hear the ambulances sign off at the hospitals.

"I hope he's okay," he says.

"Your grandson?"

He nods. The sweat beads on his skin. "Kids, they shouldn't grow up with this."

I towel his face and brow with a fresh four by four.

"Goddamn," he says under his breath.

The EMT Sports Pages

I read the obituaries every day looking for names I recognize.

❖

Oscar Levin, seventy-six. We were called to his apartment a few weeks ago. He was lying on the floor against the wall with a lampshade near his head and a tall lamp fallen across his legs. His glasses were askew on his face. He was sweating and his hands were shaking. He didn't want to go to the hospital. He said nothing was wrong. He denied that he had fallen. He got so nervous, he urinated on himself. It took us forty minutes to talk him into going, then we had to carry him down the narrow stairs strapped to a safety chair. The obituary said he was a member of the Temple Israel Church and had been a cabdriver for fifty years before retiring.

❖

Elston "Moonman" Lewis, thirty-nine. We were called to intercept with a basic ambulance. The patient was in late-stage cancer, suffering decreasing consciousness. He had a pressure of 70. His face was neon yellow. He was thin, emaciated, hardly weighed more than eighty pounds. When we put him in the back of the ambulance, his feet stuck off the end of the stretcher. Neither Glenn nor I could get an IV in him. The paper said he was captain of an area high-school basketball team in 1974.

❖

Gilda Dempsey, fifty-six. We found her facedown in the bathroom in a pool of vomit, with her pants around her knees. She'd pitched forward from the toilet. Her teeth were clenched and her pupils pinpoint. Her lungs were thick from aspiration. She'd been an administrator of a local college, and the mother of four, grandmother of six.

❖

Austin Jones, fifty-one. Father of six, grandfather of ten. Friend of many. Veteran.

❖

Call it depressing, but you like to know what happens to the people you meet and maybe a little bit more about who they were.

Worry

It's Tuesday morning, the start of my three-day shift. I awake at 5:29 A.M. I arise and turn off my alarm before it rings. I have slept fitfully throughout the night, gazing at the clock at 2:38, 3:20, 4:46, 5:07. I go into the bathroom and feel a retch in my throat. I hold my hands against the bathroom counter as I cough. I spit into the basin. The feeling gets worse and I have to kneel before the toilet. I retch but nothing comes up. I wipe the drool from my lips and stand weakly. My eyes are watery.

I shower, shave, and dress in my navy blue uniform with the patch of the American flag on my right sleeve. I drink a little cranberry juice and eat a banana. The retch comes back over me and I am again on all fours.

This time I throw up the red juice and the white ooze of banana. Again, I wipe my lips and eyes.

Driving to work in the darkness, I both dread and welcome the day. Let me make it through till midmorning, when I can eat something to gain strength. If I am to be tested today, let me do well. Let me not fail.

The traffic is light. I maintain an even pace in the slow lane. I wonder what will happen to me. Will I marry and father children? How will I support myself? How will I ever support them? Will my wife get cancer? Will my children be injured? Can I hold up to life? What will happen to me when I get old?

I drive on and wait for the darkness to lift.

CHILDREN

Message

When I was riding in Waterbury during my paramedic class, we went to a call for a "hurt leg" and walked up the splintered wooden steps of a roach-infested apartment building to find on the third floor a fifteen-year-old mother crying because her five-month-old had skinned her knee. The paramedic had to show the mother how to clean the wound and put on a bandage and assure her it wasn't life threatening. As we walked out of the apartment building amid a throng of kids, a girl maybe ten years old, tall with long black hair and deep black eyes—a child of stunning beauty—looked right at me and pleaded to me like I might be some kind of savior. "I hate it here," she said.

I took her words back with me, east on I-84 then north on I-91 to my townhouse in East Windsor and then back south to Hartford, up the steps on the capitol and up to the second floor, through the doors of the governor's office. I waited with her words by the secretary's desk, while the governor talked on the phone to his own son early in the morning before the boy went off to school and before the office was filled with staff and visitors and meetings and bill signings. When he was off the phone, I stuck my head in the door and, on his acknowledgment, proceeded into the great room where the governor sat behind his wide desk with his hardbound copies of *A Connecticut Yankee in King Arthur's Court* and the U.S. Constitution. We chatted for a little bit, and when he asked me about my paramedic course I told him about the little girl and what she had said, and about all the horrors of the inner city I was seeing and how tough it was for kids. He nodded and looked concerned and seemed to take it all in.

I am sure that girl had no idea where her words had been carried. She probably did not even know there was such a person as a governor, but I like to think that she believed somewhere there was a person who was fair and wise and could send hope her way.

❖

When I first started working for Weicker it was in 1976, shortly after his rise to national prominence in the wake of the Senate Watergate hearings, where he played the role of the young Diogenes, the Republican searching for truth even if it meant turning on his president. His campaign slogan was "Nobody's man but yours." He was reelected by a landslide, but the truth was, he hadn't accumulated much of a record as a senator. In 1978, he and his wife had a child with Down's syndrome. In the ensuing year both on the floor and in his office, Weicker was erratic, directionless, and subject to fits of rage. One day on the Senate floor, he called Senator Heinz of Pennsylvania an idiot in violation of all protocol. The account of the exchange as recorded by the *Congressional Record* after staff editing is interesting to read. There are remarks leading up to a confrontation that isn't there and apologies for something that can't be found. At the same time his wife told me how Weicker would lie in bed at night, holding the baby on his stomach for hours at a time as if they were the only two people in the world.

Eventually, I think the birth of this child was one of the best things that happened to Weicker. His disabled son gave him direction, and when the Republicans took control of the Senate in 1980, Weicker had the power to follow that direction. With Reagan proposing massive cuts in human-service programs, Weicker now had the clout of a high-ranking committee member to stand up and fight them, which he did, succeeding repeatedly in blocking Reagan's proposed cuts and restoring millions of dollars in funding for education, the disadvantaged, and the disabled.

The birth of his child let Weicker in on something I believe he had not truly felt before. His son represented the defenseless in the world and Weicker was the strong. Weicker, in my opinion, became a great senator, not just because of his seniority and leverage, but because he had something concrete to fight for that gave him the strength to stick those fights out. He was one of the few who time after time pushed the interests of kids. When everyone else in Washington was pushing for catastrophic health-care coverage for senior citizens, he was pushing it for kids. Even as governor, when making deep cuts in the state budget and angering nearly every special-interest group, he was pushing for expanded programs for kids, community-health centers, after-school programs, lead-paint removal projects.

In his 1993 state-of-the-state speech, which I drafted for him, he shocked the legislature when he unveiled a plan to desegregate Connecticut's schools, declaring, "the racial and economic isolation in Connecticut's school system is indisputable. Whether this segregation came about through the chance of historical boundaries or economic forces beyond the control of the state or whether it came about through private decisions or in spite of the best educational efforts of the state, what matters is that it is here and must be dealt with. . . . When we walk the streets of our cities and look into the eyes of our children and see hopelessness, it is our loss and our failure. From innocence, bitterness is born, and at great cost."

He never avoided the tough issues. Kids growing up in the city get a bad break. Most of them are, in fact, doomed. Hartford is one of the poorest cities in the nation because its city boundaries are so tightly drawn. If it were like Los Angeles, Newington, West Hartford, Simsbury, and all the wealthy suburbs would be a part of Hartford, and their wealth would be shared. Instead there are two Connecticuts—one of promise, the other of despair. I was proud to help write the words, proud to have an orator of his tremendous ability give them life, and prouder still to work for a man who became a champion because he believed he was one, where other men wouldn't have even bothered with the fight.

Weicker used to say his job was to speak for the powerless, to bring their voices to the rooms of power they could not reach by themselves.

Once, in 1982, we were on the way to a black church in Hartford. It was just Weicker and me in the car. I was driving, and we weren't certain of the way. When we saw a school crossing guard, he told me to pull over so he could ask directions. "Excuse me," he said, and asked her how to get to the church.

She pointed and started to give directions, then she looked back at him and said, "I know you from somewhere. I've seen you on TV."

He said, almost embarrassed, "Lowell Weicker."

"Oh, bless you," she said. "Bless you for the things you've done."

That moment made everything worthwhile. Often I hated him. He was at times a rich arrogant man, who one minute could treat you like a son and the next like a loathsome servant. But God, there were times when he could make the tingles run through you. He at least had a sense of the heroic, a sense of how it ought to be. That is no small thing.

It seems to me that too many politicians know of the plight of children only through photo ops at soup kitchens and day-care centers. I can't help but think that if they saw what we see in the city every day, their policies would be different. It would be children first, above all else. Weicker used to say the real problem was kids don't vote.

❖

We're called for a seizure in Stowe Village. The mother meets us outside and leads us up three floors to an apartment. She starts to open the door, but we hear barking and she slams it. "Put that dog away!" she shouts. "Get that damn dog away!"

She opens the door a little bit, then opens it all the way.

"Is the dog away?" I say.

"He locked up. He all excited: the cops were just here ransacking my place. Got my boy all excited. I told them leave us alone. I got a sick boy. They didn't find no guns here."

The house is a mess, but I doubt it is because it has been ransacked. In the living room there is a giant king-sized mattress. There are six kids in the apartment. Lying on the bed is a nine-year-old boy, who looks like he is sleeping. He is breathing. His skin temperature is normal.

"What happened?" I ask.

"He just started bugging," the mother says. "I seen that and I want to run away."

"He was having a seizure?"

"I don't know. He got a history of it."

I look to the oldest kid—a girl of about twelve. "Was he shaking?" I ask.

She nods and says his whole body was moving.

I check his pupils, but he tries to roll his eyes into the back of his head, and he starts crying.

A little boy of about eight wearing only shorts starts yelling at me. "Take him to the hospital. Take him right now." He looks like he wants to fight me.

"Whoa, little man," I say. "We're going to take care of him."

"He just in the hospital this morning for dehydration," the mother says. "I told the police I had a sick boy, but they went ahead and messed up my house."

I pick the boy up in my arms and carry him down the stairs. He is crying and says his head hurts. Cockroaches scatter on the floor in front of my feet.

In the hospital, we put him in bed 9. The first thing the mother says to the nurse is "They got anything to eat around here?"

My childhood wasn't like that.

Albany and Main
after Dark in the Rain

It's night. A brisk wind sweeps the driving rain up Albany Avenue. We're parked in front of Bridgestone Tires. The cops have something going on in the area and want an ambulance close by.

Glenn has country music playing on the radio.

There is a large puddle by the curb formed by a depression in the road. Four kids in hooded dark raincoats squat on the curb like gargoyles. A car drives by, hits the puddle, and casts up a tsunami that crashes down on the four children, who get up laughing, slap high fives, then hunch back down to wait for the next car.

Fixed and Dilated

It is a clear spring day, a little after three in the afternoon. We're parked in front of the Farmington Avenue office having a late lunch of subs, chips, and cold sodas.

"Four-five-one. Respond to 950 Asylum for the pediatric struck. On a one. Our switchboard's lighting up in here with calls on this."

Glenn hits on the lights and I strap myself in. Asylum is parallel to Farmington.

As we approach, we see a large nervous crowd in the street and on the sides of the road. School has just gotten out.

"This could be bad," Glenn says.

"Let's be quick," I say.

We get out and break through the crowd. Lying in the middle of the road on his side, is a small boy with a pool of blood under his head. A bystander is holding traction on the boy's head to keep his spine in line. He has blood coming from his nose and mouth. He is breathing, but he appears lifeless. He has no response to pain.

"He flew twenty feet through the air," someone says.

Glenn checks his pupils. "Fixed and dilated," he says quickly.

I put on a cervical collar and roll him onto a spinal board. Shawn Kinkade, another paramedic, appears at my shoulder and asks if I need a hand or if he can set up my intubation kit. Behind me I can feel the crowd surging. Someone is struggling to get through. They are hysterical. They touch my shoulder but are pulled away. There is screaming and crying all around us. I tell Shawn I am just going to boogie with the kid. We are in sight of the hospital. We put the board onto the stretcher, wheel it quickly to the ambulance, and lift it in. I get in back with our paramedic student, and Glenn pulls away. In the back we immobilize the head with towel rolls, strap the boy to the board, and put on high-flow oxygen. We're at Saint Francis thirty seconds later.

We come through the doors. "Pediatric, hit by car, thrown twenty feet. Pupils fixed and dilated," I say as we wheel him past the triage desk straight to the trauma room.

The room is empty. We lift the board and lay him on the trauma stretcher. Other than his respirations there is no life in his little body. His arms lie at his sides like a baby Jesus. It is a terrible few moments while we wait for the trauma team.

They arrive quickly and converge on the boy, while we step back. His blood pressure is 160—sky-high for a kid—a sign of massive intracranial pressure. They get an IV line. He has no other injuries but the head. They give medications, take X rays. Dr. Morgan arrives. "Hyperventilate him," he says. They intubate. The more oxygen they get in, the more they can stop the swelling. They put him on a respirator.

I tell the story over and over. "Thrown twenty feet. Fixed and dilated at the scene. Right out here on Asylum."

❖

In the hall I learn that Shawn and Art in 453, who arrived on scene shortly after we did, took in the kid's mother and brother, who were also hit. The mother hurt her leg, the brother was hardly scratched. She was walking them across the street holding their hands.

We get the word that the CAT scan shows a massive bleed in the brain.

"He probably tore a meningeal artery the moment he hit the ground," Shawn says.

"He was fixed and dilated on the scene," Glenn says.

❖

The Life-Star helicopter crew accompanies the stretcher as it's wheeled back from CAT scan. He will be transferred to Hartford Hospital, which has a pediatric intensive-care unit. The mother is wheeled out into the corridor. They stop the boy's stretcher next to hers so she can see him. We watch from down the hall. She struggles to rise from the board that she is strapped to. A primal wail rises from her. He lies there, his eyes swollen shut, a tube in his mouth, a machine breathing for him. "I'm sorry!" she cries. "It's my fault! It's my fault!" She calls his name over and over.

❖

At Hartford a brain scan confirms what we suspected at the scene when we first lifted his eyelids and saw his spirit gone. The boy is brain-dead.

❖

We return to the scene. It is an hour later. The police have three blocks taped off with their yellow tape. We tell an officer we took the boy in and they let us pass. We get out of the ambulance and take our radios. We stop at the next set of yellow tape. Television cameras are there filming the scene. A purple van with a smashed bumper is still in the road. We try to piece together what happened. The school is on the left. The boy's apartment building is across the street on the right. At that hour, Asylum is a busy dangerous road with cars racing home to the suburbs. Yet the mother led her boys across the street in the middle of the block. I can still see the small pool of blood in the pavement. Glenn guesses from the position of the car, the driver must have swerved to the right, clipping them with the left front bumper.

An unmarked police car is allowed to pass through the yellow tape. A policewoman gets out of the police car and walks toward the purple van. She opens the front door and helps a woman out. The driver has been in the van all this time. She is in her late thirties, early forties. Her face is sheer pain. It looks like broken glass. She walks unsteadily, as if each step takes her into a new world that is nothing but grief, and gasps for painful air.

Politicians and Parents

The lead story on the eleven o'clock news is the release of the Baby Emily report, concerning the case of a nine-month-old who was sexually abused by her mother's boyfriend, resulting in her death. The anchors announce a feature on why, unlike traffic accidents, many deaths caused by abuse are never investigated. The promo clip shows a brief shot of the purple van at this afternoon's accident scene, blocked off by police tape.

The released report on the baby's death has blame for everyone, particularly the overworked caseworkers and the hospitals who allegedly missed earlier signs of abuse. They show clips of the family members blaming the state and clips of politicians vowing to hold people responsible so this never happens again. There is a lot of blaming going on. All the newscasters look appropriately concerned and disquieted by the issue of child abuse that they are now hyping as their only-on-our-channel-do-you-get-the-inside-story series. Despite the earlier clip, they don't mention this afternoon's accident. I hear later it was highlighted on the six o'clock news, but by eleven it is old copy.

Later in the broadcast they show a rally of welfare mothers protesting proposed cuts in welfare payments. "It's not our babies' faults they were born into poverty," a mother complains.

I turn the TV off, upset with all I have seen. The politicians say we have to get these kids out of harm's way, no matter what the cost, as if it is only five or maybe six kids who are left unprotected due to an overworked or mismanaged system.

What I know is that day in and day out I go into houses unfit for human habitation. On nearly every street, in nearly every building, children are living at risk from drugs, violence, neglect, poverty. I've been in filthy apartments with cribs in every room, even one apartment where they had to move a crib so we could open the door, and move it again so we could leave. All over the city kids are being brought into a world they'll share with cockroaches, rats, syringes, and stray bullets. To make them all safe, you cannot talk about taking one kid out of a house here and there. To make them all safe you'd have to bring in a caravan of buses and take them out building by building. Tens of thousands. You're talking a mass evacuation. You'd need the National Guard or the Pied Piper of Hamelin. That's the rock truth.

Within two months, the mother of the baby who was sexually assaulted will be arrested for dealing heroin.

The Ceiling

It's three in the morning. I'm wide awake looking at the ceiling, my mind full of doubts. Maybe I should have spent more time on the scene and intubated the kid right there; more deeply oxygenating him might have helped slow the rapid swelling in his brain. Maybe when Shawn asked me if I needed any help, I should have said, call Saint Francis and let them know we're coming. It would have given them another minute's notice so they could have been ready for us when we burst through the doors. Maybe I should have taken the boy crosstown to Hartford Hospital, where they have pediatric specialists who might have known some new experimental technique that could have grabbed his departing life back by its small ankle and pulled it back into his body. I don't know. Failure haunts me.

I see the face of another kid hit by a car, six years earlier. When we arrived he was lying just below a rise in the middle of the road. He had an altered respiratory pattern. He was crying and then going out, crying and then going out. We were quick on the scene then, too, but I'd had to ride all the way in with him to Bay State Hospital, and all the way I was saying, "Come on, little buddy," as I hovered over him. The right side of his head was swollen. His left femur was broken. I'd tried to put in an airway, but his teeth were clenched. I put him on high-flow oxygen, but I should have hyperventilated him with a bag mask then. I'd been working only a few months and didn't know any better. When we got to the trauma room, I felt they were looking at me like I was the one who had run over him. He started seizing and then they intubated him. My partner said she didn't think he was going to make it.

I went to a basketball game that night and was silent through the whole game. I don't remember a moment of it. When I got home and turned on the news, I expected to see my face on a "Wanted for Murder" poster. I used to drive back to that scene, hoping to see a kid with a cast on his leg and crutches laughing and playing Simon Says with the other kids on the street. He lived, but he had a closed head injury. I still don't know if he has a regular life. He should be sixteen now. Maybe he slurs his speech and drools and doesn't have a clue about what happened to him. Maybe he's fine and healthy and handsome and has his own girlfriend, who he makes out with on the family-room couch when his parents aren't at home. I don't know.

I keep staring at the ceiling.

I want to be better at what I do.

Bad Start

I'm in at six-thirty the next morning, a half hour early as if to say I'm not afraid of coming to work. I've just met a paramedic student, a rider, when I hear over the radio, "Four-six-two, Peter?" I'm parked outside the garage, checking supplies. I answer on the radio.

"Can you respond to a cardiac arrest?"

Glenn isn't in yet, so I grab an EMT I don't know and the rider I have just met, and we tear out lights and sirens headed into Hartford to meet a basic crew at the scene.

The call goes badly. The woman is in v-fib, and I shock her into asystole. The rider tries for a tube and puts it in the esophagus. I try to get the pacer working, but it won't capture. The rider still can't get the tube, so we switch places. I can't see anything but vomit and blood in the airway. The basic crew's suction unit isn't working. The rider gets an IV in and we start a round of drugs. I still can't get the tube. I realize we've been in the house too long, so we pack up and carry the woman out of the house on the board. Her arms dangle and bang against the porch door. The woman is heavy and my back feels like it is going to explode. In the ambulance, I try again for the tube, but I can't see the chords. Another dose of epi puts the woman in v-fib. I let the rider shock her. She returns to asystole. I try for the tube again but see nothing. I get a whiff of her dead breath and fight to keep from puking.

We wheel her into the cardiac room. It takes them several attempts to get the tube, but they finally get it.

They work her five minutes and call it.

At the desk, a nurse notices the Band-Aid on my neck. "You cut yourself shaving, then go out and save lives," she says.

"I'm not having much luck at that," I respond.

❖

I feel again that overwhelming burden of failure that I try to ignore for fear the sheer weight of it will crush me to the ground.

❖

I get back to the office to pick up Glenn and finish resupplying, only to find the word of our "cluster fuck" has preceded me. The basic crew has been telling everyone how badly the call went.

"What do you mean, you couldn't find the epi?" Glenn says to me.

"Get out, we found the epi. The rider didn't know where it was, and I had to tell him while I was trying to tube, and it took a minute for him to get it out. Give me a break. Don't they have anything better to do?"

Daniel Tauber, the chief paramedic, calls me into his office. He is somewhat of a legend, having been a paramedic for nearly a decade and done just about everything. His competence is unquestioned. "Two things," he says, closing the door. "The pediatric call. I want you to know you did everything perfectly. Vinny Cezus of Hartford Hospital called yesterday upset that the kid hadn't gone directly to Hartford, but you were entirely appropriate to go to Saint Francis. Your scene time was excellent. So don't worry about that."

We talk about the call and my questions about whether I should have tried to tube at the scene, but he reassures me of my choices, and I am grateful for his support.

"How did the code go?" he asks now, shifting from the good news to the bad.

I hesitate. "It went all right. I learn from every call I do. I have never done a perfect call. I guess I was in the house too long, and I spent too much time trying to get the tube. I had a rider with me, and he did real well. He was good. He missed the tube, but so did I and they had a hard time with it at the hospital. He got a difficult IV and generally knew his stuff. I'd do it differently if I had it to do over."

He is silent for a moment, sizing me up. "Well," he says finally, "as long as you learn, that's important."

He assigns the rider to another paramedic for the day. I understand.

I walk out of the office and feel people's eyes on me.

When

Glenn and I get sent to Charter Oak Terrace for an asthma. I am glad to be getting a call. After the botched code I want to prove myself. We get in the apartment and see a little girl playing with a doll and a young woman sitting on the couch smoking a cigarette. We look around. We don't see anyone having an asthma attack.

"Who's sick?" I ask.

"She is." The mother points at her kid. The mother is maybe seventeen. She has short hair and a sneer that I don't think ever changes.

"She doesn't look sick," Glenn says.

"She got a sore throat and hasn't been eating all her food. They saw her last week and she isn't any better."

"Did you take her temperature?" Glenn asks.

"I don't got a thermometer."

I feel her skin. It is normal. Her lungs are clear.

"You take her to the Charter Oak Clinic?" I ask, referring to the community health center located about two blocks from her apartment.

"No, I don't like them there. I go to Hartford. Take us there."

I drive. All the way I think about the kid hit by the car and then the code and not getting the tube and the basic crew saying it was a messed-up call.

When we get to the hospital, Glenn says, "Where was your mind at? You were tossing me all around the back with your stop and go."

"Sorry, I guess I wasn't paying attention."

"Yeah," the mother says, sneering at me. "I got a headache from it."

I feel my temper flare. I almost say, "If you want a smooth ride, take a fucking cab or a limo, and quit abusing the system."

She has brought a stroller with her, which she lets the little girl push. The girl pushes it into the ED, and the nurses smile at her. Glenn gives a quick rundown, and they say just go on down to the pediatric clinic. The little girl putters all the way down the hall. Watching her makes even me smile. I look at her, then I look at the sneering mother, then back at her. What happens? When does the change occur? How do you go from being so wide-eyed and wondrous to having a cold sneer? Is it taught or does it just sink in through the skin?

I think about another recent story in the news that happened just off Farmington Avenue on South Marshall Street. The first reports were of a mother gunned down in cold blood while walking back from the candy store with her two small children. Then the real story comes out. The mother, walking back from the candy store, sees two rival drug dealers cruising by in a car. In front of her children, she pulls out a knife and confronts the rivals for being on her turf. They pull out nine-millimeter guns and blow her away. The paper said she made it home to collapse on the kitchen floor of her own mother's house, her dying words, "Help me, Mommy."

I watch the little girl push her stroller down the hall, everyone smiling at her. We stop at the nurses' desk. She just keeps puttering on alone.

Whose Kids Are These?

I have just read this book, *Amazing Grace*, by Jonathan Kozol. It is about the life of children in the South Bronx, one of the poorest sections of the country. Kozol wrote a book about unequal education called *Savage Inequalities*, which I quoted for Weicker's speech on ending the segregation in the state's inner-city schools.

"We are children only once," Kozol writes, "and after those few years are gone, there is no second chance to make amends. In this respect, the consequences of unequal education have a terrible finality. Those who are denied cannot be 'made whole' by a later act of government."

In *Amazing Grace*, he talks about kids in school being taught to drop to the floor when they hear gunfire. He describes the death of a boy killed falling down an elevator shaft in a grimy apartment building, and the parents being blamed for letting him play in the hallway. He points out they don't let him play outside where he might get shot. He talks about how the brightest kids in school dream of becoming X-ray technicians or security guards, for these are truly great jobs where these kids come from. And how can a teacher put down these limited aspirations when to do so would put down their entire world?

The world he writes about is grim—urine-drenched, rat-infested apartments; no jobs; numbing bureaucracy where you wait all day in line only to be told you need another piece of paper that sends you across the city for another all-day wait in line; toxic-waste dumps being put in the neighborhood; decayed schools; drugs and gunfire—and these bright little kids have to grow up in it.

The current rage in America today is to come down hard on welfare, and I see many reasons for doing so. You see healthy young men sitting on stoops, drinking out of bottles inside paper bags or dealing drugs. You go into apartments where a woman is smoking cigarettes, and her kids all have asthma, and you give them a two-hundred-dollar ambulance ride rather than saying walk the four blocks to the hospital or take a cab for two dollars.

When I worked for my friend Brad, who was running for Congress as a Republican, I wrote a press release for him calling welfare "a morally bankrupt system that erodes personal responsibility and contributes to the breakdown of family and the rise in crime." His plan called for requiring all healthy welfare recipients to work thirty-five hours per week in a private- or public-sector job, replacing cash payments with services like child care and health, requiring mothers to establish paternity to receive benefits, denying additional benefits for more children, tracking down fathers who do not support their children, aggressively pursuing welfare fraud, and instituting random drug testing of welfare recipients.

Here in Connecticut, they are now requiring people to pick up their checks rather than sending them through the mail. I have seen the lines — they are enormous, snaking out of the building and stretching across a school athletic field, old people and mothers standing with children. Medicaid patients are now being required to join HMOs that they must call before going to the Emergency Room. When the patients show me their state cards, I ask them if they have contacted the gatekeeper at their HMO. Most, even those who now have an HMO, have no idea what I am talking about. I explain how it is okay now, but in the future they will have to get permission to go to the emergency room. While I think it is a great idea, just sending these people a letter in the mail is not going to get the message across. Many can't read or don't speak the language.

When Weicker ran for governor, he had a great ad about kids, in which he said that the state really belonged to them, and they were the ones for whom we should be working. In his first year, he raised taxes by $1 billion and cut services by $1 billion to balance the state budget. In the next year he cut taxes for business in an effort to stem the exodus of businesses from the state and the resulting decline in the tax base, and started a modest number of programs for kids, including expanding school-based health centers, childhood lead screening, Head Start, and extended-day kindergarten — programs he called a cost-effective investment in the future. He used to say unless you were fiscally sound, you couldn't do anything for your people. In the following years he offered more programs for kids but never at the levels he wanted. In the speech about desegregation, he talked about how the average cost of keeping someone in prison was twenty thousand dollars a year, enough to provide a Head Start program for ten kids.

When I worked for Brad, we put out a release about the need for more prisons. "The average violent criminal serves on average only thirty-seven percent of his term. The median time served for murder is five and a half years, for rape three years, for assault fifteen months. Three point two million convicted felons are out on parole or probation rather than in prison. Sixty-two percent of these prisoners will be rearrested within three years of their release. According to a 1990 U.S. Department of Justice study, if fifty-five percent of the eight hundred thousand violent criminals now in state and federal prisons served eighty-five percent of their terms, 4,400,000 crimes would be prevented every year. The costs of incarceration are small compared to the $452,000 a year the Heritage Foundation estimates a violent criminal costs society on the street in terms of law enforcement, property damage, and human terror."

❖

So what do you do? Put the money in kids' programs, build more prisons, or cut taxes for business? Ideally you would do all three, but you don't have the money.

In his book, Kozol has a conversation with a mother about why the city is cutting back on services. He tells her the idea is to keep taxes down so people won't flee to areas where they would be taxed less. He says they complain that the taxes are killing them. The lady replies, "There's killing and there's killing."

I guess the reason why becoming a politician lost its appeal to me is that I don't have the courage or gall to say I know the answer. In my mind the real answers are too painful and controversial and may not, in the end, be answers at all (and most assuredly wouldn't get me elected).

What is so unsettling about Kozol's book and about what I see in the city every day is the children. They are like all children to start with—happy, wide-eyed, hopeful—but you know it will get beaten out of them.

VIEWPOINTS

Two Calls

We're at Mount Sinai Hospital when we get dispatched to a difficulty breathing call on the far side of East Hartford. It is a private call, meaning the person picked up a phone book and called for an ambulance from the Yellow Pages rather than dialing 911. We are dispatched to too many difficulty breathing and chest pain calls that turn out to be nothing to get excited by this call. We use lights and sirens, but it takes us twenty-three minutes to navigate through Hartford out onto I-91, then take I-84 across the river to Route 2, get off at an exit, and race out past Pratt and Whitney Aircraft to arrive at the street where the call was made.

The son meets us in the driveway. "He wasn't feeling well and was going to go see the doctor. But he got so tired walking, I thought I should call for an ambulance," he says almost apologetically.

We get into the house and find the man sitting on the couch. He says he has been having pain in his upper stomach since last night. His voice is very weak. His pulse is thready. He is pale and sweating and says he vomited a half hour ago. I take his blood pressure. It is 88/60. I put him on a 100 percent oxygen mask, and we lift him onto the stretcher and move quickly toward the ambulance.

I put in a sixteen gauge in his AC and run a bag of saline wide open. His heart is beating fast and irregularly. Glenn drives lights and sirens.

I am thinking he is either in cardiogenic shock or has an aortic abdominal aneurysm that is leaking. His stomach is only slightly distended and I can feel no pulsing masses. I check his ankles for distal pulses but can't feel any. The road is rough and the sirens are loud. I try for another blood pressure but can't hear above the sirens. I keep asking the man how he is feeling. He nods to me, mumbles okay.

I call the hospital and tell them what I am bringing them.

I try again for the blood pressure and can't hear anything. I can't even feel a pulse, but he is still conscious. When we arrive at the hospital and are parked, I feel again. Nothing.

We hurry him inside, where he is triaged to the cardiac room.

Using a Doppler stethoscope, they get a pressure of 50, which soon drops to 30. The man is barely responsive. They run more fluid and call for dopamine, a vasopressor to contract his veins to increase his pressure. They intubate him. I leave the room to write my report and when I return they are doing CPR. They get a carotid pulse back, but five minutes later, they lose him again. He has suffered a massive infarction. His old heart is so beaten up, it just can't pump enough blood to keep him alive. Even though he is intubated, the color in his head and extremities slowly turns cyanotic. After half an hour they quit working on him.

❖

This is a call where the system failed. The guy should have called as soon as he felt the pain. First of all, people need to know if you're having pain, don't deny it. Call an ambulance or get to the hospital and get checked out. Second, they should have called 911. The East Hartford Fire Department paramedics could have been on the scene at least eighteen minutes faster than we were. Another eighteen minutes and maybe he would have been stable enough to get to surgery for an angioplasty to clear the blockage in his heart. It might have kept him alive. When the call came to our company for difficulty breathing, we should have passed it back to East Hartford. The problem is, so many people cry wolf that our level of skepticism is very high. I can't tell you how many difficulty breathings I've been to where the person has turned out to have a runny nose or to be hyperventilating about something, how many chest pains are just colds, and how many severe bleedings are cuts not worthy of a Band-Aid. Doing calls like this old man too proud to tell anyone he's in pain, too proud to call 911, and who only calls for an ambulance when he can't take another step—these are the calls that you think about when you get called for BS, for someone too lazy to make a doctor's appointment, or who wants to save cab fare so they call an ambulance that their state card pays for. Sometimes the system sucks.

❖

Later that day we get called for an unknown in the south end. On the second floor we find an elderly woman complaining of abdominal pain and a headache. Her granddaughter translates for us. She went to the doctor a week ago for the same problem but doesn't know what the doctor told her. She has no apparent medical history. She has been in Connecticut just two weeks, coming from Puerto Rico. Glenn tries to find out why she called for an ambulance instead of just going back to her doctor. She is sick, the granddaughter translates. Glenn is upset. The woman is not in any acute crisis. She is all dressed up ready to go, holding her pocketbook. We walk down to the ambulance.

En route I try to find out her birth date. "Nineteen seventy-eight," the granddaughter tells me.

"Not yours. Hers."

"Nineteen seventy-eight," she says.

"Try again."

She asks the grandmother then says to me, "Nineteen sixty."

"I don't think so," I say. "She would be younger than me."

The granddaughter looks at me blankly.

I ask for any ID that might give me the answer. She hands me her shiny new state medical card. It is less than a week old.

I should be nice to all my patients, but I am in a rotten mood. They are playing dumb with me. They know I disapprove of them, but they don't care. They are getting their ride to the doctor and it is not costing them a penny.

Over the radio we hear a basic car dispatched for a man down. A few minutes later, a panicked voice comes over the air. "Four-six-three. We need a medic. We've got a working one hundred."

I hear Glenn swear in the front.

"No medics available," our dispatcher says. "You're going to have to do it on your own. Sorry."

We continue crosstown. I say nothing more to my patient and her granddaughter. We stare at each other coldly. I write my run form.

❖

When I was working at the state, the Department of Income Maintenance (DIM) tried to pass a proposal that said it would not pay ambulance companies for ambulance trips that on review of the run forms were determined not to be true emergencies. I used my position to help kill the proposal, which had outraged doctors and ambulance companies alike. The problem with the proposal was severalfold. One, once an EMT makes contact with a patient, a medical relationship has been established. If the EMT doesn't transport, he is legally abandoning the patient, unless he gets a signed refusal from the patient. EMTs are not allowed to diagnose. They can make clinical impressions, but only doctors can diagnose.

The doctors on whose license the system runs did not want this liability. The ambulance companies, who by law are required to transport people regardless of their ability to pay, did not want to get stuck with the bill for thousands of transports that a bureaucrat would deem unnecessary. What's an emergency? Sometimes indigestion mimics a heart attack. Who would decide? Instead of going after the people abusing the system, the so-called patients, the state was going to make the ambulance companies pay and put the EMTs and doctors at medical risk if one of the nontransports later decided to sue. Also, by denying the ambulance companies payment for these trips, they would cause prices to rise for everyone else.

I think what the state needs is a clear set of guidelines that the EMTs can use to determine whom they can refuse and to provide some liability coverage. And maybe give them taxi tokens they can give to patients so the patients can take cabs to see their doctors. Clearly, people with small cuts don't need an ambulance. Nor do people with runny noses. They should be made to appreciate the cost in some way, instead of taking it as a right. It is a complicated issue. Inevitably, in any triage scheme, errors would be made. The elderly man, not feeling well, given the taxi token, drops dead in the backseat of the cab. It is the lead story on the six o'clock news. Legislators panic and the triage plan is scuttled, and we go back to the current system, where paramedics are tied up on BS calls while people are dying of cardiac arrests and bad trauma with no medics available.

Using my position in the health department, I argued well enough to kill the DIM proposal at least for the time being, but I didn't change the situation. The problem is still there. I didn't like government because almost every issue was difficult, every solution caused a new problem, and it was impossible to get people to agree on common solutions. And it was always easier to stop change than to make change. Whatever you did, you were pissing someone off.

I know that top people in government and civic groups can have a bigger positive impact on patient care (they can also do far more harm) than a single paramedic. Maybe someday I will be back in a role where, fortified with what I have seen on the street, I will have greater strength, patience, and moral authority to make change. But right now I need to be at this level. I like things simple. You call 911. I come and I take care of you, or at least try to. And notwithstanding an occasional bad mood, I like being the good guy.

Viewpoint

We're sent on a three to Mather Street for severe leg pain. It is a second-floor apartment of an old house that has an outdoor porch. The ceilings are high and there is a fireplace that is closed off. One of the big windows has a plywood board in place instead of glass.

A thirty-year-old woman is lying on a dirty black leather couch. She is wearing a "doo-rag" on her head. "My leg is killing me," she says. "I got this pain that runs from my side all the way to my toes. I went to the hospital yesterday and they gave me some pills, but the pain just wouldn't go away. I got to get some relief."

I examine her. Her vitals are normal. There is no pain on palpation, and she has the full range of movement.

"Where'd you go yesterday?"

"To Mount Sinai."

"What did they tell you?"

"They didn't tell me anything. They just gave me these pills, and the pain didn't go away. I was up all night. I got to get some relief. I want to go to another hospital. They got to fix me."

She sees something in our faces.

"You don't understand," she says. "I'm in pain."

"All right."

We walk her down to the ambulance and drive her crosstown to Hartford Hospital. They put her in the waiting room.

❖

I am worried about my attitude. I have talks with others about it. A friend of mine, an ER nurse, had to leave the ER because she saw it happening to her. After seeing so many people of certain races and ethnic backgrounds abusing the medical system, having multiple kids and then not caring for them, coming in addicted to drugs or cut up from fights, she had to get out. She felt she wasn't a bad person, but she started stereotyping.

My girlfriend Michelle, who is black, said she started feeling the same way toward her own race after working as a paramedic in the city for many years. I see it in a lot of EMTs. They are not inherently bad people, but when they work for a living and see others living off the dole, they get angry. Not that they would really want to change places, but they see something is clearly wrong. It's too easy to sit behind a desk in a lawmaker's office, proclaiming all sorts of stuff about peace on earth and love thy brother. It is unsettling when you deal with it face-to-face.

Weicker used to cite the Episcopal hymn "Once to Every Man and Nation." He'd quote: "Then it is that the brave man chooses, while the coward stands aside till the multitude make virtue of the faith he had denied."

I want to be that kind of a paramedic, where I can say it is my job to take care of the sick, to stand like Horatio on the bridge against all the hate, prejudice, and scorn that society—and sometimes I myself—feels.

❖

We're called for a woman with low blood pressure in Newington, a nice suburb south of the city. In the upstairs bedroom, we find a large woman lying in bed with a washrag on her forehead. She had surgery the day before on her hand and the pain pills have made her nauseous. Glenn rolls his eyes at me and I agree the lady is a mental case. Still, we help her onto our stair chair and carry her down the carpeted stairs.

"Where is my granddaughter?" she asks dramatically. Once the granddaughter appears, she says, "Don't let her see me like this. Oh, Kathy, Nana will be all right. Don't you worry."

We get her on the stretcher and tuck her in, under the watchful eyes of a police officer, who is on the scene to help out and who, in checking for the paramedic patch on my left shoulder, makes certain our company has sent a paramedic and not a basic unit as the terms of our contract with the town state. Feeling a strain in our backs, we lift the woman into the ambulance and head to the hospital.

I know if she lived in the inner city we would have at least tried to make her walk—because she probably could. But this lady might have lodged a complaint against us, even though she was well enough to walk.

It bothers me that I seem to have two standards.

Brave Attempts

In 1994, my best friend, Brad, decided to quit his job as an assistant U.S. attorney and run for Congress. It was quite a risk for a father of four with a big mortgage on his house, but he said he was tired of watching his fellow law-enforcement officers go into the streets under-manned, underarmed, and without the support of their government. He saw too many criminals go through the revolving-door justice system and get back on the street to commit more violent crimes. He asked me to help him, and I could not say no. He is a good, decent man who wanted with all his heart to make a better world for his kids. I will always remember on election eve standing with him and the four kids in the twilight, holding his campaign signs as cars drove by. Each toot of a horn thrilled him, and as it got darker, he was reluctant to leave, believing that each car that came by was another vote, and maybe the one that would put him over the top. We stayed until we faded completely into the darkness.

Some of his views were different from mine, but I understood where he was coming from. He called for tough sentences, an end to welfare giveaways, and balancing the budget. He became one of Newt Ging-rich's protégés, a breed of young Republican who lined up behind the Contract with America, a platform of term limits, less government, and stiff criminal sanctions. While I love my friend and agree that changes—big changes—need to be made, I fear a selfishness behind this conserva-tive movement and an ugliness at its fringes. At the same time, I cannot say the old way has worked, and it may in fact have done more harm than the tough love the new Republicans preach. And there is an awful truth behind Gingrich's mantra during the campaign: "Twelve-year-olds are having babies. Fifteen-year-olds are killing each other. Seventeen-year-olds are dying of AIDS. Eighteen-year-olds are receiving diplomas they can-not read."

ne of Weicker's big achievements was the Americans for Disabili-
es Act (ADA) that he wrote but which passed after he had left office.
The ADA was a wonderful idea to help the disabled have full access
to society, but it also came at great cost in terms of implementa-
tion. Small businesses claimed compliance would cost jobs, and maybe
even put them out of business. There is a price to be paid for all
laws, and sometimes the price is so high, in the end the law does more
harm than good.

In a debate, Brad's opponent spoke about all the wonderful things he
had mandated as a congressman for the government to do to help the
people. Brad was able to respond: well, we're stuck paying for all those
mandates. He was right. Yet I felt there was something restraining the
spirit of that argument. It was cold realism, not the soaring inspiration I
felt with Weicker. But maybe sometimes you have to let realism go to
achieve greater possibility. I think maybe we are at our best when we
refuse to set limits.

This year Connecticut hosted the international Special Olympics,
which Weicker chaired. It was a big success not just for the athletes, but
also for letting the person on the street see what these people are capable
of doing and for bringing everyone closer together. Weicker often liked
to cite the Special Olympics pledge in his speeches: "Let me win, but if I
cannot win, let me be brave in the attempt."

❖

I am working with John Hart, who works full-time as a technician in
Hartford Hospital's ED and only part-time now on the ambulance. He's
been in EMS and firefighting for over ten years. He misses the streets, he
says, but the other job pays better and he's got a wife, kid, and mortgage.
We're sitting outside Saint Francis, passing the time between calls, just
bullshitting. We're talking about how the job can affect your views on
things.

Our conversation turns to the races. He says before he started working
in the city he didn't care for Hispanics or blacks, but now after seeing
where they live and dealing with them, whether in the back of the ambulance or taking their blood pressures in the emergency department, he
feels differently. He says he's screwed up a lot in his life, and through
sheer luck, he's where he is today and not in some dark place. He has
some sympathy for misfortune. They're all just people, he says, living in
different circumstances.

I like what he says.

Incident Report

We do a minor motor vehicle accident (MVA) in Hartford. There is little damage to either car, but a little girl sitting in the backseat without a seat belt has a cut on her forehead that a passing EMT has already bandaged before we arrive. The mother wants us to take her to John Dempsey Hospital in Farmington, where the girl, who has a brain tumor, has just come from the doctor's office. The mother says she will follow in her own car, but the cop tells her the car is inoperable. The left front tire is flat. We have her ride in the back with the daughter, whom we have c-spine immobilized. We go to the hospital on a three—no lights or sirens.

The girl is alert and oriented, suffered no loss of consciousness. Her pupils are equal and reactive, and she has the full range of feeling and movement. Her vital signs are fine. At the hospital we get her transferred to a bed in the ER, while her mother goes to the registration desk to check her in. I leave my run form with the nurse.

"Did you get the mother to sign her refusal?" Glenn asks when I return to the ambulance.

"I'm sorry," I say. "I thought you'd gotten it."

"I got the others. I told her I'd get her to sign on the way or at the hospital."

I take the form and find her just getting off the phone in the waiting room. "I need you to sign this refusal form for yourself," I say, putting an X where she should sign her name.

"I ain't signing that," she says. "I didn't refuse no treatment."

"Ma'am, this is to prevent you from getting a bill. It does not prevent you from seeking treatment now. It just says you didn't want us to treat you, so we transported you as a nonpaying passenger rather than as a patient."

"I ain't signing my rights away," she says. "I didn't refuse treatment. I was talking to the policeman and I can't talk to two people at once. I know what you're trying to do, and I ain't signing no rights away!"

"Ma'am, you don't need to shout."

"You can't force me to sign nothing!"

A secretary, who is also black, comes out and tells me to stop upsetting the woman.

I look at her, and say, "Excuse me, I am not upsetting her. I am in a legal position where I must obtain her signature."

"You are upsetting her. Now let her go see her daughter."

"This is not your business. I am trying to get her to sign a refusal of treatment, which will spare her a bill and legally protect me."

"You lying!" the woman shouts. "I didn't give away any rights."

"There is no need to shout," I say. "Please act like an adult."

"You the one who's not acting like an adult. Trying to take away my rights and lie about me."

A nurse comes out and in a calm voice tries to find out what is going on.

I start to speak, but the woman shouts over me. "He's lying about me! I can't talk to a policeman and them at the same time! I didn't refuse nothing!"

The nurse listens to her rave, and then asks, "Are you injured?"

"I hit my head," she says.

"We're going to have to put a cervical collar on you then."

"I want to see my daughter. Where's my daughter? She got a shunt in her head. Maybe they don't know what that is."

"We know what that is," Glenn says. "Your daughter is fine. She has a cut on her forehead."

All during this I am thinking I hate black people like this. The lady is ignorant. She is trying to make herself into a victim, and she is trying to turn all her problems—her poor driving, her daughter's plight, American evil—on the two of us. I almost say this to Glenn as we sit at the hospital writing lengthy incident reports to document the episode. But I don't say it because I know it is a bad thing to say, and because I know that if the lady was white I would not have said I hate ignorant white people. I would have said, what a fucking bitch, but it would not have been racial.

I am pissed off at the secretary for assuming I was the one instigating the shouting and that I was terrorizing a nice black woman whose poor little daughter was injured. I am tempted to take her aside and lecture her about how unprofessional it was for her to attack me, to tell her how I

We get a call for a person not feeling well. When we arrive, a teenager meets us outside and says his mom's not feeling well. "What's wrong?" Glenn asks.

"She's been lying on the floor for three days."

"What?"

"She been going to the bathroom on herself."

"Does she respond to you?"

"She don't say nothing."

"You waited three days to call?"

The woman is tottering on a chair in the middle of the living room, while six family members look on. The woman is in her forties with thick track marks on her arms.

I look at her pupils, expecting to find them constricted, but they are dilated and barely reactive. She is very hot and can't squeeze my hands or respond to any commands.

"She does heroin?"

"Yeah, but not for three days."

She has shit and vomit all over herself. Her pressure is high, and she is definitely out of it. Once we have her in the ambulance, we look for veins. Her track marks run the length of her arms, like surgical scars. I have never seen them so long and so pronounced. I flip her wrist over and try for a narrow vein, but it blows. I feel the hand and find a tiny spot of sponginess. I use a twenty and get a flashback. I draw bloods and fill all four tubes. Glenn hands me the line and it runs. I try some Narcan to see if there is any heroin in her system, but there is no reaction. I am thinking either she got so conked out she became hypoxic and fried her brain, or else she has wicked out-of-control hepatitis. I run fluid through the line, and we head off to Saint Francis. Her temperature at the hospital is 105. She is very sick. The nurse cringes looking at the track marks. "You got a line?" she says. "Did you get bloods?"

"Yup," I say.

"Nice job."

Later in the EMT room at Hartford we are telling another paramedic about the call—the point being a lot of people call for an ambulance if they stub their toe, and these galoots didn't have the sense to call with the lady lying there in the living room shitting on the carpet for three days. We tell about the track marks, which are the biggest, toughest things either of us has seen.

The other paramedic says, "Translation, no IV access."

Glenn doesn't say anything. I think he is waiting for me to say, "Oh, I got the line."

But I am feeling so good, I say nothing.

I think it's like Michael Jordan having to say, "I made the shot."

As if anyone doubted. Nothing but net.

Tricks of the Trade

W e're called to Farmington Avenue for "something in the eye." The address turns out to be an insurance company, where the guard tells us there is a man inside who got grease into his eye. As we wheel the stretcher down the hall, I am thinking: "Grease, grease. Now is that something you irrigate with water, or is that something that causes the eye to explode if you irrigate with water?" There are so many things in the paramedic textbook that when you are reading, you sometimes say, I'll never get that one. There are twenty zillion substances that can get into eyes. Grease. Grease. Irrigate or leave alone. I am starting to get a little nervous, but I decide that, when I see the patient, I'll look him over, and if it doesn't come to me, I'll call Medical Control or Poison Control and get the information that way.

The nurse meets us in the hall and says he has greasecutter in his eyes. She has already called Poison Control, and they told her to irrigate, which is what she is doing with saline. She hands us a printed pamphlet describing the greasecutter chemical.

"Great," I say, relieved.

The man says his eyes burn. A nurse is putting a few drops at a time in each eye.

"We might want to up the flow," I say.

Just then another nurse comes in. I recognize her as the nurse who was present when we did a diabetic there several weeks earlier. She smiles at me and says to the other nurse, "He's the one who got the excellent IV that day."

The nurse looks at me and says, "I thought you looked familiar."

We get the man on the stretcher and take him down the hall. I run water on his eyes as we go. In the ambulance I have the nurse run water in his eyes while I hook up a device I heard about at the state EMS conference years ago. I spike a one liter bag of saline and attach it to a basic two-pronged oxygen cannula, which I tape to his nose. This creates a perfectly spaced flow of water into both eyes simultaneously. The nurse thinks it is a great idea. I thank her again for her help, and we're off to the hospital.

When we come through the ED doors, the triage nurse stops and looks at my device and says aloud, "Look at that. Now I'm impressed."

I am feeling pretty good about myself after this call, like I am already a pretty darn good paramedic.

My next call I stick my patient three times without getting an IV.

No rest for glory.

WHIPPED

Baby Girl

A paramedic student asks me if I ever had any calls that kicked my butt. I think he is expecting me to give a reassuring answer—to say that I haven't, that as long as you do what you're taught, you'll be all right. Instead I say, yeah, I've had a few that whipped me good.

❖

It's late in the afternoon when they call our number. It's for a miscarriage within blocks of the hospital. Glenn shakes his head. Miscarriage is a routine call that often turns out to be nothing more than a little spotting or a stomachache. We don't even bother to put on our lights and sirens.

I grab the blue bag and start walking up the steps of the apartment building when a woman comes running out. "You're going to need the stretcher," she says.

"She can't walk?"

"The baby's coming out! Hurry!"

I turn and shout to Glenn. "Grab the OB kit. The baby's coming out."

"There's one in your bag," he says.

"Get the stretcher. I'll see you inside."

I follow the woman who is running ahead of me now. We go in the front door. I tell her to hold up while I prop the lock open so Glenn can get in. We race up three flights of stairs then down several corridors. When we reach the apartment, she points to the bedroom. "She's in there."

It is a well-kept apartment. I enter the bedroom and find a woman lying prone on the bed, with a man holding her hands and comforting her. "What's going on?" I say.

"The baby's coming out," he says.

She is wearing a dress. I lift it up. The sight stuns me. I see the motionless legs and behind of a baby hanging out of her.

"It's coming out the wrong way," I blurt out.

"She's six months pregnant," the friend says. "They should never have let her out of the hospital. They should never have sent her home."

I am in near panic, uncertain what to do. "Go help my partner in," I say.

The baby is blue. I try to remember what it said in the book to do about a breech delivery. The baby isn't making any progress. It is stuck. I am worried that the baby's head is pressed against the umbilical cord, cutting off his supply of oxygenated blood. I try to put my gloved fingers in the mother to try to create a tiny breathing space for the baby.

The mother screams, and I say, "I'm trying to make an airway for the baby."

The man says to her, "He's trying to make an airway."

Glenn shows up. "It's a breech," I say. "We're going to need backup."

He takes the radio and calls the company for another unit.

"We're going to have to deliver here," he says. Even though we are just blocks from the hospital, the baby is too far out to put the mother on the stretcher and try to make a run for it.

He takes the baby's back and legs. As I tell the mother to push, I try to press her skin back and away from the baby's head.

"Push," I say.

I can hear her strain. I still haven't seen her face.

"Push."

Nothing is happening.

"Push."

I see tiny toothpick arms now. Blue, lifeless.

"Push."

It seems an eternity. I push her skin to the side.

Suddenly the head pops out and the baby falls onto the bed. I hold it in my hands. It is wet, slippery, and lifeless. Its eyes are fused together. I start doing compressions. The baby's head is at the top of my fingers. Its feet dangle limply on my wrist. It is blue. Its skin is almost transparent. It looks like a creature from the movie *Cocoon*. It is a girl. "We need suction," I say to Glenn.

He takes the bulb suction out of the OB kit and tries to suction the mouth and nose, but the tube barely fits into it.

"We need to get some oxygen going," I say.

He hooks up a nonrebreather mask, which I try to hold over the baby's face. We have told the other crew to bring up our pediatric kit, which has intubation supplies, but I don't think I can get a blade in the baby's mouth because it is so small. Even the pediatric ambu-bag we have in our blue bag is way too big to fit the baby's face.

Suddenly, I feel it move. "She's alive. Cut the cord and let's boogie out of here," I say.

Glenn clamps it in two places, and hands shaking, makes the cut. The other crew is just coming in the door.

"We're taking the baby to the hospital," I tell the mother.

The friend gives us a towel to wrap the baby in. It swallows her up.

We move quickly down the hallways. The neighbor holds the door open for us by the stairways, and we begin our descent. We go down four flights. We are in the basement and can't find our way out.

"This way," the neighbor shouts. "Up here."

We retreat toward her voice, back up a flight of stairs. A trip that should have taken forty seconds is taking minutes. We are losing time.

"That way," she says, pointing us down a long corridor. We race down it. Ahead I can see the door. We're out.

In the ambulance, I put the baby on the stretcher and take the child ambu-bag and attach an infant mask to try to pump air into the lungs, but the seal is too big. I can't get any air in. The baby moves again, a desperate agonal movement. "Come on, little baby," I say. To Glenn, I call, "I can't get any air in."

"We're two blocks away," he shouts to me.

Moments later we're out at the hospital. I climb out holding the baby in my hand, still doing tiny compressions with my fingers, the oxygen mask back over her face. We move into the ED, past the triage desk, and into the cardiac room. I am six foot eight; the baby can't be more than ten inches. I lay her on the bed. Two doctors are there. They see the little thing and start shaking their heads. "No, no," one says. "Look at it."

I am still doing compressions.

"It's too blue. When was it born?"

Glenn looks at the clock. "Seven minutes ago," he says.

"But it has a heartbeat," a nurse says.

"No."

My compressions slow to none. My fingers linger for a moment on her chest.

It is the tiniest thing I have ever seen. Her legs are as blue as the darkest ocean. Her face is purple. She moves again but can get no air.

I feel the room staring at me.

"If it had been intubated, maybe, but look at it."

They get a tiny stocking cap and put it on her head. They pull a towel up to her neck. Lying on the huge stretcher, she looks like a mouse.

"It hasn't a chance."

A few people rush in the room with an incubator, but the doctors shake their heads.

Glenn and I stand there, looking at the baby. While we know she doesn't have a chance, it is hard to just stand there and not do anything. I feel dazed, like we've just raced across the country to catch a boat and we're too late. It's already left shore—still in our sights but unreachable. No words come from my mouth.

We walk down the hall together, silently.

I sit in the EMT room and stare at my blank run report. I am distraught, overwhelmed by the baby's death. I feel responsible. A half an hour before I was sitting in the ambulance, bullshitting with Glenn, and now I have experienced the most horrible of events—a baby, entrusted to my care, who came into the world directly into my hands, lies on the hospital stretcher, blue, cold, her tiny heart beating slower, her lungs unable to get air. I failed at saving her. It could have been, it should have been the most joyous of calls. I should be jumping about like Rocky, lighting cigars and passing them out, proclaiming, "It's a girl! It's a girl!" thrilled at having brought life into the world, feeling as alive as twenty men. Instead, I sit with head in hands, beaten.

Shawn Kinkade, who is writing his own run form, looks at me and knows something is wrong. He puts down his pen and starts talking to me. He gets me to tell him what happened, and we go over what I did, and in quiet kind tones he tells me about similar calls he's had. It is not that he makes me feel better—but he keeps anguish from overtaking me, keeps me from feeling completely alone.

❖

"You think we'll get stork pins?" Glenn says later when we are just sitting outside by the ambulance. They give tiny pins shaped like storks to EMTs who deliver babies in the field.

"I don't want one," I say.

❖

When we leave the office that night after turning in our run cards, we shake hands.

"Maybe we'll have a better day tomorrow," he says.

"You're a good partner," I say.

❖

I have a bad night. I get home and call Michelle, but we haven't been getting along great, and she has a lot of work to do for her PA school. I want to tell her about the call, but it's not a good time, and I don't want to use it to get sympathy to get back in her good graces. I keep quiet about it.

I have a bad night. I can't sleep. I stare at the ceiling. I keep seeing the baby pop out and lie there lifeless in my hand. I wonder what the mother thinks of me. I wonder if she holds me responsible.

❖

The next day I ask Debbie Haliscak about the call and whether I should have intubated. She says I did the right thing. I probably wouldn't have been able to get the blade in the mouth anyway. I did the right thing. A lot of preemies don't even have lungs developed enough to breathe.

I see one of the doctors who was there, and she tells me I did a good job. She said her only regret was that medicine hadn't advanced enough emotionally to help the baby die. She wishes someone could have held the baby to help her over to the other side.

Glenn and I talk about it. It was the first delivery for both of us. He says, "We were with the little girl when she came into the world. She spent most her life with us."

As the days go by, I read what I can, even go to the bookstore and buy a book that has pictures of babies in various stages of development.

I am still bothered. I sit at my computer. I feel my body start to shake. I weep.

At my request, Debbie sets up a meeting for me with a neonatologist so he can answer the questions that stay with me. I tell him I want to know what I could have done better so that next time, if the baby has a shot at all, I can give it one. He tells me I was right not to intubate, unless I was sure I could do it. He says bagging is the most important thing, even more important than compressions, because if the baby gets more air, it will stimulate the heart. He shows me the proper equipment. There is a tiny neonate mask and a tiny ambu-bag, neither of which we carry. He says it sounds like I did the best I could under rather traumatic circumstances.

Though I am not religious, I feel I need absolution.

They have all told me that I did the best I could, but I know different. I was there. I held a tiny new life in my hands. I felt it try to breathe like a little fish out of water. I know I didn't keep her warm enough. I moved too quickly to get air into her new blood. Another

medic—a Michelle Gordon, a Shawn Kinkade, or a Tom Harper—
might have let her lungs better know the soft feel of pink air. I hear the
mythic story of a paramedic who, on delivering a baby of twenty-six
weeks, intubated that newborn, the light from the laryngoscope blade
lighting up the entire baby through its translucent skin. I don't know if
that baby lived or died, but I believe it got better care than I gave this
child. I sit alone for hours, dwelling on it. No other medics are there.
Only me. Not that I could have saved you, but I know I could have given
you a better chance. I should have been able to get more air into you.
Please, forgive me.

Paramedic Amputates Leg on Scene to Save Life

On Monday, the day before I begin my three-day shift, I get a
phone call from Michelle, who asks me if I heard about the call
in West Hartford that morning. I haven't and she says something
about a dump truck running over two women, killing one instantly and
the other had to have her leg amputated on scene. We both wonder who
was there working the call and what the situation would have been like
for a surgeon to come out and amputate the leg.

Later on the news that night it is the lead story. They show the woman
being taken by Life-Star helicopter. I can see a Professional Ambulance
on scene but do not see any of our people. The newscaster says the
woman's leg was amputated on scene by paramedics to save her life. She
is in serious condition at Saint Francis. The other woman was taken by
ambulance to Hartford and pronounced dead on arrival. They devote
most of the newscast to determining whether or not the driver of the
dump truck who backed over the ladies, and who was hospitalized for
shock, had any previous driving violations.

On Tuesday I am in the EMT room at Hartford Hospital writing a run
form when I hear one of our paramedics, Sandy Balboni, talking about

the call. She says the driver backed over the ladies, then hearing everyone screaming and yelling at him, pulled forward again, and basically
ran over them twice. She was the first medical responder. The one
woman was dead, the other's leg was hanging on only by skin. There was
blood everywhere.

"Hey," a medic says, "I hear they are going to offer you a surgical residency here. Didn't you see the doctors talking about you in hushed tones
as you passed? She's the one who saved the woman's life. She amputated
at the scene."

She shakes her head and laughs. "I know. I was into my third beer last
night when the news came on, and all of a sudden I heard them saying I
amputated the leg—the truck did that. I looked down at my beer and said
I may have had too many of these."

"I heard you performed neurosurgery last week and saved two lives by
performing a kidney transplant on scene. You may not even have to do
your residency. They're talking about just making you an attending
[physician] here. Some of the residents are upset by it, though."

She laughs and then lets out her breath. She is quiet a moment then
says, "In ten years of doing this job, it was one of the worst things I've
seen. The supervisors wanted to know all the details and my scene time
and why I'd called Life-Star. None of them asked me how I felt about
it. . . . It was a tough call."

We are all quiet.

"You did good," another EMT says softly to her.

She nods. Her eyes are faraway.

Another Code

We're dispatched for a man down not breathing. A few minutes
later, we get an update. The fire department is on scene and
it is a cardiac arrest.

When we arrive, we see a ten-year-old boy standing on the front steps, crying and holding the door open for us. We learn later he went out on a walk with his father, and when they returned he went into the kitchen to get something to eat. When he came back to the living room, he found his father on the floor. He called 911 and asked for help.

The fire department is doing a good job of CPR. The man has been down about seven minutes. He has a history of multiple bypass operations. I attach the defibrillator pads and turn on the monitor. He's in v-fib. "I'm going to shock him," I say. Everyone backs off. I hit the yellow charge button, then press the red fire buttons. A jolt of energy goes through the man. He's in asystole, or ventricular standstill, where only the atrium beats. I hand Glenn the med box. "Get a line," I say. To the firemen, I say, "Continue CPR."

I set up my intubation gear. I unzip the kit. I stare at the selection of metal blades and plastic tubes. For a moment, I feel panic coming over me. I haven't had a tube for two months. I wonder if I can do it. I hear this voice in my head saying, "Give it up. Quit. Zip up your bag and walk out the door." I grab the laryngoscope handle, attach the number three miller blade, snap it into place. The light is on. I set it aside. I take a number eight endotracheal tube and stick in the aluminum stylet, which is bent and gives me a little problem shaping it as I curve the tube into a hockey-stick shape. I attach a ten cubic centimeter syringe to the port so I can inflate the cuff once I am in.

"Okay," I say to the fireman doing the bagging. "I'm going to tube."

The man's face is gray with a blue tint. His eyes are open, fixed, and dilated. He has a white beard and protruding upper teeth. I spread his teeth apart, sink the blade in, sweep the tongue to the side and lift up. Lying on my belly, I look into his throat. It is clear of puke or secretions. I see the chords hanging down silently. I slide the tube in the mouth and move it forward, watching it pass through the chords. I hold the mouth open longer, making sure I am seeing what I am seeing. I am in. I pull the blade out and go to pull the stylet out, but it is stuck. I yank, and finally get it out. I attach the bag valve to the top of the tube. I reach for my stethoscope to check for lung sounds to verify placement, but it is not around my neck. I look to Glenn, but he doesn't have his stethoscope with him either. I reach back into the blue bag and pull out blood-pressure cuffs, but no stethoscope. I yell to a fireman to go out and get my scope from the front seat of the ambulance. I put my ear under the man's arm and listen. I hear lung sounds. I know I am in. A firefighter returns with the scope, and I check again. Positive sounds under the armpits, nothing in the stomach. I secure the tube with tape and wrap it around the man's head.

Glenn has the line in and bloods drawn. We slam in an atropine and an epi. I look back at the monitor. The man is in v-fib. I shock again. Back to asystole. We do another round of drugs.

A second crew has arrived. With the help of the fireman we get the man on a board and strapped down, and carry him out of the house and down the steps, past the crying boy, across the lawn, and over to the ambulance.

They lift the man into the back. I recheck the lung sounds and they are less audible on the left side now. The tube has slipped into the right main stem of the lungs. I have Glenn listen as I pull back and retape. I shout to one of the EMTs to drive. I look at the monitor and the man is back in v-fib.

We shock him at three-sixty. The charge zaps the man and there is the smell of smoke, from singeing the hairs on his chest. The man is still in v-fib.

I push lidocaine and another epi, then go back to bagging while Glenn keeps up the compressions. We really need a third hand. The man is still in v-fib, so we shock again. He's still in v-fib, so we give another lidocaine. I recheck the lung sounds, and while I am hearing them in the left, they are still fainter than the right. I pull back and retape. We're at the hospital now. The man is dead, lifeless, purple from the shoulders up. We hook him to the portable oxygen, pull the stretcher out, and wheel him into the ER. Glenn is standing on the stretcher rail doing CPR. I'm bagging as the others steer, but just looking at the guy, I wonder what the point is. As we go through the ER, everyone turns to look. They shake their heads as we pass. The man is beyond saving.

I give the report as we enter the cardiac room. "Down about thirty minutes. He's been back and forth between v-fib and asystole. We've given him three epis, two atropines, and two lidocaines."

We transfer him onto their table. The respiratory therapist says to me, "I'll take over," as she attaches her own bag to the tube. The doctor checks lung sounds and says, "Equal lung sounds."

They make a halfhearted effort to work the guy, who clearly has no chance at this point. We stand watching.

They call it.

No one says anything to us.

ATTACHMENTS

Change

"You're taking her to the hospital," the daughter says.

"I'm fine. I'm not going anywhere," says the woman sitting on the shag carpet with her back against the couch.

"Yes you are," the daughter says. "You don't have a choice. Tell her you're taking her," she says to us.

"Hold on a minute," I say. "I need to examine her. If she doesn't want to go, I can't take her against her will. That's kidnapping."

"That's right," the mother says. "I don't have to go."

"She needs to go," the daughter says.

"I am not going, you ungrateful daughter. I'll never do anything for you again."

"Let's just calm down," I say. I kneel by the woman. "What happened? How long have you been sitting here?"

"Just a few minutes," she says, avoiding my eyes.

"She has not," the daughter says. "She's always falling. She's been there all day."

"Just hold on," I say.

"Bitch," the mother says. "Get out of my house."

Glenn takes the daughter into the kitchen. I examine the woman, who I discover has not seen a doctor for ten years. She has an irregular pulse and sores on the bottoms of her legs. She tells me she falls a lot, but she is okay and can take care of her house better than her ungrateful daughter can. She says she has only been on the ground a little while and enjoys sitting here. She turns and looks at her cat sitting on the stairs watching us through the railing. "Come sit with me, Stanley," she says. "Give Momma some company."

The cat doesn't move. I can hear the daughter telling Glenn that the mother was on the floor on Sunday when she came and wouldn't get up then either. She can't take care of herself, she says. She crawls around all day on the floor.

"You have a very nice house here," I say. "But I think it's best if you come with us to the hospital and get checked out. Then you can come back and live here healthier than you have been. You're not going to be able to stay here if you keep falling."

"Fuck you, I'm not leaving. Not today. Maybe tomorrow. I don't want to go now. Leave me alone."

A police officer has come and he tries to persuade her.

"I don't have my makeup on," she says. "And look at me. No, I'm not going. Maybe tomorrow, but not now, please. I'm quite happy here."

"Make her go," the daughter says. "Look at her."

"Get out of my life, you ungrateful daughter! All you cause me is misery in my old age."

Glenn pulls the daughter back into the kitchen.

"If you can stand up by yourself, then we'll go," I say. "But if you can't, then we'll take you to the hospital and get you checked out so you can come back here, okay?"

"No," she says. "I'm not going today. Look at me."

"You look fine. So we're going to bring our stretcher in and get you comfortable and we'll take a nice easy ride to the hospital. No lights. No sirens."

"All the neighbors will be looking at me."

"No, no. It'll be fine."

"Not today, I'll go tomorrow."

Glenn brings in the stretcher, and we each take an arm and lift her up. "Unhand me, fucking goddamn assholes." She can't stand on her own without our holding her. "Get your cotton-pickin' hands off me. I can't believe I have these boys here in my house, not that I don't like boys or haven't had my share of them once upon a time."

"I bet you did. I bet you were a looker," I say as we ease her down onto the stretcher.

"You should see the pictures of me then. But look at me. I can't go out without my makeup. Really, I don't need to go. Please leave me alone."

"Yes, you do, Mother," the daughter says.

"Bitch," she says. "You'll get nothing from me. Nothing from me, you hear."

I have taken two photos off the bookcase and show them to the woman. "Is this you?" I ask.

"Yes, that's me and that's my husband. He died a year and a half ago. Forty-two years we were married."

"You were a looker," I say. The photos are black-and-white and she looks like a long-legged beauty from a 1940s movie. "Beautiful. You have any bathing-suit pictures?"

She slaps my hand gently. "You're very kind. I was a beauty, though, and I had lots of fun. Frank was a good husband. He was handsome, too."

"You made a nice couple."

"We did," she said, "we did."

Glenn tucks the blanket in around her and carefully buckles the straps.

"This is all so unnecessary," she says.

"We'll drive in slow, then the doctor will check you out, and hopefully, you'll be back here soon, at this lovely home of yours."

She looks around. "It is a nice home, isn't it?"

"Yes it is, ma'am," I say.

We wheel her out to the ambulance. The neighborhood is quiet. "I do all my own gardening," she says.

The bushes need some trimming. The grass is getting a little long.

"It's very nice, ma'am. Well kept."

"I've worked hard," she says. "I really don't need to go. This is so unnecessary."

Fear

If there is one thing that has affected me in EMS it is dealing with old people. Before I started this I didn't think too much about getting old—it was too far off—but here you can't escape it. You go down the hall of a nursing home and see the people lined up—the Os, the Ms, and the Qs—and you know that you are going to end up there someday. (The Os have their mouths open perpetually. The Ms go *mmmmm* all day. The Qs are Os with their tongues hanging out of the corner of their mouths.)

I lived with a woman twelve years older than me for almost ten years. She was smart and beautiful, could grow a garden of bright colored flowers, read two books a day, talk baseball like a pro, cook a killer steak, and despite being five three and a hundred and ten pounds, she could match me beer for beer. We'd party till four in the morning and end up standing on the couch singing along to Elvis's "Suspicious Minds." She was as healthy as a horse, but she chain-smoked and had a bump on her collarbone that she wouldn't have checked out. She wouldn't ever go to a doctor. We broke up for lots of reasons, good and bad, but I always worried what I would do if she got sick and old.

❖

We take a man from the hospital to a nursing home where he will undergo rehabilitation for a stroke that has left him with some partial right-sided weakness. He is a big man—six feet three, in his late sixties, with distinguished gray hair and the solid jaw of a corporate leader. He is wearing blue flannel pajamas. His wife is in her late thirties, an attractive well-dressed blonde. She seems very uncomfortable around him. We have barely gotten him into his bed at the nursing home when she says a brief good-bye from the door. I see his jaw tense, then loosen. He looks toward the window, but his gaze is not fixed. I hear a wild moan in the hall from one of the residents, the elderly woman in the wheelchair we passed on our way in, a woman with a permanent O shape to her mouth.

As we wheel our empty stretcher out the main door, I see our patient's wife in a crimson BMW pull out into the street. The back wheel kicks up sand as she accelerates in front of a moving station wagon. Soon she is gone from sight.

Mothers

We respond to Newington Children's Hospital for a person having seizures outside the front door. When we arrive we see several nurses and doctors kneeling and standing over a young woman who lies flat on her back, her eyes staring straight up. She is crying and shaking. They have her attached to a blood pressure cuff and pulse oximeter. A crash cart is by her head. She is on an oxygen mask. A nurse is writing the latest set of vital signs on a chart.

"What's going on?" I ask.

A doctor says he is not sure, but he thinks this might be a psychological crisis. In a hushed tone, he tells me she has just been told that her child is suffering from adrenoleukodystrophy, a terminal disease. "A very lethal disease," he says. He says she walked out of the hospital, then passed out. I ask if she had a seizure. He says no.

I kneel by the woman. She is looking straight up. Her body is tense, on the verge of breaking out into full-scale trembles. I ask her to squeeze my hands, which she does.

"Her vitals are stable," the doctor says. They are in fact perfect: blood pressure 120/80, pulse 80, and respirations 20 with a pulse saturation of 99 percent. Her pupils are dilated, but they react to light.

We lift her onto our stretcher. I tell her in soft tones that we are taking her to Hartford Hospital, where they will have someone she can talk to. A nurse hands me a sheet of paper that has the woman's name and number and another sheet of paper that records the entire course of the code blue they called for her.

En route to the hospital she begins to shake again, her jaw quivers, tears flow from her eyes. She wails, a piercing flesh-tearing wail. The sound is primal, a deep, chilling, inconsolable grief. I think if there is a God, he must be hearing this sound, and parting the clouds in heaven to look down on our ambulance, moving north on Route 15.

❖

We have been briefed in advance. The fourteen-year-old boy's best friend committed suicide two months earlier by hanging. The boy has been distraught and increasingly difficult to deal with. The mother is afraid he is going to harm himself. When she suggested that he get help, he said he did not want to talk to anyone and would run away. She has made the decision to have him committed to the Institute of Living (IOL). Because she has worked with me on the ambulance, she has requested that I be the one to take him. Glenn is out sick, so Toniah Abner from the night crew stays over to do the call with me, while they try to find me a partner for the day.

We arrive at the house in Newington, a modest three-bedroom on a quiet street. The boy's mom comes to the door and leads us into the kitchen. The boy is sitting at the breakfast table. He is thinly built with weirdly cut hair and wearing a Megadeth T-shirt. "I'd like you to meet some people," she says. "This is Peter. He's a paramedic. He goes out with Michelle."

That causes him to take a second look at me. "Cool," he says. "Are you going to marry her?"

"We're not quite at that point yet," I say.

We shake hands.

"This is my partner, Toniah," I say.

And they shake.

The boy's father is also there, and he also shakes our hands as we exchange introductions.

"Christopher, there's something I need to tell you that's going on," his mom says. "Remember how I asked you if you wanted help, and you said you'd try to run away?"

"Yeah, I don't need help," he says. "I'm not talking to anyone."

"Well, we love you and don't want to see you hurt yourself."

"I never said I'd hurt myself, you lying bitch," he says.

"Remember when Marion was sick and she said she would have loved to have had someone to get her and help her, but she couldn't ask?"

"I don't care. I'm not talking to anybody."

"Well, that's why Peter and Toniah are here. They're going to take you to Hartford Hospital and then to the IOL in Hartford, where there will be doctors who can help you."

"Uh-huh," he says. He crosses his hands over his chest. "I'm not going."

"Well, we're your parents, and we love you, and you don't have a choice in this matter."

"I'll run away."

"No," she says. "We're concerned about you. Just the other night, you took some of that Vivarin."

"That's legal. It's like vitamin C."

"It's caffeine," I say. "But it's powerful stuff. I used to take it when I was in high school to stay up late studying. It exhausted me. I'd end up walking around with my fly open and not know it."

The boy laughs but keeps his guard up.

"Christopher," I say. "What your mom is talking about is a good thing. You've been through a tough time, and there are good people there who can help you."

"I'm not going," he says.

"Christopher," she says. "They are going to take you."

"I don't care. I'm not going, I'll fight."

I am looking at him. He is a little wiry kid, but though I am nearly twice his size, I am not looking forward to a wrestling match, particularly in front of the boy's mom.

"We do this all the time," Toniah says. "We will restrain you. It's your choice."

He looks up at me, maybe weighing his odds.

"We don't have to go lights and sirens. It'll be a nice ride. Toniah will drive, and I'll sit with you in the back. So you'll come with us, okay?"

"Can I take my Walkman?" he says.

"Sure," I say, surprised by the quick turn of events.

"I've got to brush my teeth."

"All right."

I accompany him upstairs. His room is a mess. Tapes, clothes, books, papers are scattered everywhere. There are posters and hand-drawn signs, all with images of death. I watch him closely to see that he doesn't pull a knife out of his drawers. He finds the Walkman and a few tapes.

When he is ready to go, his parents say, "We love you."

"I never want to see you again," he says, then turns and starts toward the door. Toniah and I walk on either side of him. Toniah motions for me to grab his arm, but I don't. I don't want him to feel he is being taken by force. I let him feel my presence, but don't hold his arm. I wonder if he tries to run whether I will be able to catch him. He doesn't try to bolt. I have him sit on the bench. He has his tape on full blast.

"Is that Megadeth?" I ask.

He looks at me blankly, then turns the volume down.

"Is that Megadeth?"

"No, just Death," he says.

"You like metal."

"Yeah," he says.

We talk about music. He doesn't care for Guns N' Roses, but when I mention Alice Cooper, he likes that. He also likes Ozzy Osbourne. I tell him the story about Alice Cooper biting the head off a chicken, and he is very interested. He says he's going to get an electric guitar after Christmas and his mom is going to pay for him to have lessons.

"You know, I know you're pissed at your mom now."

"She's a lying bitch," he says. "I never tried to hurt myself."

"Well, sometimes people can see the same thing differently."

"She wanted me to go to a private school, and I didn't want to so I carved an X on my arm."

"You painted an X on your arm or you carved it?"

"Carved it with a knife," he says.

"Well, I can see how she would think you were trying to hurt yourself. That's a reasonable—may not be right—but it's a reasonable interpretation."

"I just didn't want to go."

"I didn't get along with my mom either. She didn't understand me and was also doing stuff I didn't like. She died when I was thirty. We never made it right. Adults don't always know what they're doing. Sometimes they need people to talk to, too."

He is listening to me.

"Me, I'd love to be a rock 'n' roll star. I'd like to be like Eric Clapton, but I'm not musical. I mean, I love to sing around the house, I sing all the time, but I'm not good. I still like to do it. I've got one of those CD players that holds twenty-four CDs, and you can hit random and it'll play just like a jukebox."

"Cool," he says.

"I just come home and put it on, and have a beer and sing along. It gives me strength. I do this three days a week, then I write on the others—that's what I really like to do. But I'm thirty-seven years old. Sometimes I don't know what I'm doing with myself, but I have this dream, and I don't want to give it up."

"You're, like, an author?"

"It's what I try to be."

"Cool. What are you writing about?"

"This—being a paramedic—and I like to write fiction, stories about real people. I guess I hope I'll write a bestseller, and I'll make a million dollars and sell it to the movies, and I'll get a big house with a swimming pool on the ocean, and sit around and smoke cigars. I tell you what—I make a movie, I'll give you a role. You can be a rock guitarist."

"Yeah."

We're almost at the hospital now. "Hey," I say, "I forgot to take your blood pressure. Can you take your coat off for me?"

"Sure." He undoes his coat, and I take the pressure.

"How is it?" he asks. "Am I okay?"

"One twenty over eighty. Perfect. It's good. You'll live to be a hundred years old."

We go into the ER. He's got his headphones back on—the volume is so loud I can hear the pounding guitars. The triage nurse comes over and I lead her away from him.

"Get away from the music," she says.

I explain that he's a sweet kid and that his best friend killed himself and his mom is worried he might hurt himself. I give her the number of the doctor at the institute who will come down to see him and get him transferred to the IOL. I say there is a lot of tension between him and his mom right now.

"Poor thing," she says.

The nurses all take to him instantly. They put him in a room with an attendant watching the door. A nurse goes in and talks to him, and they seem to be getting along great. I look in the waiting room and see his mom. She is on the other side of the divide, now, helplessly looking into the ER, barred by the locked gate.

❖

I think sometimes the reason I haven't settled down and fathered is because I am worried I could not bear the pain of my child's hurts. I told my friend Brad once that I thought he was courageous to have four kids. He said it wasn't courage. Being a parent gives you strength you thought you might not have.

❖

We're called for a three-week-old who fell, hit his head, and is not breathing.

We pull to the curb behind the fire truck. I see a mother emerge from the front door carrying a small infant, surrounded by large firemen in full turnout gear. "The baby was breathing when we got here," a fireman tells me. "He's got a bump on his head."

I look at the baby, a tiny baby, who looks fresh out of the womb. I see the hematoma on the back of the skull. The baby is so tiny, I am concerned, but the baby is crying and that is a good sign. I take the baby from the mother's arms and examine it as I carry it to the back of the ambulance. The mother climbs in next to me on the ambulance bench. I lay the baby on the stretcher and the mother instantly reaches to pick it up.

"No, no," I say. "It must be on the stretcher." I do not want any sudden stops to send the baby flying. It is safe on the stretcher.

The baby lies there crying. I listen to its heartbeat with my stethoscope. The crying makes it hard for me to hear.

The mother reaches for the baby again, and I say no. "*Es bueno,*" I say, "that the *niño* is crying. *Bueno.*"

I pick up my clipboard and start asking for information. We are already en route to Hartford Hospital.

The mother is crying and can barely tell me the baby's name and birth date. She tries to pick the baby up again, and again I say no.

A wild look comes in her eye. She reaches under her shirt, removes a huge bare breast and throws herself on top of the tiny infant, whose lips and tiny hands go right to the stiff nipple. He is instantly quiet and peaceful, lying there sucking under his mother who is now prone above him on the stretcher.

I look to the front, but Glenn is oblivious to the scene in back. He is just driving along listening to country music. I look back at this scene, at the tiny baby lying under this huge breast, and the mother lying awkwardly on top of him, doing the only thing she knows will make him stop crying. In EMT school they teach us not to let patients have anything by mouth. I say nothing, speechless.

A Couple

It's the end of our shift, and we're sent to cover Newington. Normally I hate being out in Newington, but I'm bone tired, my back is killing me, and I've sweated clear through my uniform. There are white streaks on my black T-shirt showing through from all the salt that has come out of me. We've done eleven transports since seven this morning and two refusals, so being out in Newington for the last hour of our shift is something of a relief. Newington is a sleepy town with a young population that helps keep its call volume low. We are under contract to keep a paramedic rig in town twenty-four hours a day with a five-minute response time whenever called. As soon as we respond to a call, the company has to send another medic unit out to cover. The crew covering can be out there seven or eight hours without a call and nothing to do but drive

around town or sit in the park and watch the young mothers take their
kids to swim practice, or soccer practice, or baseball or football practice.

We're out there ten minutes when we get called for an MVA at Cedar
and Russell. We pull up, and it looks like a BS call, like a few refusals
and we'll be able to clear. It's a fender bender. One car hit another from
behind, and that car clipped another car, but the damage looks minor. A
cop waves me over to the middle car. There is a smashed bumper, but no
damage to the windshield. I see an elderly couple in their seats with
shoulder belts still on. I go to the passenger side, where the woman is sitting. "How are you?" I say.

"My chest hurts," she says, "right here where my belt is, but I'm worried
about my husband. He has high blood pressure and has had heart surgery."

"How are you, sir?" I ask.

"I'm okay," he says. "My wife's chest hurts."

"He's got high blood pressure, and he had heart surgery," she says.
"I'm all right, really. Will you check him out?"

She is seventy-five and he is eighty-three. We get them both boarded
and collared and into the back of the ambulance. I kneel between them,
taking blood pressures and doing a full physical assessment. I put them
both on oxygen by cannula as a precaution. I put the husband on the
heart monitor. He has a normal sinus rhythm. His blood pressure is high
at 230/120, but he tells me he always runs high. His wife's chest hurts
right along the path of the belt, but I am not overly concerned about her.
There is no crepitus or bruising. She has pain only if I press down hard.
We go to the hospital without lights and sirens. The wife on the bench, the
husband on the stretcher, they hold hands. I get their full medical histo-
ries. He has prostate cancer, I learn. I run a six-inch strip from the heart
monitor and give it to the wife. "This is your husband's heart," I say to
her. "From watching the two of you, I know that it beats for you."

He squeezes her hand.

At the hospital I try to have them put in the same room, but because of
the husband's heart history and high blood pressure, they put him in
Room 11, where he can be put on a monitor, while she goes into Room
20 on the other hallway.

After I have written my run reports, I stop by to see them. I tell the wife
her husband is doing well, and hopefully, they will be back together soon.

"I am so worried," she says. "It is his birthday today. Eighty-three years
old. I wanted to take him to a lobster feast. He insisted on driving. He

couldn't stop in time. He doesn't have the reactions anymore. He won't be able to drive after this. They will take that away from him. He is dying of cancer. The poor man is dying."

❖

He is still on the board, hooked up to the monitor when I check on him. I tell him his wife is doing well and sends her love.

"Is she all right?" he asks.

"Yes, she is doing well."

"It was my fault," he says. He starts to cry. "I hurt her. I didn't mean to hurt her. It was my fault."

He brings his hands to his face and weeps. His entire body shakes. "Don't worry," I say. "She is okay. She will be all right. Don't worry."

"It was my fault. Who will take care of her?"

"She will be all right." I hold his hand.

"I love her," he says.

He cries.

❖

It is dark when I get home. I live in a large apartment complex, a restored carpet factory that rents out to young professionals. It is a little more than I can afford, but I like living there. The ceilings are high, the outside walls are brick, and there is a health club on the premises. I get out of my car and walk to the door of my building, carrying my briefcase. It is the same briefcase that once held briefing papers for senatorial debates and draft copies of the governor's state-of-the-state speech. It is now old and beaten, ripped in the corners. It holds my protocol book, my clipboard, copies of my run forms, cough medicine, deodorant, a paperback novel, my stethoscope, and assorted items. I nod to my neighbors in business suits and dresses, whose names I do not know. "Evening, how are you?" I check my mailbox. Grocery-store flyers and bulk-mail credit-card applications.

In my apartment, I set my briefcase down on the kitchen counter. I take some cold potatoes and chicken out of the refrigerator. I open a beer and turn on the stereo. James Carr, an old forgotten soul great, sings "To Love Somebody."

I stand by the window and look out through the blinds at the gray-black sky to the north. I wish my apartment were not so empty.

CHANGES

❖   ❖   ❖   ❖   ❖   ❖   ❖   ❖   ❖

Changes

My friend Brad is going to be on the "CBS Nightly News" with Dan Rather in their Eye on America spotlight. Several months after he lost his bid for Congress, he was appointed sheriff of Middlesex County. Every year on opening day at Fenway Park in Boston, we go to the Cask and Flagon on Landsdowne Street for a few postgame beers. I am unable to attend this year because the Monday home opener is rained out and I am working on the ambulance on Tuesday. Brad goes with another good friend of ours from our younger years. "Hey, everybody," the friend declares, raising a beer in toast, "there's a new sheriff in town!"

Comparing my life with Brad's, I feel like Falstaff in the *Henry IV* stories in which Prince Hal goes on to become king. I think of all the beers Brad and I drank together, the highways traveled and women chased. Now Brad is a father of four, a church vestryman, and a pillar of his community. Though I have had long relationships with women, I am still single, driving a car with over 120,000 miles on it, and a source of concern to my father as to why I have not settled into a stable job with a retirement plan.

It seems there is a serious overcrowding problem in the Middlesex County prison, and Brad has been ordered by the court to release prisoners, but he is refusing. He says he has let out everyone he can, but the remaining prisoners are not candidates for release. He has appeared on the front page of the *Boston Herald* declaring, "I'd rather go to jail then let them out." Both the *Herald* and the *Globe* have written positive editorials. There is a clear irony in the sheriff having to go to jail for refusing to let out the prisoners the court ordered him to jail. This is the story CBS News is covering.

We are at the Farmington Avenue office at six-twenty, waiting for the news to come on, when we get a call for a drunk. We drop the drunk off at Saint Francis and clear by ten of seven. I'm hoping to catch the show when we get another call—shooting on Brooke Street. We respond on a one. They update us—shooting to the neck. A crowd is gathered outside the apartment building. They point inside the door. As I go through the narrow corridors and into the apartment, cluttered with furniture, I am saying to myself, please don't be lying on the ground, dead in a pool of blood. It will be a nightmare getting the person out of here. In the back room, I see a woman standing with a red towel around her neck. She is alert and oriented. I ask her to remove the towel. She has bullet holes on both sides of the front of her neck—the cop wants to ask her questions. "At the hospital," I say. "She's coming with me." I walk her quickly out of the apartment and get her into the back of the ambulance. I put in an IV as we go, lights and sirens, to the hospital. She asks me if she can have a cigarette.

"No," I say, "you're lucky you're not dead."

"Why can't I smoke?"

I am tempted to say, "Because you will be blowing smoke rings out of your neck."

They have the full trauma team awaiting her. Dr. Morgan says he's never seen anything like it. A through-and-through bullet wound to the neck without taking out her trachea or esophagus.

I look at my watch. It is 7:01. The show is over. I think if I had gone and worked for Brad I would be sitting in his living room now with his kids all around, celebrating his being on TV. I'd be drinking a beer, my tie loosened, and fielding calls from reporters for him, spinning the story like I did in the campaign. Instead I'm tired, beat, blood on my shirt. Still, I feel good about myself. I like my job and I'm getting better at it.

On Guard

They say if you stay in EMS long enough, you will see everything once. They also say everything is unique; you never see anything twice. When you are sitting in the ambulance and you hear a good call go out or sitting in the EMT room writing your report and another medic tells you about his interesting call, you feel a little twinge of jealousy that you missed that one. On the other hand, sometimes circumstances dictate that you get that special call. When it comes you try to be ready for it. No matter what the call, extraordinary or mundane, you try to be a good paramedic and never let your guard down. Any call can make or break you.

❖

We're called for a chest pain on Martin Street. A man with dreadlocks meets us at the door. "Who's sick?" I ask. "You?"

He nods. "I'm feeling a little weak. I had some discomfort in my chest earlier. I just don't feel quite right."

He walks out to the ambulance with us, and I have him take a seat on the stretcher. I tell him that since he's complaining of chest pain, I am going to do a full workup, put him on the monitor, give him some oxygen, put in an IV and draw bloods. I help him take off his jacket. The man is quite dirty and smells.

I take his pressure and find it elevated at 200/120. I ask him again if he is having any discomfort in his chest and he says a little. After I get the line, I give him a nitro, which helps ease the pain. He is a normal sinus rhythm going about 90 on the monitor. I get a complete history from him en route to the hospital. When we get out of the ambulance at the ER I keep him on the monitor, even though his discomfort has abated. It is awkward to carry the monitor and the IV bag. Sometimes medics will disconnect the person from the monitor in the rig because they will soon be hooking them up to the hospital's monitor. I keep it on. Wheeling him in the door, I watch his rate start to climb: 120, 130, 140, 150. I have a different patient. They take his pressure: 240/120. He goes to the cardiac room. I think I would have looked like an asshole if I had reported his pulse at 90 when the triage nurse felt it at 150. I did my job.

❖

The forty-two-year-old woman from the north end of Hartford with a history of gastrointestinal problems and diabetes has been vomiting since four in the morning, but just a few minutes ago vomited blood. She called her physician, who told her to call an ambulance and go to Hartford Hospital. He'd call and let them know she'd be coming in. She is a thin, emaciated woman. Her pressure is 130/80 both lying down and sitting up, which is a good sign, but her heart rate is 130, a bad sign. I want to put in a precautionary line, but she has no veins and tells me they'll have to go in her neck or groin at the hospital. I do a finger stick to check her blood sugar and find it almost 800. While driving to the hospital, I ask her if she has been checked for TB or HIV. She says no. She doesn't have them.

When we get to Hartford Hospital, there is a slip on the bulletin board with a message from her doctor. I take it off and hand it to the triage nurse. I give my report. I hear Glenn say, "I thought so," as the nurse writes on his form. I look at him and he points to the notation "HIV positive." After we unload the patient, he says she looked like she had it. I tell him I asked her and she said no. This startles him. "It's against the law for a person to lie to us about that." I'm not certain if he's right about that, but I am bothered by it. Normally, I have found that white homosexuals have been the most elusive about their HIV status, but no one had ever denied it when I asked about it point-blank. Most minorities or IV drug abusers have no problems telling me. Often it is the first thing out of their mouths. I think about making a notation on my report that I asked and she denied it, and I think about asking her again and giving her the business for lying to me, but I don't. When I go in, she is on her side. She looks so tired and weak there, the sheet giving her no warmth at all. I put a blanket over her and ask if that is better.

"Thank you," she says.

❖

We get called for an unconscious in West Hartford. Before we arrive we get an update—the person inhaled gasoline. When we arrive, both West

Hartford medics are already on scene along with a police officer. The medics are kneeling by a man lying on the grass. He is a disheveled man with a dirty T-shirt and jeans, and bits of grass and debris in his tangled hair. "He's not really out," the female medic says. She rubs her knuckles on his sternum, and he jerks awake.

"Leave me the fuck alone!" he says.

"Calm down," she says to him. "You have some scissors?" she asks me.

"In the ambulance," I reply.

When I come back with them and the oxygen, she has already gotten a pair from the other medic and is cutting the man's sleeve so she can take his blood pressure.

He swings his right arm and connects with her jaw. In an instant, we are on top of him. They hold his arms down, and I put a knee on his chest, a little harder than I intend to, as I feel the air go out of him.

He is spitting and swearing at us. I put an oxygen mask on his face. He tries to bite me, but I keep my fingers clear. I lift his head up and strap the mask around him.

"Get this goddamn mask off my face!"

"It's a felony to hit an EMT," she tells him bluntly.

"I don't care. Get the fuck off me."

"We need to check you out, so be still," I say.

"You ain't doing nothing to me!"

"We'll leave you alone if you answer a few questions we have to ask you."

"I ain't answering nothing!"

"What day is today?"

He gives me the date properly except that he is shouting it at me.

"Where are you?"

He shouts out the address.

"Who's president of the United States?"

"Bill Fucking Clinton! Now get off me!"

We hold him down until the tension in his muscles subsides. With the help of a police officer, we get him up.

"You think I'm crazy. You afraid of me?" he says to me.

"No," I reply.

"How tall are you?"

"Bigger than you," I say. "Now would you be still enough to let us check you over?"

"I ain't talking to you."

The man jerks his arm at the cop, who tightens his grip on him. We all move closer, ready to pounce on him if he strikes the cop.

The other medics try to reason with him. I ask a friend of the man what happened. He says he was working with a gas saw in the basement and came out every fifteen minutes to get away from the fumes. The last time he came out he lay down on the grass and they couldn't get him up. He tries to talk to the man, who is shouting at the officer. But that just gets the man more upset. "You all leave me the fuck alone!" he screams. "Get out of here and let me be. I ain't going nowhere."

"You're coming with us or the officer is going to arrest you," the female medic says. "You've already broken the law by swinging at me."

"I don't give a good goddamn. You think I'm crazy?"

He looks like a complete madman.

"You have to be checked out," the officer says. "Let these people do their job."

The man goes into a tirade.

"Look," I say to his friend, "we're trying to figure out whether he inhaled something that is making him act like this or if he's just being an asshole."

"He's being an asshole," his friend says.

"You've seen him like this before?"

"Yeah," he says, then starts toward the man. When he can't get him to calm down, he tells the officer to just leave them alone for a minute. The officer tells him to back off or he'll arrest him, too.

"Let me just talk to him. Let me reason with him. There's no need for this."

The officer calls on his radio for backup.

The scene is getting out of control. More officers arrive. One of them takes out his pepper spray, which causes us to back off, not wanting to get sprayed by accident. I think that maybe if I were alone with the man, I might be able to calm him down, but then again, he is all hyped up and my few attempts have failed. I still want him to come in and get checked out, but as long as he knows where he is and what day it is, we can't take him against his will.

The cops eventually cuff him and lead him off to the cruiser as he swears and cusses at us all. The female medic says she will press charges against him for hitting her. The guy's friend just stands there shaking his head.

When we clear the scene, I think that a week rarely goes by that one of my patients doesn't take a swing at either me or Glenn. I'm usually good at deflecting the blows and calming the patient down. I wonder if the day when I truly get socked is ahead. I have heard of EMTs getting the shit kicked out of them. (The worst I ever got hit was by an old lady, who slapped me and grabbed my hair when I was trying to give her an IV.) You have to be ready to fight or at least not let on that you're scared if it comes to a fight, but you can't initiate one either. At least half the EMTs in the company wear bullet-proof vests. I don't. Maybe I'm foolish to believe I don't need one, that even though I look like a cop in my paramedic uniform I feel the fact that I am a paramedic shields me like a white flag in the middle of a battle zone.

Completing my run form, I fill out the section that grades a patient's level of consciousness based on eye opening, muscle response, and verbal response. Under verbal response, I check "obeys commands," but write the prefix "dis" in front of "obeys."

"He was an asshole," Glenn says.

"An asshole who's going to jail."

❖

We're sent to the Newington VA Hospital for a stat transfer to John Dempsey Hospital for a woman who needs a pacemaker installed. Most patients we transfer are relatively stable. In most cases the patients are going for cardiac catheterization and are on nitro and heparin drips that keep them pain free. This woman has passed out four times in the last hour. The nurse claims she went into cardiac arrest once and CPR had to be done for two minutes to revive her. She shows me the cardiac strips. The woman goes into a rare rhythm called torsades de pointes, an abnormal beat of the lower heart chamber that produces a rhythm that looks at first glance like ventricular tachycardia but is not. And unlike ventricular tachycardia, if you give the person lidocaine, it will kill them. The treatment of choice is magnesium and ventricular pacing. It is a rare rhythm that you may never see.

The woman passes out again, and just as the nurse gets ready to start pumping on her chest, she revives by herself. I ask if they can spare someone to accompany us. If she is an imminent code, I will need the extra hand. The company sends us another EMT and the VA gets a doctor to come along.

Glenn drives to John Dempsey with lights and sirens.

"I think I feel one of those things happening," the woman says, then passes out. I look at the monitor. She is in torsades.

"Let's wait," I say. "Just a little. She'll break on her own."

I reach to hit the monitor record button to preserve the episode. From the history the nurse gave of the woman passing out repeatedly for the few preceding days and the one event I witnessed in the ICU, I believe she will come around. I don't know if the supposed two-minute cardiac arrest was real or not. It may have seemed like two minutes to the nurse. But given the woman's rhythm, banging on the chest might knock the rhythm into ventricular fibrillation, which is much harder to recover from. I wasn't there, so I can't judge. I just have a hunch it will break. After fifteen seconds she hasn't broken the rhythm, so I reach to attach our external pacemaker. A moment later, she opens her eyes, and the rhythm clears.

I keep her on the monitor at the hospital. We go directly to the ICU unit. As we are getting ready to move her over to the bed, she goes into the rhythm again. This time I hit the record button right at the start and capture the entire episode, which lasts for thirty seconds. A group of doctors and nurse practitioners crowds into the room. The doctor traveling with us gives his report, and I make copies of the strip for them, which they are all interested in.

Later I show the strip to several other medics. They all say v-tach on first glance. I explain what it is and point out the changing amplitude of the rhythm that distinguishes it from v-tach. I say I don't think I would have been able to call it right if it had just popped up on the monitor on a 911 patient I found at a private home. I might be too quick to shock or give lidocaine. Now that I have seen it, I will know what to look for. Every call teaches you something you save for later use.

❖

When I see Michelle that night—she is studying for a big test in her physician assistant class—I show her the strip and ask her to guess the rhythm.

"Torsades," she says.

"I'm impressed."

Later when I recount my day, I tell her, "I was a good paramedic today. I treated my patients with dignity and respect. I kept the monitor on."

"I know you're a good paramedic," she says.

"Well, there's a lot that I don't know, but I try hard."

"Yes, you do," she says, and goes back to studying her book.

❖

In the morning, we're parked outside of Saint Francis when we see Daniel Tauber and Mike Riggs, one of the supervisors, park in Medic Three. They get out and come over toward us, which I regard as an ominous sign.

Daniel is all business. "You know that call you did yesterday," he starts. "The lady with torsades," I say.

"No, the one in West Hartford," he says. "Your patient was Life-Starred to Norwalk. He had near-fatal carbon monoxide levels."

"You're kidding," I say.

"No. You, the other medics, the company, the PD, and I, because I am in charge of your medicine, all stand to be sued. Did you write a run form on it?"

"Yeah, but it was real short because we were canceled by the officer once he arrested the man."

"You ought to write a detailed incident report, documenting everything."

"He was alert and oriented."

"They will say you should have known he was under the influence of carbon monoxide, had him restrained, and taken to the hospital."

"I'll write a report."

"Make it good."

❖

When something bad is happening to me, I am pretty good at keeping it at a distance. I grow quiet and shut down the feelings, but my mind sometimes runs a little wild. I wish that I hadn't been assigned this call. After all, with all the calls that go out, it is a fluke which ones you get. I could have been on a colds and flu when this one came in and I wouldn't be worrying about this now. Or I could have been delivering a pair of healthy bouncy twins, and right now I would be passing out cigars, rather than contemplating my ruin. I wish I had malpractice insurance. I had it for a while as a condition of my internship in Bridgeport, but I let it lapse. Not that I own a house or anything, and my car is old and dented and has a rope holding the hood down. I do have some savings, and I have a computer and a stereo, and over three hundred books and four hundred CDs and records that I treasure. I imagine having to go to court, and seeing the guy there, who instead of being dressed like a complete wildman is wearing a three-piece suit, with a trimmed beard and mustache. He's talking in a clipped Yorkshire accent, and he's represented by O. J.'s lawyer, Johnnie Cochran, who will say, "The way my client was treated by this man—why, Judge, it was an outrage! He was treated like an animal, not the fine upstanding citizen he is now, sporting that finely tailored Pierre Cardin suit, which he worked hard for, despite having to battle discrimination and rogue paramedics ever since he was a little baby boy in his sweet mother's arms. Why, this man who denied him proper care, if you trimmed his mustache and shrunk him down a few sizes, he'd look just like the author of *Mein Kampf*. This is an outrage, judge."

All during the O. J. trial I thought any one of those lawyers could put any paramedic on the stand and drill them on any call and find fault with them in some way. It is like putting a running back on trial and finding fault with him for not scoring an eighty-yard touchdown run every time he is given the ball. "Why, judge, this man has a record. He killed a little baby, and he killed a little boy he found lying in the middle of the road, and he killed all those people who had just a little bit of chest pain. They lay down and closed their eyes and waited for their constitutional right— for the heroes of *Rescue 911* to come in and save their lives—but this man failed. He has a record of failing. Why, his days are littered with sick people and dead bodies. He's got no business being out there on the streets. This is an outrage, Judge."

I think, let him take everything. Maybe that way I'll find true freedom. I will pack up my most precious belongings—my sperm-whale tooth, my Tony Conigliaro baseball card, a dog-eared paperback copy of the *Odyssey*, and a tape of Elvis Presley singing "Kentucky Rain"—wrap them in a polka-dot bandanna and tie them up on the end of a stick, and start walking along the railroad tracks that have always run by wherever I have lived since leaving home as a teenager. I'll go to New Mexico, or Oregon, or Alaska, or somewhere in America where they will give a hardworking stranger a chance. At least till my face appears on "America's Most Wanted" and they tree me with a pack of dogs.

❖

We are sent out to cover Newington, and I stop at an ice cream parlor and go in for a cone. I haven't had a cone for years, but think I should start enjoying life. They have piña colada ice cream, and I think what the hell, I might as well go for the experience. It's not bad—it tastes like a cold piña colada. I eat it purposefully as if I am saying go ahead and try to take the ice cream cone from my hand, you weaselly scumbag lawyer. I feel better about not having amassed a fortune, and having squandered my money on more immediate pursuits of women, beer, and good times.

❖

That night I tell Michelle about maybe being sued, but she says I have nothing to worry about. I can't do blood gases in the field. As long as the guy was alert and oriented, I couldn't take him in. I tried to initiate treatment, but he refused. I imagine sitting in court and Johnnie Cochran saying, "Isn't it a fact that you could have had this innocent man taken to the hospital under protective custody and gotten him the health care that he needed to live a free life as is his constitutional, God-given right, whether he is white or black or whether you like his face or not? Isn't that right?"

I respond, "If I had, then the odds are I would be sitting here being grilled by you for kidnapping. Give me a break."

"Judge," Cochran says. "Judge, this is an outrage!"

And then Judge Ito finally tells him to sit down and shut up.

❖

I read my textbooks on carbon monoxide poisoning. I am hoping they will say nothing about patients being combative as a sign of carbon monoxide poisoning. My textbook says: "Signs and symptoms of carbon monoxide poisoning include headache, instability, errors in judgment, vomiting, chest pain, confusion, agitation, loss of coordination, loss of consciousness, and even seizures. On physical examination, the skin may be cyanotic or it may be bright cherry red (a very late finding)." The words "agitation" and "errors in judgment" catch my eye. But then I think he didn't have loss of coordination, chest pain, difficulty breathing, or seizures. And as Michelle tells me, agitation and errors in judgment are as likely a diagnosis for an asshole as they are for carbon monoxide poisoning.

I read the section on liability and consent. Under the heading "Problem patients," I find reassurance: "If the patient refuses and still remains alert and oriented, then he or she cannot be forced to accept treatment."

❖

I hand in my incident report the next morning. When I see Daniel in the afternoon, I ask if he got a chance to read it.

"About which incident?" he asks.

"The one where the guy was going to sue everybody. The carbon monoxide call."

"Oh, that one. There are so many."

He hasn't read it yet, but he doesn't sound too concerned today. He says he read something on carbon monoxide himself last night and couldn't find violence as a side effect, unless you counted it as a side effect of hypoxia.

He puts his feet up and starts talking about carbon monoxide. Daniel is one of those few medics who has come as close as possible to having seen and done everything at least once. He tells me about a call he went on where he and his partner were unknowingly exposed to carbon monoxide. They learned that it was a problem only after they had left the scene with their patient. He says he was enjoying inflating and deflating the blood pressure cuff. His partner was driving the ambulance eighty miles an hour. When they hadn't arrived at the hospital a half an hour later, their dispatcher called to see how they were doing. The driver yelled at the dispatcher, then threw the radio out the window, and kept on driving. The company had to get the cops to find them, and they were eventually run off the road, and taken into the hospital as patients themselves.

One thing I know is I'll be more on guard next time.

Long Day

It is the last day of our shift and we are getting hammered — call after call. It's been in the nineties all week with the humidity index at the soup level. We can't get a Gatorade and drink it before we get another call. By the time we clear the hospital, the thirst quencher is as hot as tea. We drink it anyway, go to the convenience store, buy another bottle, then hear the dispatcher say, "Four-five-one."

"Leave us alone," Glenn shouts at the radio as I reach to pick up the microphone.

He says he's getting pissed off, but I don't mind it. I like being busy — I just want time to drink my drink when it's still cold.

It's eleven and we've already done five calls, one refusal, and two wild-goose chases where we are sent crosstown, lights and sirens, for a "man down," only to arrive and not find anyone.

We're sent for the "unknown." Again, we race through traffic, lights and sirens wailing. I try to time my sips of the Gatorade with the bumps in the road.

Ahead we see five police cars in a circular driveway. A police motorcycle is lying on its side, a few feet behind a parked car. It looks like the car probably backed out and clipped the bike, which has little damage to it.

The cop who was driving the bike is strutting about, saying he's fine.

"Get me a Band-Aid," he says to me. "I cut my finger."

He has a small cut on the tip of his finger. "Did you knock your head or anything?" I ask.

"No, just get me a Band-Aid."

I go back to the ambulance and get one four by four, which I hand to him when I return.

"We don't carry Band-Aids," I say.

"What, you don't have an alcohol prep so I can clean it?" he says to me. He turns and looks at the other cops like I don't know what I'm doing.

I go back to the ambulance and get two alcohol preps. Glenn, who has applied to be a cop, stays with the cops and tries to bullshit with them about how hot it is today.

I come back with the alcohol preps and give them to the cop. "Here's one for your finger, and one to keep for next time you cut it."

He looks hard at me while he opens the prep, like he is trying to figure out whether or not I am dissing him.

"I need your name and address and you have to sign this form, stating you are refusing treatment and transportation to the hospital."

"You ought to go get checked out," one of the other cops says to him.

"It's fine with me either way," I say. "But you come with us, you get collared and strapped to the board."

"I don't need to go."

"Your buddy here can drive you."

"Yeah, maybe I should get checked out."

"What's your name?"

Another cop tells me his name.

I write the name down. "Address?"

He thinks a second then says, "Fifty Jennings Road," which is police headquarters.

"Sign here," I say.

He signs, then I start back to the ambulance.

"See you, guys," Glenn says, but none of them says anything.

"Was that BS or what?" I say when we're back in the ambulance. "Sending us crosstown, lights and sirens, for a cut finger."

"That was BS," Glenn says.

"Five cop cars for a cut finger."

"Four-five-one," the radio calls, and we're off for a chest pain.

❖

As soon as we clear the hospital, we stop at the Charter Market, where Glenn buys some hamburger rolls and bologna. "I got us lunch," he says, but before we can even get all the way into the ambulance, they call our number again, and we're sent to West Hartford for a possible dead body.

"Well, it'll either be a code or a no transport," I say.

"I just want to eat," he says.

Our West Hartford medic, Bob Gionfriddo, is already on scene. When we enter the apartment, which is suffocating with heat, and enter a tiny cluttered bedroom, I am expecting to see Bob either doing CPR or looking over a stiff, but the woman on the bed is moving, though she is out of it. "Your guess is as good as mine," he says. "I just got here."

We put her on oxygen and the monitor. She seems to have left-sided weakness. She gazes to the left. On the monitor she's in atrial fibrillation, a disorganized beating of the upper chambers of her heart that can cause blood clots. We're suspecting a stroke at this point, but Bob checks her blood sugar anyway, and it comes out normal. Glenn gets the stretcher while I search through the cluttered room for a name or prescription drugs to give us a clue. All three of us are sweating. There is a fan on, but the room must be over a hundred degrees. The lady is lying on the far side of a large four-poster bed. The stretcher cannot fit entirely in the room, due to the heavy dressers that keep us out.

"I might as well just pick her up and carry her out," I say.

She is not light, but I figure it will be quicker than moving the heavy dressers. I just want to get out of the hot room. I bend my knees and put one arm around her shoulders and one under her legs. I lift her and start toward the door.

"She's letting go her bladder," Bob says.

"Great," I say, feeling the growing dampness on my leg. I get her over to the stretcher and look down at my black pants. There is a visible wet patch.

"Great," I say again.

We wheel her out and get her into the back of the ambulance. Glenn drives, lights and sirens, while I put in an IV and draw bloods. We have her on full oxygen. She starts to come around but cannot speak or move her left side. She squeezes my hand and looks up into my eyes with desperation. "My name is Peter," I say. "I think you have had a stroke. You're in an ambulance. We're going to the hospital. Do you understand that?"

She squeezes my hand. Her eyes are filled with terror.

I squeeze her hand back. "I'm here with you," I say. "I'm here."

After we get her taken care of and I write my run report, I call the office for our run number and our times. "Can I make a quick stop back at the office to do some laundry?" I ask.

"Huh?" she says.

"I got peed on," I say.

❖

We get an hour to eat our lunch while my pants whirl around in the laundry machines. I wear a green hospital sheet wrapped around my waist. "See what a good partner I am," I say to Glenn. "Willing to do anything so my buddy can get a break and eat his lunch in this air-conditioned office."

"I ain't complaining," he says.

❖

While we are there, Daniel Tauber comes in and laughs at my hairy legs sticking out from under the sheet. "Let this be a lesson: you should always carry a spare uniform," he says.

"Yup," I say.

Glenn asks about our stork pins from the baby we delivered who died a couple months before. Daniel had promised them to us, but we hadn't gotten them yet.

Daniel has us follow him into his office.

"Boy or girl?" he asks.

"Baby girl," we say together.

"She even has a name," Glenn says. "They named her."

The stork pin is a small gold pin of a stork carrying a baby in a white diaper in its mouth. The stork is pink.

We both put them on. "I wavered a lot on this one," I say, "but I don't feel bad about wearing it."

"We did the best we could," Glenn says. "We were there with her."

"Yeah," I say. I look at him and know how much it affected both of us. "Papa Glenn," I say.

He smiles.

❖

We're back on the road within the hour, responding to the Community Health Services on Albany Avenue for a possible fractured skull.

When we get there, we wheel the stretcher inside along with equipment to c-spine the patient. The fractured skull turns out to be a seven-year-old boy who fell and cut his head, which has been elaborately bandaged by the clinic's PA. It is not fractured, she says, but she wants Saint Francis to do a head film of it before it is sutured to make sure there are no foreign bodies inside. We have the boy hop up on the stretcher, and we belt him in. His mother sits in the back of the ambulance with me.

"Where we going now?" he asks.

"We're going to take you to the hospital," I say, "and have the pretty nurses look at you."

"What are they going to do to me?"

"Well, you might have to have a few stitches," I say.

He starts to cry.

"Be good, Tyrell," his mother says.

He undoes his seat belt and tries to scamper off the stretcher.

"Whoa, little man!"

"I don't want no stitches. Let me out of here. Let me out of here."

I belt him back in.

"Tyrell!" his mother says.

"But, Momma, I don't want no stitches."

❖

No sooner are we out of the hospital than we're sent priority one for a man unconscious on Brown Street, third floor.

We find him facedown against the wall in the corridor. I kneel next to him to check his breathing, and the first thing I feel is the wet carpet on my knees. I am kneeling in pee.

"He knocked on my door, and he was shaking when I opened it," a woman says. "He takes Dilantin."

He is breathing fine, but he is totally out of it—in the postictal phase that follows most seizures. I turn him over on his back and do a full assessment while Glenn gets the stair chair.

"No air-conditioning in here," I say to the lady as the sweat runs off me.

"It's on," she says, "but it don't work too good."

"Tell me about it."

The patient is a stocky young man, and we have to secure him tightly to the chair because he is still out of it. I take the foot end, and as we go down the flights of stairs in the suffocating stairwell, I feel like my back is going to explode.

"I've got to put this thing down," I say, pausing on one of the landings.

Both of us are sopped.

"Let's get moving. It's too hot here," Glenn says.

I pick it back up, but the pain won't go away. We make it outside, and I have difficulty straightening up. I feel like I need a stiff kick in the back to set me straight.

As I do an IV and draw bloods en route, my sweat drips onto the face of the patient, who finally opens his eyes.

"You know what happened?" I ask.

"No."

"You had a seizure."

He shakes his head as if to say not again.

At the hospital as I am walking back out to the ambulance, the nurse who will be caring for him calls to me and thanks me for putting in the IV and drawing bloods, and that makes me feel good. She is nice and pretty, and I like her. I am glad she thinks well of me.

❖

"Well, I got pee on me again," I say. "But I don't think they'll let me launder again, seeing as it's five o'clock already."

Before Glenn can comment, they call our number and we're sent to the "man down" on Main Street, which turns out to be a guy who fell running after his bus. He has a bloody nose but doesn't want to go to the hospital. We give him some cotton five by nines and an ice pack.

As soon as we clear the scene, they send us to West Hartford for a general weakness at the walk-in clinic. They are about to start an IV, the dispatcher tells us. When we arrive the doctor meets us outside the examining room. She explains the man is a diabetic who has been feeling poorly since this morning and has a blood sugar of 90. "Do you carry fluids?" she asks.

"Yes," I say.

"Oh, wonderful," she says. "Would you like us to do the IV?"

In the room there are two nurses with latex gloves on, standing by a table that has a tray with IV supplies on it.

"No, thanks anyway, we can do it."

The nurses seem relieved to hear this.

One says to the other, "I do want to learn how to do it."

The man is alert, though slightly confused. His skin is very hot. We get him on the stretcher and take him out to the ambulance. I tell the wife we are going to wait in the parking lot for a few minutes, while we get him an IV and some dextrose.

"But he's a diabetic," she says. "He has to be very careful with his sugar."

"Yes," I say. "This should help him, but it won't hurt him."

"Shouldn't you wait till we get to the hospital?"

"His hospital experience is starting now. We're an extension of the emergency department. This will speed his visit. We're also going to draw blood."

"Oh, you're going to draw blood. Well, he should be checked for Lyme disease. We played golf all day yesterday, and one of our neighbors had Lyme disease, and just collapsed, and it turned out he had Lyme disease."

"I'll mention that to the doctors," I say.

I let Glenn do the IV. I have already done five today and am feeling guilty for hogging them.

He puts in a sixteen and draws four tubes of blood while I spike the bag of saline.

"D fifty?" he says.

I nod.

He knows how to do it. I trust him. While he can be a pain in the ass at times, he has good skills. Though he does most of the driving and cleaning up, he is thinking about applying to paramedic school, and I think I should let him do as much as he can, and help prepare him to be a medic. He pops off the yellow tops, screws the D50 into the injector, attaches it to the medication port, turns off the line, then we slowly inject the sugar. The man perks up a little, but I am suspecting his problem is more exhaustion than diabetes.

When I am giving my report to the triage nurse at the hospital, the man's wife starts to give his whole medical history and insists that he be checked for Lyme disease.

"Do you want her to go over to admitting and get him signed in?" I ask the nurse.

"Yes," she says. She points her to the waiting room, and we head down the hall.

"You again," the nurse says to us when we wheel the patient into Room 9.

"One of those days," I say.

On the phone to dispatch to get our times, I am tempted to clear the call as "Lyme disease," but I just call it "Exhaustion/hypoglycemia."

It is 6:45 now and they send us to area nine, on-line with HPD. We get more Gatorade at the Charter Food, and after sitting for about ninety seconds, we are sent to a possible fractured leg in the north end.

There is a crowd gathered around a young girl and her mother who both lie in fetal position on the sidewalk. Nearby is a pink bicycle fallen on its side. I kneel by them. "What's wrong?" I ask.

"My leg hurts," the little girl says with a sniffle. She is seven years old. Her mother, who could be in her middle twenties, is crying.

I look at the leg. It does not look misshapen. "Can you move it?" I ask. She shakes her head no. I touch it and feel she has a good distal pulse. I reach under the leg and then see blood on my gloves. With Glenn's help, I turn her over and see she has a cut—a three-inch avulsion that is oozing blood and is dirty.

"Mom, you're going to have to calm down," Glenn says.

"You wouldn't be calm if this was your daughter," she says.

"Mom has to be calm so daughter can calm down," Glenn says. "Do you understand what I'm saying?"

I get some five by nines and tape but have to return to the ambulance to get some sterile water so Glenn can wash the wound. Since most cuts and small fractures are basic calls, I let Glenn handle them. Besides, blood and broken bones give me the willies. Not that there is any fracture here.

Glenn washes the wound by pouring water on it. The girl starts crying and the mother says, "Don't hurt my baby. Why aren't you taking her to the hospital?"

"I've got to wash the wound first," Glenn says. "Remember what I said about calming down?"

Glenn puts a five by nine over the cut then wraps it with tape.

I go back to the ambulance to get the back set up while Glenn carefully picks the girl up and carries her over to the ambulance.

"How come you're not putting her on the stretcher out here?" the mother asks.

Glenn passes the girl up to me, but the mother gets between us. The girl starts crying.

"You're hurting my baby," the mother says.

We finally get her on the stretcher, and Glenn gets in to tech the call while I drive.

At the hospital, I go around to the back to help Glenn lift the stretcher out.

"Can I help?" the mother asks.

"We got it," Glenn replies.

We lift the stretcher out and wheel it in, the mother walking next to us, holding her girl's hand and wiping her own tears away.

The triage nurse comes over and removes the bandage to inspect the cut, then retapes it. "You can put her in the wheelchair," she says.

I wheel a chair over.

"Aren't there any doctors available to see her?" the mother says.

"They're all busy right now," I say. "It's just a cut. You're going to have to sit in the waiting room for a little while. They're very busy tonight."

Glenn comes over to help lift the girl up, but the mother pushes him aside and picks her up. Instead of putting her in the wheelchair, she starts toward the waiting room.

"Ma'am," Glenn says.

She whirls around to face us. "Fuck you, goddamn honkys!" she says. "You won't put her on the stretcher. I'm not putting her in no wheelchair. Where's the doctor! I won't let you treat my daughter like dirt. Fuck you! Fuck the both of you!" She walks into the waiting room and turns around again. "My daughter's hurt. Fuck you, assholes! I'm going to report all of you!"

Glenn and I are stunned. People are looking at us like we are criminals.

"You can have my name and work number, lady. I don't care," Glenn says.

The woman has already turned her back, and for a moment I think she will walk out of the hospital altogether with her daughter, but instead she takes a seat at the far end of the waiting room. "It'll be okay," she says to her daughter, then glares back at us.

"What was that all about?" a security guard asks us.

We shake our heads.

Our relief is waiting for us back at the base, so as soon as we finish the paperwork we head in. Driving back, Glenn says, "I thought picking her up in my arms was nice, a personal touch."

"You'd think so."

"I mean, her leg wasn't broken or anything. The only reason she was crying was because her mother was getting her all excited."

"I know."

"I don't care. I don't care what she thinks. I'm going home. I'm going to take a shower, then I'm heading out to the bar, and I'm going to drink some cold beers. Screw her."

Waiting for Weicker
So I Can Say No

I've been in a bad funk lately. Normally it is only on Tuesday mornings when I ride into work for my first shift of the week that I feel the doubt and wonder why I am doing this, but this week the doubts last all week long. I just turned thirty-seven. I have no pension built up. I have no law degree or medical degree or business skill to fall back on. I am barely living on what I make, borrowing from savings to buy books. I will have to borrow again to get a new used car, as my trusty old Plymouth has a limited future. I think if I get married and have a kid by the time I am forty, I will be sixty when he is twenty, seventy-seven when he is my age. That's old. I wonder how I will be able to send him to college or help him out with pocket change. My body is stiff and sore now. What will it be like then? Will I be able to throw a baseball around with my grandson, or will I have to be led on a walker to his Little League games on day-leave from the nursing home?

❖

We're sent to an HMO for chest pain. We are directed to an exam room where a tall gaunt bearded man sits on an exam table, with a woman standing next to him holding his hand. I do a quick visual on him. He looks pale and unwell. "Are you having chest pain right now?" I ask.

"No," he says. "I just have a headache."

"He's been dizzy," the woman says.

A nurse sticks her head in the room and says, "The doctor wants to talk to you."

She leads me down the hall where I enter a small room and see the doctor sitting at his desk. He is a young man, probably not thirty. "Yes, hello," he says, looking up at me. "He needs to go to Hartford Hospital. He's orthostatic. Pressure of one twenty lying down, eighty sitting up. He's very dehydrated. At the hospital, he'll need a liter of normal saline and should have blood work done."

"I can run a line on the way in," I say.

"Great," he says.

He hands me an envelope with his orders in it, but he seals it first with tape. I take it and put it in my back pocket.

We get the man on the stretcher and into the back of the ambulance. I have Glenn spike the bag of saline while I look for a line. No veins are visible. I have Glenn put a tourniquet on the other arm and he looks as well. I take my glove off so I can palpate with a more sensitive bare finger. I think I may feel one in the AC area, so I go in with a twenty, but get no flashback. I decide to screw it and we just head in. I am learning that unless they desperately need a line not to stick more than once if I can't see or feel a vein.

En route, I redo my physical assessment and question the man on his medical history and his current condition. He says he has Hodgkin's disease and has been unwell for the last week. He is a little evasive in his answers, but I chalk it up to nervousness.

We are only a few minutes from the hospital when I open the sealed envelope, looking for insurance information (which I don't like to ask the patient for directly as I prefer to be a medical giver and not a bill collector). I glance through the papers, and a small notation at the bottom catches my eye. The patient has AIDS.

This is important information for me to know and I am angry that both the doctor and the patient refused to share it with me. Very angry. I treat everyone alike. I have no hesitancy about sticking someone with AIDS. When I was in my internship at one hospital I had to elbow my preceptor out of the way so I could stick a person with TB and HIV. I wanted all the lines I could get. I have been asked by a nurse at one hospital why I bothered to put in a line and draw bloods from an HIV-positive male who had the crap kicked out of him by a man with a stick. I answered I treat all patients the same, and this man who had three bags of heroin just before his beating was in intense pain despite the heroin. He had been hit in the head and the ribs. While he was hemodynamically stable, I felt he might have significant injury. She wondered why I would risk my own health to do the IV in the ambulance which is a much less stable environment than the ER. I answered because it was my job.

I normally wear gloves on all patients, but if I know they have AIDS I am extra careful. The doctor should have informed me. Imagine how a surgeon would feel if he learned the patient's doctor had neglected to inform him the man he was to operate on had HIV. He'll operate on anybody, but he needs to know that information. I am not a chauffeur. I am a medical professional. I deserve the respect and information I was denied.

❖

All week I go out and pick up patients, in nursing homes and in dirty tenements. I take them into the hospitals, where I transfer them to the hospital stretchers, and give my report to what sometimes seem like uninterested ears. We remake the stretcher and go back out for the next call. Drunks, colds and flu, back pain, small cuts. I do few calls that challenge my medical knowledge or skills. No Room 1 traumas, no bad chest pains with lethal rhythms on the cardiac monitor, no cases of congestive heart failure with flash pulmonary edema requiring Lasix, nitroglycerin, and morphine from my drug box. And nothing to challenge me emotionally. And no funny kids to make me laugh. Not for weeks.

❖

I watch the doctors in their offices or at their workstations as they consult and hobnob with each other. There is a real class system here. The doctors are at the top, then the nurses, then us at the very bottom. I tell the nurses what I get for vital signs. They retake the vitals themselves and write them down on their pads. I tell them the story, they say thanks, then turn to the patient and ask what is the matter. They need to do it, but it makes me wonder what the point is sometimes. I might as well just pick them up, put them on the stretcher, and deliver them. I write my run forms, but they seem just like pieces of paper that will go unread.

❖

I am cramped sitting in 451. My back hurts. The sun is beating down on the ambulance, a tin can in the sun.

There is a story in the paper about Weicker running for president as an independent. It says he may announce in October. I have believed all along that he would run because he is a political animal and can't stand to be out of the spotlight. While he has no chance to win, he can have a great time traipsing about the country, speaking his mind, and ridiculing those who have a chance and must therefore bend constantly to the wind. I have talked with many of my Weicker friends about what we will say when he calls us. Most of us have worked for him for ten to twenty years, and in the past, when he summoned us, we always answered the call. I started working for him when I was seventeen. I worked for him in Washington during his 1976 campaign. I worked in Connecticut on his 1982 and 1988 campaigns with a year and a half in between in Washington.

In 1988 I drank champagne with him as we flew back from a debate to Washington in a private Lear jet. He said then that if there was one person who would make the difference in his being reelected this time, it would be me. A month later I watched him walk across the darkened yard of his campaign manager's house to board his campaign bus for the last time, as his victorious opponent announced over the radio, "The American Dream is alive and well in Connecticut." When after his defeat he was living in exile in Virginia, I traveled down twice a month to write the newsletter for the new medical research public-interest group he was running. I was there when people wouldn't return his calls, when he spent his time reading aloud to his faithful few excerpts from a Winston Churchill biography.

When he called me at Eastern Ambulance in 1990 and told me to be at the state capitol to hear his announcement, I answered the call and busted my butt to get him elected governor. And when he was being hung in effigy for his stance on the state income tax, I traveled to Greenwich where he was holed up like a Mafia chieftain in a small apartment on his estate, protected by plainclothes cops, to work on a speech for him to give at Yale, a proclamation of the righteousness and inevitable logic of his course. I sat in the audience as he called on the people of his state to put children and the future first. He used my Walt Whitman quote: "I am the teacher of athletes. He that by me, spreads a greater breast than my own, proves the width of my own." I stood with the crowd and cheered in a standing ovation. What a magnificent speaker he was, what life he gave to the words.

"If he calls, I'm going to say no," I tell my friend Tom Dudchik, Weicker's former deputy chief of staff. "I'm going to point to the patch on my shoulder and say see what it says here: 'Paramedic.' That's me. I have my own life now."

I am down on Weicker. While I think he would be just what the country needs as president because he is a decisive, unafraid man, he has no chance to win, and it would be another year out of my life with nothing gained. When you work for someone you believe in, you are a part of them, and their glory is yours, but then when it is over, you are left alone.

After Weicker won the governorship he hired a former aide, now a big-time lawyer, to run his office, and I found myself faced with the choice of a diminished role in his office for less pay than I asked or the job at the health department with a bigger salary. I took the money and that shocked him, I think. For over ten months he never called me, and all the bigwigs in state government who didn't know me, and all the lobbyists who were so nice to me when I was his campaign issues director, but who felt I was on "the outs" now, would walk by me as if I were nobody. Then I started writing speeches for him again, and all the people who wouldn't return my phone calls or say hello to me when I walked by started treating me great. For two years I was back to being somebody. I wrote five major speeches, including two budget addresses, a state-of-the-state address announcing his plans to desegregate the state's schools, and an address at the Harvard Kennedy School of Government, after which he publicly said we were a great writing pair, like Gilbert and Sullivan.

Then one afternoon, he gave me two days to write a graduation speech for him at the same time I was taking my paramedic exams. I wrote a dog-shit speech. He stopped calling me to write for him, and I was back to not having people return my phone calls again. He bumped me from his final budget address, saying he needed a numbers speech, not a passionate speech. "I can do numbers speeches," I told him. "Just give me the numbers and I'll write a better speech than anyone." But he had already made up his mind. I told him I was quitting then, earlier than I had planned to. I was going to work for my buddy running for Congress and would start in February, instead of May or July. He told me I was being foolish, that my friend wouldn't need me until September, and that besides, given the long-term incumbent who my friend was running against, he didn't have a chance. I should stay and collect my paycheck, and he'd have some more speeches for me to write. I reminded him that when he was running for the Senate in 1970, his best friend and old college roommate Hank Harper came to work for him without asking what his chances were. Besides, nobody thought his opponent had a chance against him in 1988 and look what happened. Sting! Still he smiled and shook his head and genuinely wished me well. After the election, and before I started working as a paramedic, I saw him again, and we talked about our respective plans for the future. He told me he thought our paths would cross again. What he was saying without saying it was he was thinking about running for president.

Weicker recently published his autobiography, which is more a political tract than a serious examination of his life and the choices he made.

He had actually asked me to write it with him back in 1989, but his then publisher wanted a name writer with a better vocabulary than mine. He decided to put off the book himself, telling me he wasn't certain his story was done yet. When it finally came out, written with a former newspaper editor, I was disturbed there was no mention of me. Not that there really should have been. What was he supposed to write? "Entry 1976: A new intern started working for me today. A fine young fellow, who when I ask to run and get me potato chips, gets them for me in record time. My suspicion is he keeps a cache in his desk rather than running down three flights of stairs to the Plastic City. What ingenuity! I see big things ahead for him." "Entry 1987: Summoned Canning to my office. He came in as he always does, hopeful I will ask his opinion on policy. Tennis I declare. Noon. Be there. He played well and we won. Don't know if the high point was Canning dropping Dan Quayle to his knees with a volley to the groin or my outstanding backhand." Or "Entry 1992: I worked through the day with Canning on the state-of-the-state speech. Later, when the crowd finished its thunderous applause, I thought about asking him to stand and bow, as I'd say, 'Let's give a hand to the little people who write the songs that make us all sing.' But I didn't."

When he left office, a reporter for the *New York Times* recounted that Weicker had told him he wrote every word of his speeches himself.

❖

It is another smoldering hot humid day. At four in the afternoon, we're called for an overdose off Huntington Street. "You're going to need the stretcher," the guy who flagged us down out front says. "He's laid out on the floor."

"What'd he OD on?" I ask as Glenn gets the stair chair out.

"I don't know, man. He's just some guy who's staying with me. I can't believe he did this, man, I'm late for work."

In the third-floor apartment we find a man lying on his back, soaked in water, barely breathing.

"I threw water on him as soon as I found him. That was good, right?" the guy says.

It is commonplace for people to throw water on people who OD.

"No," I say, "all that's going to do is give him a cold. Does he do heroin?" I check the guy's pupils, which are constricted.

"Hey, man, I don't know. He's like, just staying with me."

"Does he do heroin?"

"Well, yeah . . . yeah, he does."

Glenn notes fresh track marks on his arm.

"Yeah, yeah, he injects it," the guy finally says.

"He looks real diaphoretic," the cop who has shown up says.

"That's 'cause his buddy here threw water on him," I say.

"Hey, I didn't know, man. That's what everybody does. I was just doing my best, man," the guy says.

"Don't do it next time."

"Okay, okay."

I get a line in his left forearm while Glenn spikes a bag of saline. After the line is set, I draw up one point two milligrams of Narcan and inject it slowly. Heroin depresses the central nervous system, which includes breathing. Narcan reverses the effects of heroin and other opiates. If pushed too fast, it can make a comatose patient suddenly alert, violent, and violently ill. As I push slowly, I note the man's breathing is improving. His pupils are no longer constricted. I give him point eight more. He opens his eyes.

"Did you shoot up?" I ask.

He says he did two bags. He looks like he's going to puke, so we give him a garbage bag when he sits up, but he just dry heaves then lies back down on the floor and closes his eyes.

We get him up on the stair chair and strap him in. He is deadweight. All of us are dripping sweat. We have to carry him down three floors, which turns out to be seven flights of narrow stairs. I take the foot of the stair chair and Glenn takes the head. The cop stands behind me holding my belt to keep me from tumbling backward. The guy's feet are hitting my knees. Both Glenn and I are irritable. The small of my back feels like it's going to explode. I look at the guy we are carrying with revulsion. I have done countless overdoses and drunks and though I have never said it to a patient of mine, I want to say, "Scumbag." I think I should have given him more Narcan. I gave him enough to put his breathing back to normal and put him on the verge of nausea. I could have slammed a heavy dose right into his veins without even bothering to do an IV, "hot-wiring" him, bringing him from deep heroin bliss to puking nausea. If he got violent, the cop could have smacked him with his billy club. I think I should have at least given him enough so he could stand, however wobbly, and we could have dragged him along, step by step, so we wouldn't be carrying him in this heat, with our backs threatening to explode, and the two of us yelling at each other to go slow, or speed up, or lift better. I look at him and think, Scumbag.

❖

I have thought that maybe I'll become a PA or even a doctor. That would be great. Dr. Canning. Nice sound. Dr. Canning will see you now. Dr. Canning, stat! Oh, thank you, Dr. Canning. How can I ever repay you? I have no money. We're poor, but I can bring you fresh milk every day from our one old cow. We're going to name our baby Dr. Canning, Dr. Canning.

But I think I really don't like sick people. Nothing against them personally, but I don't like vomit, I don't like the smells of infection, sickness, and age. I hate the sound of suctioning, I hate the terror I see in the eyes of people who are losing their health. I am realizing that I am a soldier who doesn't like war. I look at all these doctors. In one sense I think that they are great—they are all incredibly bright—but do I want to spend my life inside a hospital, my complexion eternally pale? Do I want to spend six years of my life studying? I'll be forty-four before I am done. I don't think so.

Maybe I'll go to law school and become a tax lawyer. Make a load of money, but tax lawyers have to work long hours, too.

I am having a crisis here.

❖

The call is for a baby with a fever in Bellevue Square. The mother is diapering a baby on her lap. Another baby is lying on the couch. Three small children wander about half-dressed. A man in a baseball cap stands by the wall. There are two cribs in the living room.

"Which one is sick?" I ask.

"Him," she says, pointing to the baby lying on the couch. "He got a fever that won't go away. I give him Tylenol twice, but he's still hot. He just not right."

I pick the baby up. He is warm. His eyes look right up into mine. He is fifteen months old.

"He hasn't been breathing right today. I gave him two of my asthma treatments, but he still not breathing right."

"Your medication?"

She nods, not picking up my tone implying that maybe it was not the best idea to be giving a baby an adult's medication.

"All right," I say, disgusted with her. "Let's go then. Which hospital?"

"Saint Francis, but I'm not going. He going to go." She points to the smiling man in the baseball cap. "He the baby's uncle."

"Do you have the medical card?"

"No, I can't find it. They have all the information at the hospital."

"Okay, fine."

I carry the baby out. The uncle follows us.

In the back of the ambulance, I take the baby's vital signs and complete my assessment. His lungs are congested and he is hot. His pulse and respiratory rate are up, but not dangerously so.

"What's the baby's name?" I say to the uncle, who sits next to me on the bench.

"I think it's Leonard."

"What do you mean, you think it's Leonard?"

"Leonard, yeah, it's Leonard." He nods.

"What's the last name?"

He shakes his head.

"You don't know the last name? This is your nephew."

"Garcia," he says. "No, wait a minute. Gonzales."

"Which one is it?"

He shrugs and holds his hands up.

"I don't suppose you know the baby's birthday?"

He shakes his head again and smiles, as if to say he is sorry.

I look at my chart and all the empty lines I am supposed to fill in. Baby's medication, allergies, family doctor, birth date, name.

At the hospital, I deposit Leonard on the triage desk next to the computer. "This is Leonard," I tell the nurse. "He is about fifteen months old and has a fever. His mom gave him Tylenol twice and also decided to try two of her Ventolin treatments on him. Unfortunately, that's about all I know. His mom is at home at this number and she should be able to tell you his name and birth date. The uncle here doesn't know. Sorry."

The nurse calls and gets the information. We get a wheelchair and sit the uncle in it, so he can hold Leonard. We leave them, uncle and nephew, in the waiting room.

❖

I am worried that I am prematurely burning out, that all my grand statements about being a paramedic are going to dissolve in my growing distaste for the people I meet, my aching back, my declining savings, and my fear of dying alone and unknown and unloved.

❖

We respond to a motor vehicle accident on Broad Street. The police are already on the scene. A quick survey shows a minor accident. A woman in a fur coat paces outside her Saab. There is a scratch on the bumper. A few feet away sits a Dodge, with a small dent in the driver's-side front.

There is no starring of the windshield, no damage to the steering column or car interior.

There are three passengers in the car. I open the driver's door. The driver is slouched in his seat, holding his head and moaning.

"You all right?"

"My back is killing me. I got shot there last week. My head hurts, too."

"How about your neck?" I feel his pulse. It is steady and regular.

"It hurts bad. I need her insurance card. Did the cop get that?"

"I'm sure he did. Did you have your seat belt on?"

"Yeah, yeah, but I took it off."

"Did you get knocked out?"

"For a little bit," he says.

I look across at the woman sitting in the bucket seat next to him. She has one hand on her head, the other rubbing her knee. "How about you?"

"I hit the glass with my head and my knee hurts."

"Wearing your seat belt?"

She nods.

The man in the backseat has his eyes covered with his hand. He, too, is slouched down.

I ask, "How long were you unconscious for?"

He thinks for a moment, and then says, "I just woke up. I just woke up now."

"Right," I say, not quite containing my sarcasm.

We have to call for a second ambulance. All three get cervical collars to keep them from moving their necks. They are placed on hard wooden spinal-immobilization boards. Three straps secure them to the board at the knee, waist, and chest. Rolled towels are placed to the sides of their heads. A strip of heavy cloth tape secures their heads and neck rolls to the board.

"Goddamn, how long am I going to have to be on this thing?" the driver asks.

"Until they determine your neck isn't broken," I say as I roll the tape across his eyebrows.

En route to the hospital, his beeper keeps going off.

"Popular man," I say.

"Goddamn," he says, reaching to shut it off for the third time.

❖

The dispatcher tells me to call one of the supervisors in operations. I do so and she asks me about a call I did the week before—an elderly woman in diabetic ketoacidosis. She lived alone in a dark apartment in a Hartford high-rise for the elderly. Her son had found her confused and called us. She was dehydrated, breathing deeply to try to blow off the deadly acid building in her system. She had peed all over her thin slip and her bed. I got a line, ran in some fluid, and checked her blood sugar, which was too high to measure. I read in the paper that she had died a day later. The supervisor wants to know if I know anything about her wallet that had one hundred and twenty dollars in it. She says the police are inquiring. I say I don't have it, and the son was there the whole time. The cops should check with him.

❖

I don't even want to do any more calls. I am tired and frustrated and in a bad mood. In a few days I will snap out of it. I will remember that I love this job. I will start doing challenging calls again. I'll give nitro, Lasix, and morphine to a man in congestive heart failure (CHF), and it'll chase the suffocating fluid out of his lungs, and he'll be able to breathe, and relax and live for a while longer. And I'll be on scene just six minutes at a bad car wreck— I'll get my lines, make the patch, and get the patient into the trauma room. And I will gently convince an elderly woman suffering from gangrene to leave her north end home which she loves for the medical treatment she desperately needs. And I will goof with some kids in Stowe Village, who gathering around me will gawk at my great height and say, "How tall is you? You seven feet? No, you eight feet tall? You a giant!" And feeling like Gulliver among the Lilliputians, I will puff out my chest and compare myself to the idol of all little basketball heroes, the mammoth Shaquille O'Neal. "Who's bigger, me or Shaq?" I will challenge. And we will all laugh as they say, "Shaq way bigger than you. Nobody bigger than Shaq!"

But today, as I sit in the ambulance cramped and hot, I think of all the wrong turns I have made. I could have married my college sweetheart and we'd have a family and I'd be a mild-mannered insurance salesman living in a house with a picket fence and taking my kids to Red Sox games. I could have stayed with the political game, bought an eight-hundred-dollar suit and become a lobbyist, making big bucks by selling influence. But no, I wanted to see the world. I didn't ever want to be old and sitting there in my chair, feeling cheated that I hadn't at least tried to seek my fortune. My childhood companions were Paul Bunyan,

Huckleberry Finn, Boone Caudill, and Ishmael. They are not the stuff of insurance sales and influence peddling. I wanted— I still want—to be a hero. Working for Weicker was great—I felt like I was doing some good—but it was he who was the real greatness, not me.

I want to find my own greatness. I believe that this work, this city, this life is my battleground.

When Weicker calls, if he calls, I will say, "Thank you anyway, but this is my place now. I am a paramedic."

City Scenes

The job of a paramedic is a passport anywhere in the city. In a day, you can travel the breadth of ghetto to corporate tower, from life's beginnings to life's end.

❖

We're called for chest pain at a downtown office building. A security guard meets us at the front door and escorts us to an elevator he has waiting. The fire department is already on the scene. On top of the stretcher we have piled our longboard, oxygen bag, heart monitor, drug box, and suction unit. We watch the numbers light up as the elevator rises toward the top: 8, 9, 10, 11, 12, 13, 14 . . .

When we get out of the elevator, a fireman says he's stable. An attractive young blond woman in a red business dress leads us down the hall and through two walnut doors to a large office. A man in his late forties is on the couch with his feet up on the coffee table. His tie is loose. He is pale and ashen and on a 100 percent nonrebreather oxygen mask.

"Describe the pain," I say.

He says he feels a little bit of discomfort in his chest like a pressure or a muscle pull. His hands are shaking. His pulse is 102. His blood pressure is 180/100. He says he called his doctor and took one of his pills, but when he didn't feel any better he had his secretary call 911. On the monitor he has a sinus rhythm with occasional premature ventricular contractions. The man is having a heart attack.

As we help him onto our stretcher, I look out the full window. I can see all of Hartford. The office buildings, the capitol dome, I-84, abandoned factories, and urban neighborhoods. I feel like I am on top of the world.

"Pete," my partner says.

"Huh?"

He looks at the buckle he is holding. I grab the other half and buckle it together. We get the man comfortable and secure the monitor and oxygen tank.

"You scared me," the woman in the red dress says to the man. She hands him his jacket. "I thought I'd be looking for a new boss."

"Thanks," he says. "And call my wife."

"Anything else I can do for you?"

"You've done enough."

"You look real comfortable. I'd like to hop on for the ride."

The firefighters laugh.

Color returns briefly to the man's face.

"Not right now," he says.

In the outer office, a group of women and men stand and wave as they watch us wheel him by.

"Get back to work," he says. "I'll be fine."

In the ambulance, I start an IV and give him a nitro, which will drop his pressure and increase blood flow to his coronary arteries. I give him two baby aspirin to thin his blood and help dissolve any clots he may have in the arteries.

"You're under a lot of stress?" I ask.

"Stress, yes," he says. "I manage money. It's been very stressful, particularly lately." His hands are shaking.

My partner drives through the city streets toward the hospital.

"I just bought a new house," the man says. "I've got two kids ready for college." He shakes his head.

"You still feeling that discomfort?" I ask.

He nods. His brow is sweating.

I recheck his vital signs. I give him another nitro. "Hang in there," I say.

The emergency parking lot is filled. We park by the entrance and wheel him in. There is a logjam at the triage desk. Three crews are ahead of us. A man and a woman from a motor-vehicle accident are strapped to backboards. A homeless woman I have treated for asthma before is in a wheelchair, getting a breathing treatment.

The nurse sees us. She looks from the patient's face to mine.

"Chest pain," I say.

"Cardiac room," she says.

We push our stretcher past the others.

❖

"My heart's beating like it's gonna explode." A fourteen-year-old has been smoking marijuana. He is holding his chest and writhing with anxiety.

"How much did you smoke?" Glenn asks him.

"Just a little."

"Uh-huh," Glenn says.

We're on the front porch of a two-family duplex. The boy's mother is not home, only his seventeen-year-old brother, who is in the house talking on a cellular phone after his beeper went off.

The boy's pulse is 140. His pressure is normal. He's not sweating. His skin temperature is normal. His pupils are dilated but are equal and react to light.

He wants to go to the hospital, but since his condition is not serious, we can't take him without parental permission.

"My mouth is dry. I can't get no spit."

"Smoking'll do that to you," Glenn says.

"I need to go to the hospital," he says.

"Pretend like you have to go to the bathroom," I say. "Bear down hard. That'll slow your heart down." Bearing down will stimulate his vagus nerve, which will depress the electrical stimuli in the heart.

He shakes his head like I am crazy.

A policeman arrives and gives us permission to transport.

As a formality, I put him on oxygen by a nasal cannula and get out our cardiac monitor. I turn the monitor on and apply the patches to the ends of the three electrode wires. The boy is staring in horror at the monitor, which is showing a flat line.

"Is that bad? Is that bad?" he asks.

We stare at the flat line together. "Yes, it is, but . . ."

"I don't want to die," he says. "Oh, please God, I don't want to die."

"There is just one thing you should know."

"Don't let me die."

"It's not attached to you yet."

He looks at the electrodes I am still holding in my hand. He is still too scared to be relieved.

I apply the electrodes to his chest. The monitor shows a sinus tachycardia rhythm at 135.

"Is that bad? Is that bad?" he says.

"It's a little high, but . . ."

He is squirming in his seat. "Don't let me die. I don't want to die."

"Pretend like you're going to the bathroom."

He follows my instructions this time. The rate drops to 120.

"There," I say. "That's better."

"Is that good? Is that good?"

"It's better. You'll live."

"It's—it's going up. It's going up."

The monitor is at 125, 128, 130, 133, 135.

I turn it so he can't see it anymore.

"Is that bad? Is that bad? Am I going to die?"

I am tempted to jump about making madman devil faces and screeching guttural noises. Instead, I just say, "Kid, you'll be fine."

❖

A visiting nurse meets us at the apartment door. "She's eighty-nine years old and is a little difficult. She's been increasingly weak over the last several days. Her doctor wants to see her in the emergency room."

The apartment is beautiful. The living room is stylishly decorated with beautiful paintings, woodcraft, and abundant plants.

We enter the bedroom. The woman is lying on her bed with a pillow under her head. A woman in her fifties sits on the side of the bed holding her hand. On the wall is a painting by Gauguin—one of his works from the South Seas, a lush picture of greens, blues, and yellows.

"How are you today?" I ask, approaching her side.

"What a silly question," she says. She has a very proper accent like a movie star from the 1930s. "If I were well, you wouldn't be here, now would you?"

I smile weakly as I feel her pulse. "We're going to take you to Saint Francis Hospital so your doctor can evaluate you," I say.

"I don't want to go." She turns to her friend. "Millie, you will look after me, won't you?"

"Yes, I'll go with you."

"I'm awfully afraid," she says.

"Don't be. These young men will take good care of you."

She looks at us. "What are you doing in my bedroom?"

"We're here to take you to the hospital, ma'am."

"It's okay," her friend says.

"I've always been fond of young men, and I've known many in my life."

"You look familiar," I say. "You sound familiar. Haven't I seen you somewhere before?"

"I don't know. Have you?"

"You sound like Katharine Hepburn. You look like her, too."

"You're complimenting me, I take it."

"Yes, I am."

"Oh, dear, how dreadful it is to be old."

We lift her sheets across to our stretcher. "Will I be coming back, Millie?" she asks.

"Yes, hopefully, after the doctor checks you over."

She looks about her apartment, then her eyes fix on me. "You're taking me by ambulance?"

"Yes, ma'am," I say. "But we'll go in nice and easy. There's no need for lights and sirens."

"Oh, dear. I've always liked the sound of sirens. They make a nice ending, don't you think?"

"I don't know, ma'am. I suppose we could put them on for you if you like."

Once we have her loaded in the ambulance, Glenn sits in back with her while I drive. I pull out onto the road nice and easy, then I hear Glenn calling up to me, "Put the sirens on."

"Huh?" I say.

"She'd like to hear the sirens."

"Okay." I hit the red lights and turn on the sirens. I drive slowly and alternate the sound from siren to phaser to wail. Two cars pull to the right, making way.

"Yes, ma'am," I hear Glenn say. "They are."

❖

Sometimes when we're parked waiting for a call, I step outside the ambulance and look at the city all around us—the playgrounds, the apartment buildings, the office towers, the highways—and I hold my arms out. This is my city, my church, my garden. What life swirls around us.

❖

He stands in the middle of the alley. A tall muscular Puerto Rican with a broad smiling face. His left arm is bloody red. He pounds his fists together and shouts joyfully. "Come back and fight, you fuckin' asshole. I'll kick your ass. I'll kick your ass all over town, you fuckin' fairy."

He spots us walking slowly toward him and turns to face us. "Hey, tough guys!"

We step back. Glenn removes the HPD portable from his belt and asks for a squad car.

The door to the apartment building has been smashed, punched out. The glass is shattered with a large hole in the middle big enough for an arm to go in and come out, pulling more shards of glass with it.

A crowd stands at a safe distance, watching the scene.

"I showed him who's the tough guy. He may be a Solid, but I'm the tough guy." He shouts down the street, "Keep running! Keep running!" He laughs.

A friend approaches him and starts to walk him toward us. The man's smile, which borders on crazy, does not seem threatening. I get some five by nines and saline water from the ambulance and inspect the wound. "You really should come to the hospital with us," I say. His arm is covered with blood, but there is no arterial bleeding. In the bend of his elbow, there is a deep wide cut through which I can see tendons and bone. It is a space big enough to drop a set of car keys in. He has another gash on the side of his wrist.

"You were fighting with the Solidos?" Glenn says. Los Solidos are one of the most violent gangs in the city.

"I don't care," he says. "I like to fight. I'm the tough guy here. I kick his ass."

He winces a little when I pour the saline water on his arm, before wiping the blood off with a five by nine.

"You got any beer in the ambulance?" he asks.

I wrap a trauma dressing around the wound.

"I like to fight." He smiles broadly. "And I like to drink beer."

❖

We're sent to a tenement address in the south end for a difficulty breathing. An old woman answers the door. She has on a nasal cannula hooked with lengthy tubing to a home oxygen supply. "You think you're coming for me, huh?" she says. "Not today. Hah, hah, hah. Not today. It's him you're looking for." She points up the stairs. "It's him. Earl! Earl!

They've come for you! Get down here! He's got pneumonia. Get him out of here before he gives it to me. Hah, hah, hah."

A young man comes down the stairs. He has a nasty cough and looks awful. He says he wants to go to Hartford Hospital.

As we start out the door, we see a social worker coming up the walk. The woman sees him and smiles. "Thought they were coming for me, huh?"

"Seeing the flashing lights of the ambulance gave me a start," the man says.

"Hah, hah, hah. Not today. Not today," she says. "They ain't taking me today. Hah, hah, hah."

HEROES

TV

Now that the new TV season has started I try to watch "ER" on Thursday nights. I think it's a great show and for the most part truthful to the overall feeling of the world of emergency medicine, though missing many of the real-life qualities and details that don't work too well on TV. For instance, dying or severely injured patients need oxygen in high concentrations, something which is best attained through masks. The problem with masks is the patient can't speak clearly to make a moving dying speech, so on TV they tend to opt for the nasal cannula. In the TV world the doctors tend to spark out a little too much (meaning they get overly excited), sweating and shouting, which is needed for the drama, but in real life, with the exception of new residents, the trauma teams are much more professional and calm about their work.

In the episode I watch tonight, the plot starts to include some pre-hospital people as the alluring Nurse Hathaway goes for a paramedic ride-along as part of her recertification. It seems she has a thing for one of the paramedics. The first call they go on is for a shooting. They find the patient in traumatic arrest. They get the tube on scene, then get the patient in the ambulance. Instead of climbing in the back to help the other paramedic work on the critically injured patient, the nurse climbs in the front with the guy she likes so he can say to her, "Welcome to hell." Then when they arrive at the hospital and get the patient in the trauma room, the patient conveniently goes into v-fib and develops a tension pneumothorax so they can start shocking him and needle decompressing him, even though he has been down forty minutes. If this was going to happen to him, it is far more likely it would have happened in the street and the medics would have done it.

The nurse and the medic are walking out of the room, both depressed after the new resident has pissed everybody off by making the correct decision to end the code, and Nurse Hathaway says back to the medic, "Welcome to hell." Then a prostitute walks by and a doctor notes she has pelvic inflammatory disease. The medic cringes at the sound of the disease and says, "I just bring them in; I don't need to know what they have." This is a terrible thing for a professional to say. Paramedics want to know everything about a patient because it is their job. A good medic will bring that patient in and will tell the nurse or the doctor that his clinical impression—based on physical assessment, patient history, and vital signs—is that the patient has pelvic inflammatory disease, which is characterized by abdominal pain and painful puslike discharge and is often accompanied by a fever. Imagine how upset nurses would get if a nurse said, "I don't care what they have; my job is just to hold their hands and clean their bedpans." Or how upset doctors would get if a doctor said, "I don't care what they have just so long as they can pay their bill."

I'm being a little touchy here again, but I think it's important that paramedics are recognized as professionals. I'd hope this character would have a chance to redeem himself, in addition to possibly getting more seriously involved with the lovely Nurse Hathaway. As it turns out, they do become involved, but they split up when he is revealed as a racist burnout, unable to cope with the death of his partner and people he thinks are abusing the system.

Anyway, I do like "ER." I will never forget the episode where the good Dr. Greene has to manage a problem pregnancy in the ER that is complicated by the patient's suffering from eclampsia. He makes a couple of mistakes, and that—combined with vicious bad luck and lack of help from the attending staff—results in his saving the baby but losing the mother despite his best efforts. The young intern Carter tells him, quite movingly, that he thought Dr. Greene was heroic. But that doesn't help Dr. Greene. His grief is too great. Tortured, he goes out and gets on a subway and just rides. Whether you are a doctor, a nurse, or a paramedic, the bad calls stay with you, and nothing anyone says can make them go away. You have to deal with them yourself, alone.

❖

I don't think there are many politicians who have been in Congress for twenty years, running up deficits and building up million-dollar pensions for themselves, who have ever had to truly face the consequences of their votes in terms of the effects on real people. When George Bush was asked in a presidential debate how the national debt affected him personally, his answer was "I don't get your question." Most politicians live only with the political consequences of political decisions. Saying "Read my lips; no new taxes" won the election for Bush in 1988. Raising taxes during his first term cost him the election in 1992. I don't believe he saw the effect of those political decisions on real people's lives. Robert McNamara and his cronies weren't thinking about real human lives when they were having this country play around in Vietnam. And for all their latter-day mea culpas, they still aren't looking into the eyes of veterans in VA hospitals. Few politicians live with ghosts.

The hard part about EMS is that for all the BS runs, there are times when the patient is dying in front of you, and no one can really say whether or not the person is savable or whether death has already embraced them. You have to believe they are savable, and you do your best, but unlike TV, where only occasionally they lose, you almost always lose. And that is never easy. The consequences of your actions are inescapable.

❖

I've just gotten off from working an overtime shift in the city and am driving through Bloomfield; I plan to stop at the ambulance bay where Michelle is working. Some nights we'll have dinner together, and if the shift is not full I may sign on with her and work till eleven. Since she is going to PA school full-time, in addition to working Friday, Saturday, and Sunday overnights, it is one of the few times I have to see her. Besides, I learn when I work with her. She is an excellent paramedic.

I try a new route, cutting from West Hartford into Bloomfield. I am going up a country road approaching a stop sign when I see the orange-and-white box ambulance of Bloomfield come flying along the street, lights and sirens pulsing. I am annoyed that I have missed her and the call. I turn left, thinking the bay is in that direction. In my rearview mirror, I see the lights of another ambulance coming up on traffic. I pull to the side and see it is an L&M ambulance. A little further down the road I see the lights of police cars, fire trucks, and a second Bloomfield ambulance. A car is wrapped around a telephone pole. Jeff Quinn, the L&M medic, is out leaning into the passenger seat of the car. I think about pulling over and offering a hand, but there are more than enough people on the scene. I turn around and head in the other direction. When I get to the ambulance bay, the door is locked. I calculate the time. It will be at least an hour before Michelle is back. I decide to head home. I'll call her from there, and if she hasn't eaten, I'll drive back and bring some dinner and maybe work the night shift with her.

It is three hours before I finally talk to her. "So you did the big bad one," I say.

"Yeah," she says. She sounds tired, depressed.

I tell her that I went by the scene and saw the car. She says her patient had pulses when she took him out of the car, but they lost pulses in the ambulance and started doing CPR. He had an indentation in his forehead that you could fit a roll of quarters into and a broken neck. He was a big man with a moose tongue and when she tried to tube him, he vomited and she got splashed with blood. He didn't have any track marks on his arms, but the other passenger did. She couldn't get a line, and they called him at the hospital as soon as they rolled in. The other passenger, whom Jeff brought in, looked like he would make it. She was worried about getting splashed with the blood and questioned whether she should have taken the patient she did and not the other one. She is upset she didn't get the tube or a line, though at the hospital they said the patient would have been nearly impossible to tube given his build and the size of his tongue. She is worried that working in Bloomfield, where the call volume is lower than in the city, has dulled her skills and instincts. She wishes that she had worn a face shield. She talked with a doctor for over an hour at the hospital. The doctor was wonderful, she says, reassuring her about her decisions and skills, and saying while she would make certain they got blood results from the autopsy, the likelihood of getting infected from being splashed was relatively low.

She'd done another code early that morning and hadn't gotten the tube then either. It was on an elderly woman whom they'd found on the kitchen floor.

"You okay?" I ask.

"I just need to sleep," she says.

"I'm proud of you," I say.

"It makes me rethink why I'm even still doing this."

"You do it because you're good at it," I say. "You do it because you're the best."

Race in America

The O. J. verdict is due in at 1:00 P.M., ten minutes from now. I'm sitting in the waiting room at Saint Francis, writing my run report, and glancing up at the TV. There are eight other people in the room, all blacks, either patients waiting to be seen or relatives and friends of patients back in the Emergency Room.

As the minutes draw closer the room begins to fill with other EMTs, nurses, and security guards. O. J. and his lawyers stand to hear the verdict. Everyone is holding his breath. When I hear the words *not guilty*, I feel disappointment, then disgust. I watch the others in the room. A young black woman, who has been sitting forward in her chair, says to herself, "Yes! I knew it." Two other blacks look at each other and smile. They look like they want to stand and holler, but they are outnumbered in the room. A white nurse shakes her head and says, "Can you believe that? That sucks." "He's gonna walk. They're going to let him walk," a white security guard says. The room empties out, leaving only the original occupants.

❖

I drive down Albany Avenue and see a shirtless black man sitting on a car, holding a cardboard sign that says, "O. J. is Free." A few others stand by dancing and waving their arms. Cars honk as they pass by.

Later in the day, we transport a sixty-year-old white male down to New Haven where he will undergo a heart bypass. He is disgusted with the verdict. "It's an outrage," he says. When we wheel him into his room, his roommate is also a middle-aged white male, who says, "It's a travesty."

I talk to Michelle about it on the phone that night. I tell her I fear that the decision will harm race relations in the long run. The best thing would have been for the black jury to find him guilty because whites would have been pleased to see that blacks could put race aside. It would defy their expectations and give them pathos. But to see blacks standing and cheering will only further inflame the angry white males who have been fueling the country's turn to the right.

Michelle, who also thinks he is guilty, tries to explain to me why blacks are celebrating. Do I know what it is like to be stopped on the street and frisked for no reason? Do I know what it is like to go into a department store and be followed around because of the color of my skin? Do I know what is like to overhear people who are nice to my face refer to me as a "nigger" behind my back? They are celebrating because America is acknowledging that racist cops are bad and won't get away with it anymore. It doesn't have anything to do with O. J. It is a different kind of justice. I am grouchy and say, but he's guilty. That's not the point, she says. No, I say, my point is he's guilty and it's going to hurt blacks in the long run. They shouldn't be celebrating. Our conversation ends without its usual warmth, and I wonder whether or not I am underestimating the effect of race on our own relationship.

A week later, I am sitting in the ambulance with my partner for the day when an EMT comes up and they start telling jokes. "Did you hear about the nigger who . . ."

"Please stop," I say. "I find this offensive."

They look at me, stunned.

"Okay, can we finish the joke anyway?" one of them says.

"I really rather you didn't."

They go around to the side of the ambulance and finish the joke.

My partner, whom I have never worked with before, apologizes and says she is not a racist. A joke is a joke. It's like a Polish joke or a blond joke.

I tell her that I have told black jokes many times before, but that they bother me now. Maybe if she'd said black instead of nigger, I say, I might not have objected, although I would have tried not to laugh if I found it funny. I tell her my girlfriend is black and these jokes bother her, so they bother me.

She tells me some of her best friends are black. She admits if her daughter came home with a black person, she would be upset. While she would be happy her daughter found love, she would be unhappy and wouldn't want her daughter to suffer from society's reaction. She isn't sure what she would do. After working with her for the whole shift, I feel that she is a good, decent person. I think about my old friend, Barbara, who I lived with and loved for ten years. When she was in high school in the Midwest in the 1960s, she went out with the captain of the football team, who happened to be black. She had a cross burned in her yard for it. Though she and I did not work out in the long haul, I came to admire her over the years as I have admired few in my life—for the way she saw things as they were but lived them as they should be, for the way she listened to children, for the way she raised her own son, and for the way she enjoyed a cold beer and good songs on the jukebox. She lived an extraordinary life with verve. It is not always easy or safe to be more than just good and decent.

I grew up in white suburbia. The only black kids at my grammar school were a boy and a girl bused in from Hartford. The boy hogged the basketball and was always driving out-of-control and taking wild shots. The girl beat up all the toughest boys. I went away to a prep school in New Hampshire that had a fair-sized minority population, but most all hung out together. I was in the dumb math class, and besides two pot-heads, the only kid in the class dumber than me was a black kid from North Carolina. He got a full scholarship to Princeton, while I ended up getting turned down cold at Harvard and Princeton and only wait-listed at Amherst, where the director of admissions was my father's old prep-school roommate. I remember being really pissed off at this kid until one night I heard him on the phone talking to his mother. His father had recently died and she wanted him to come back and work on the farm, and he was trying to explain to her what it meant to be getting a scholar-ship to a college like Princeton.

My kid brother is seven years younger than I am. While I am the "black sheep," the difficult child, he is the favorite son. After I followed the family tradition of going to prep school but failed in my attempts to get into Harvard, he was kept at home at the public school, where he starred as an athlete and student leader, all the while helping to care for my mother, who was losing her battle with multiple sclerosis. When he graduated from Harvard he decided he wanted to teach and ended up in Brooklyn in a tough, predominantly black neighborhood high school. Although he finally burned out from it and is now a first-year law student thinking about becoming a corporate lawyer to make a load of money, I still respect him. He also goes out with a black woman.

My dad is a good man, even though he wishes I had not traveled the paths I have. He used to tell me black jokes when I was growing up, and I shared some I heard with him. Still, he is remarkably cool with the idea of his sons being with black women. His mother once told me she couldn't believe they put different races together as roommates at colleges. My mother's father, a timid inventor whose ideas were always being ripped off by others, thought blacks were of a different species. Times and people do change.

When I first started going out with Michelle, I remember standing in the line at the grocery store thinking I am standing here with a black woman. People are looking at me, thinking, hey, there is a white guy standing with a black girl. When I am with Michelle, I don't think about race anymore. She is just Michelle. I think if we were to get married and have a kid, I would hate for my kid to be treated badly, to be scorned because of his race. I read an article about interracial marriages and how one couple taught their children that they represented the best of both cultures. I think about teaching my son about Jackie Robinson. What a great story for a kid to learn. I think if things don't work out with Michelle and me, and I have a kid with a white woman, I will still teach him about Jackie Robinson, and how one day when he was being viciously heckled by the fans and the opposing ball club, the Dodger shortstop, a white southerner named Pee Wee Reese, walked over to him and put his arm around him, and silenced the crowd. I think about teaching him about Hank Williams, the country balladeer, and Muddy Waters, the delta blues man, and how their music together formed rock 'n' roll. I drive the streets of Hartford. I smile at the little black kids, thinking my kid might look like that someday. I see the junkies and angry black males with surly faces, and I think I don't want my kid to look like that.

I'm Open

We are sent for a leg injury on a basketball court in the north end. We arrive to find the man is a drunk known to us. He was trying to play and just fell down. There is nothing wrong with his leg. Glenn puts on his gloves and starts talking to the guy. I stand back and spot a little kid with a basketball. I guess he is about seven years old. Kids in the city are tight with their basketballs. I have yet to have one pass a ball to me. This, I sense, is my opportunity. I point to the man on the ground. "Did you do this?" I say.

He shakes his head, like I am about to yell at him.

"I heard that he went up to dunk, and you soared up there and stuffed him. Blocked his shot. In his face."

He breaks into a smile at the thought but shakes his head.

"You must be some jumper to have gotten up that high, little guy like you."

"I didn't do it," he says, laughing.

I point to another kid across the court. "He told me this guy went up for the dunk, and you soared up there and stuffed him. Rejected."

"No," he says.

"You hung in the air like a helicopter, he told me. You stuffed him. And look at him now."

"It wasn't me," he says.

"I heard different."

"How tall are you?" he asks.

"Seven feet—no, eight feet," I say.

"You tall."

"Yeah, but I won't go against you. You'll stuff me. Set me down like this poor guy."

He laughs again.

I go for it. "Pass me the ball." I clap my hands together. "I'm open."

He smiles and shakes his head.

"I won't bolt with it. I promise."

He won't give it up.

Glenn has the guy up now and we start back to the ambulance.

"I would have passed it back," I say.

He keeps hold of the ball.

"Don't you be hurting anyone else," I say.

"I won't," he says.

Paramedics

Four-five-three pulls into the hospital with a priority-one patient from an MVA in West Hartford. Their portable oxygen has run empty, so I grab mine from 451 and connect their patient up to it as Tom Harper and Kelly Tierney take her out of the back. She is in her early thirties, pale as a ghost, her chest and one arm crushed. She has defecated on the board. She is taching out at 140 on the monitor. Tom says her pressure is down to 60 from 110 at the scene. He has a bag of ringers running wide open through the fourteen gauge in her good arm. We wheel her into the trauma room. I can tell Tom is disturbed by the way he looks at the doctor and two nurses who enter the empty room with us. He gives a crisp report describing the injuries and mechanism— a head-on crash, destroyed steering column, fifteen-minute extrication.

When we leave the room, Tom lets his anger fly. "I asked for a full trauma response—that's my right as a medic, they can't refuse that," he says, as we watch the trauma team only now come running down the corridor and into the room.

As paramedics we have been given the right to call for the trauma team if our patients meet certain criteria. The hospital chose not to activate until they saw the patient themselves. The woman is critical. They put in a chest tube and ready her for the operating room. Tom is still angry. He stalks back to the ambulance, which is a mess of blood, torn medical wrappers, and gear.

I sit in the EMT room with his partner Kelly Tierney. He describes the scene of the accident. The engine was under the car, the windshield shattered. While the girl was talking, she had no idea what happened or where she was. As soon as they got her out, they boogied for the hospital.

When Tom returns from outside I say, "Tom Harper, it's good to know you're out there, doing what you do."

"Too bad I'm not better at it," he says tersely. He grabs an equipment replacement sheet, then stalks back out.

"They should have had the full trauma team there," Kelly says.

It is their second call of the day—the first they thought was going to be a code, but it turned out to be a presumption, a dead body on Laurel at the high-rise. I tell him I've been doing a lot of ALS calls, but they are all routine—put them on a monitor, give them oxygen, an IV, maybe a few drugs, but nothing life and death. He says it had been that way for them for the last month. This was their first bad one in a while.

Glenn and I do a chest pain, which we take to the hospital across town. In the EMT room there, as I start my report, Sandy Balboni and Bill Buhener are doing their paperwork from their patient, a Room 1 trauma from the same accident as Tom and Kelly's. They say the man has a flail chest and massive internal injuries. They don't think he'll make it. I tell them about how Tom's patient looked. They say both cars were destroyed. I ask if they had the full trauma team waiting for them. They said they did—they even met them in the parking lot, with a fresh oxygen tank.

Sandy's radio goes off. There is a call in West Hartford, where she is one of the medics, for a person "submerged." The call goes to Meg Domina in Medic Two. They also send a transport ambulance.

We wonder what "submerged" means—probably a drowning—and comment how busy West Hartford has been these past few days. There were fourteen calls in twelve hours yesterday, including a cardiac arrest Glenn and I worked with Bob Gionfriddo, one of the other West Hartford medics.

Glenn and I do a seizure on Main Street. A security guard found the man collapsed in the elevator. He has alcohol on his breath but has a known history of seizures. He is combative and takes a swing at me. I use my broken Spanish to try to calm him down. He says his *pecho*—his chest—hurts. While Glenn holds him down, I put in a line and draw bloods. I get him on the monitor and give him some baby aspirin and a nitro as a rule out for chest pain. At the hospital, they want to put him in a room without a monitor. I tell them while I think it was probably a seizure, he did complain of chest pain. They clear Room 5 for us, and start a cardiac workup.

We are back on-line in the ambulance when we hear an EMT on the radio tell the office they are still on scene in West Hartford. A man working in a trench was buried up to his waist in dirt, and as his coworkers tried to get him out with a backhoe, a water main broke and filled the trench, submerging the man. Meg Domina is in the trench with him now, up to her waist in water.

We shake our heads. I can't imagine being on the scene of that call. As much as I want to be challenged, that sounds like a nightmare—something I want no part of.

When we return from a maternity call, we hear on the air that the scene is now closed. The man has been declared dead. The crews won't be through for a while. They are bringing in the CISD (Critical Incident Stress Debriefing) team for everyone.

Another West Hartford call goes out for a man unconscious. We say pretty soon there will be no people left in West Hartford.

"Four-five-one. Signal seventeen in West Hartford," the radio calls. "Cardiac arrest."

We shake our heads. Dispatch sends for another ambulance to back us up. When we pull in front of the address—a nursing home—I grab the monitor, blue bag, and biotech from the side while Glenn pulls out the stretcher, longboard, and straps. Inside they are holding an elevator for us. As the elevator goes up slowly, we glove up. Glenn attaches the defib pads to the monitor. I pull out the airway kit, slide a stylet into a seven point five tube, and pull out an ambu-bag and attach it to the portable oxygen. We're ready to go.

The door opens and a nurse points us down the hallway to the right. We dodge elderly patients in wheelchairs and walkers. Another nurse points us into the last room on the hallway, right across from the nurses' station. "In there," she says.

We turn the corner into the room.

A man is lying on the bed with a nasal cannula on. He is breathing. We look at each other, then at the nurse. Just then a cop arrives.

"Is there a problem?" the nurse says.

"No," I say. "It's just that we thought that this was a cardiac arrest."

"Well, it almost is. His pressure is eighty and dropping. It's circulatory collapse. He has a history of congestive heart failure, heart bypasses, and COPD." That's chronic obstructive pulmonary disease. She is an older woman, who is visibly disturbed.

"It's okay," I say. "We just thought he wasn't breathing and his heart had stopped."

"I just wanted to get him help. I'm sorry for the confusion."

"No problem at all."

Glenn calls the office and tells them to cancel the other ambulance, while I assess the patient. His pressure is 110/60. He is a little cyanotic, so I up his oxygen, which improves his color. We go to Saint Francis on an easy two.

❖

We go nonstop all day—a burned foot, another maternity, a report of a man down in an alley who we could not find, more chest pain, asthma. I don't mind. It is the last day of my shift, and I will be able to sleep late the next day. I like being busy.

❖

We get called to the high-rise on Laurel for a difficulty breathing. In the driveway are a police car and a hearse. "It's from the presumption four-five-three did earlier," Glenn says.

"What apartment are you going to?" the office manager, a pretty young woman, asks.

We give the number.

"Oh, he's a regular," she says.

A security guard says, "It's probably just another of his anxiety attacks. We had a guy die here earlier. That's probably got him upset."

I nod that I understand.

"Which isn't to say it might not be something serious," he says.

"We'll check it out," I say.

Upstairs on the fifth floor, we see an open apartment door. As we come down the hall, we see a man walk past. When we enter he is sitting in his wheelchair.

I ask what the problem is, and he says he is having a little trouble breathing. He says he has congestive heart failure, diabetes, and had a heart attack ten years ago. His color is good. His pulse is steady and regular. His pressure is also fine. I listen to his lungs. They are clear.

"Clear," he says. "The visiting nurse told me this morning she heard some crackles, and I was worried. She said if I felt like I was having a hard time breathing, I should call for an ambulance."

"Well, they sound clear to me, but we are happy to take you to the hospital if you'd like. Only you can tell us how you really feel."

"I just get worried," he says. "I'm here all alone and I haven't been healthy."

"It's okay, we don't mind coming. You can call anytime."

I get him to sign a refusal.

"I feel embarrassed now," he says.

"Don't be."

"Okay, thanks. Good-bye, fellahs."

"Take care, sir."

At six we are sent to Windsor for a fire standby. We end up transporting one firefighter with smoke inhalation and heat exhaustion. We are unloading him when Mike Lambert, the newest paramedic to be cut loose, comes up to us. He looks a little frazzled, a little lost.

"You guys been busy today?" he asks.

"Yeah, real busy. We've been running all over the place. Nothing spectacular, but just a lot of calls."

"I've only done one."

"One?"

"Yeah, I was out at that call in West Hartford. They just finished up with it. The guy in the trench."

"You were at that?"

"Yeah," he says. "We couldn't get to him at first. He was underwater. Then we worked him. We tubed him, gave him IVs, drugs, fluid. Nothing worked."

"Wow."

"Traumatic asphyxiation." He shakes his head at the thought. "He was crushed by all the mud and he drowned. It took four hours to get him out of the pit."

"Man, sounds rough."

"We did all we could." He holds his arms out. "There was nothing more we could do."

I want to say something to Mike, like good try or you did your best, but the thought of the horror leaves no space for words. We push into the ER with our patient, leaving Mike outside, alone.

❖

After "ER" that night, the local news comes on, and I watch the coverage of the accident. They say until they got the water main fixed and the water pumped out, only the man's outstretched hands were above the surface. They don't show the man, only the rescue workers in the pit. For a time, the water is up to their hips. I can see Meg Domina and Mike. The newscasters talk about how the rescuers risked their lives, going down in there to try to save him. They talk of the helplessness people felt. Meg, who is six months pregnant, has a look of battle shock in her deep brown eyes as she works side by side with Mike in the pit.

Boots

We're sitting in the EMT room at Hartford Hospital, and Glenn is giving me crap about how I need to shine my boots, when Rick Ortyl comes in. Rick is in his early forties and has been in EMS for twenty-five years. He works full-time as a medic for Professional and part-time as the assistant EMS coordinator for Saint Francis–Mount Sinai under Debbie Haliscak. He shakes his head. "How much longer are you going to be doing this?" he says to me. "I think I'm about ready to hang it up."

"So you're just going to teach your classes and have all the young girls go 'Oh, Mr. Ortyl, you're so wonderful.'"

"Yeah, that's the life and, of course, I'll come out and ride with you guys, and bust your butts every now and then."

"I'm going to keep doing it for a while longer—at least until I'm good at it," I say, "but the truth is I have been in a funk for the last couple weeks that's making me have my doubts." I tell him how that week a doctor wouldn't give me any medical history on his patient who was having a minor allergic reaction to a drug. Just take her to the hospital, he'd said. That had depressed me.

He shakes his head. "There's no respect from some people. I'm ready to pack it in, but then again, I may do a good call, then get all fired up about it, and be ready to keep going."

"Yeah, I know what you mean."

We clear the hospital just as two MVAs go out over HPD. We're sent as the second car to an accident on Franklin, and Rick is sent on a one to the call off Maple that comes in as "patients trapped in car, fire department on the way." There are only minor injuries at our call. A patient with neck pain and a refusal. The basic unit on scene first will take the patient in. I look around for the car that hit the Jeep but don't see it. Glenn is back in the ambulance, clearing us from the call, while I help the basic crew get the refusal. I see Glenn gesturing to me to get in the ambulance. I leave the refusal with the other crew and return. "What's up?"

"They need another medic at the other call."

I strap in and we take off. It is only about six or seven blocks away. As we turn off Maple onto a side street, I can see a huge crowd on both sides of the street. There are two ambulances there, a couple of fire trucks, several squad cars, and police tape already lashed across the road. We park and get out. I break through the crowd, then duck under the yellow tape. All I see is twisted black metal, broken windows, and firemen. Rick shouts to me, "I've got two unresponsives." The fire department is helping the basic crew pull the passenger out and slide him onto a board.

"I'll take him," I say to Rick. We get the board on the stretcher and start strapping the patient down and rolling back toward my ambulance at the same time. I glance at him—he looks to be in his early twenties. He is out cold. He has a deep cut below his mouth. His color is funny— it's a purplish blue tint. I stare at him as we wheel rapidly, ducking under the police tape. I see his shoulders shake as he breathes. In a matter of seconds we are back at my ambulance. I rip out our stretcher and then help Bob Bahan, one of the EMTs, lift the patient into the back, and scramble up. His partner hops in with me. "What can I do for you?" she says. "Let's get his clothes off and secure him to the board," I say. I reach for an oxygen mask, strap it on him, then stop. I look at him more closely. He shakes as he takes a breath, but he doesn't take another one. He has stopped breathing. "I'm going to have to intubate him," I say. I get out the intubation role, slide a stylet in a number eight tube, attach the syringe, take out the laryngoscope, open up the blade. I detach the front collar of the patient's cervical collar, slide the blade in. He has no gag reflex. I look for the chords, but see nothing but blood. I drop the laryngoscope, suction the airway, and shout that I need a driver. Bob is getting a blood pressure.

"I'll have to move my rig," Bob says.

"Do it and come back quick," I say. I am tempted to just have his partner drive, but I don't want to be alone with this patient. I have too many things to do. I drop an oral airway in his mouth to keep his tongue from obstructing his airway, and start bagging. With each squeeze of the bag his chest rises. His color improves almost instantly. I tell the partner to take over.

Glenn is nowhere to be seen. Over the radio I hear someone say there are two working one hundreds—cardiac arrests. Glenn must be helping Rick with the other patient. The partner is bagging while I am putting the guy on the monitor. I get on the radio and say, we don't have a one hundred, but a critical patient. Should we go to Saint Francis? I ask. Hartford is only blocks away, while Saint Francis is a five-minute drive, but two critical patients is a lot to handle even though a trauma center is equipped to take two. The dispatcher says Hartford is expecting two patients. "Okay, Hartford," I say.

The guy has a normal sinus rhythm at 80. His pressure is 100/60. The man is stripped except for his briefs. He doesn't seem to have any other injuries, but it is hard to tell because he is totally unresponsive. The other ambulance backs up past us. "Where is your partner?" I say aloud as I spike a bag of Ringers Lactate. "I may need you to drive."

"Tell me what you want me to do," she says.

Just then Bob appears in the back door. "Drive," I say.

I strap a tourniquet around the patient's arm, and sink a large bore fourteen into his AC. We're moving now and as we go around a corner, I am tossed. I lose pressure on the vein and blood spurts from the catheter. By the time I get it shut off, my gloves are soaked in blood. I attach the line, run it wide open, then try to tape it down, but the tape sticks to my gloves. I grab two strips of the spare tape I have hanging above the cabinets. I attach the two strips and secure the line. Still there is blood everywhere from everything I have touched. I reach back for the laryngoscope, but we are already at the hospital. It is just a two-minute trip. I reach for the spare oxygen, unhook the bag from the wall supply, hook it up, and set it between the man's legs. I hear him gurgling and tell the partner to suction. Bright red blood again fills the suction tubing.

"Let's move," I say.

We pull him on the stretcher. I grab the monitor and bag of fluid. The partner is doing a good job bagging. We hurtle through the ER doors, headed for the trauma room.

"Hold on a minute," the triage nurse says. "Did you radio?"

She steps in front of us and tries to stop us. She is dragged several feet before we can stop.

"We were told you were expecting two. This is the second one."

"You didn't patch. What's the story? I see he has a heartbeat." She is looking at the monitor. "Then you have time to talk to me. What's wrong with him?"

"He's unresponsive, not breathing, and his airway needs to be suctioned."

"What's his name?"

"I don't know."

I am angry at this woman right now. She has no idea what we have just gone through. All she wants to do is show that she—the triage nurse—is the boss. She finally says, okay, you can take him in. We wheel him into the trauma room where a full second team stands around the trauma table expecting us, while another team works Rick's patient who is in traumatic arrest. "They didn't radio," the nurse says.

The doctor ignores her. "What's the story?" he asks me as we lift the patient on the board onto their table.

"Unresponsive, car demolished. One hundred over sixty, eighty, and respirations of about two. He's got a lot of blood in his airway."

They try twice to intubate but are unsuccessful. Rick Ortyl, who is standing against the wall, steps forward and taking a laryngoscope in his hand, sinks the tube.

"I don't think you're in," a doctor says.

"Pulse SAT one hundred percent," a nurse says, referring to his blood oxygen saturation.

"I'm in," Rick says.

The room is crowded so all the prehospital people are kicked out. We stand outside talking about the call. Almost everyone says they have never seen a car so destroyed. Glenn, who rode in with Rick and Joel Morris, another paramedic, says the car was so horseshoed, the front end and the back bumper were almost touching. The crew who rode in with me are sent off to get their rig, which they beached at the scene. I thank them for the good job they did.

I sit down back in the EMT room to write my run form. I have a name for the patient now, and as I write it in the blanks, the battered body takes on a new form. Twenty years old. Just a half an hour ago, as I sat in this very room, he was driving around with his buddy in a muscle car, enjoying the day, listening to music, maybe checking out the babes on the avenue, driving a little too fast, a whole life to live, immortal. They bang one car and spin away, racing off the scene, hollering with youthful craze as they peel away. They hear a siren behind them and step on it even more. The car handles great as they cut up a side street, everybody on the street turning their heads. The radio pumping. A car is coming at them. They swerve.

I think about all the times I drove too fast in my youth. In Colorado driving down the Rockies, stoned out of my mind, thinking I was in a pinball machine. In Massachusetts, the passenger this time, breaking the windshield with my head, not getting medical attention, spending the next day vomiting. I think about the friends of mine who didn't make it. One sticks in my mind more than the others. A twenty-year-old girl, whom just a couple of months before I had escorted home from a bar in a beautiful white snowstorm. She'd told me to come see her, and I didn't, though I often thought to. I woke up one morning, got the paper from my door, and saw the photo of a body under a sheet on the dark, wet road, with her name listed in the small print of the story about a car coming back from a party in the country, going out of control, and hitting a bridge abutment, killing the passenger instantly. I thought how maybe if I'd gone and seen her, she might not have gone to that party that night, but might have been with me instead, sitting in a cloth robe, fresh out of the shower, sharing fresh fruit, home-fried potatoes with sausage, and the comics.

I break out of my reverie. I quickly write:

Pt. 20 y/o male passenger unbelted in head-on into telephone pole MVA. Car horseshoe shape around pole. Pt. unresponsive, cyanotic. Rapidly extricated. C-spine immobilized. Intubation attempted X 1. Airway suctioned of blood. Oral airway inserted. IV #14 in L AC LR Wide open. Pt. ventilations assisted. Pt. n. sinus on monitor.

Pt. transported to HH, airway monitored and suctioned and airway assisted with bag valve mask. Pt. turned over to ED staff with full report.

He gets a Glasgow coma score of three, the lowest score. No eye opening, no verbal response, no motor response.

❖

Then I go out to look at the ambulance. The car is trashed. Blood is everywhere—on the floor, on the seat, on the cabinets, on everything I touched. The airway kit is scattered on the floor. The main oxygen is still running. I turn it off. There are IV dressings and wrappers and a broken blood tube on the floor, along with the needle.

It takes an hour to clean and restock the ambulance so it is ready to go. Every time we think it's done we spot some more blood—on the stretcher bars, on the stretcher straps, on the monitor casing, on some trauma dressings in the cabinet. We finally clear the hospital. One dead, one critical.

"Well, that call ought to last us for a couple weeks," Glenn says.

"Yeah, I guess."

Scenes of the wreck are on the ten o'clock news, though I miss it because I am too tired to stay up. In the morning a picture of the wreck is on the front of the *Courant*'s Connecticut page. The call went so fast I never really got a chance to look at the car, but Glenn was right—the front and back ends are only feet from each other, wrapped around the pole like a ring. I learn later in the day that my patient has succumbed to massive brain injury.

That night I take off my boots as I sit on the couch with a beer already opened. With the reading light on high, I notice something on my boots. Dark red splotches run down both boots from the ankle to the sole. I shiver.

Whiffle Ball

G lenn is out for a few weeks with a strained ligament in his knee, so I am working with Darren Barsalou. It is a beautiful day. We're playing whiffle ball by some trash heaps in area two. Darren has taped a strike zone on the side of the ambulance and laid a longboard against the rig to keep the balls from going under it. He stands back forty feet and fires the whiffle ball at high speed. I foul it off. There is no score in the top of the fourth. A short but strong and limber athlete of twenty-three, Darren plays on league softball and football teams. Glenn and I used to play Darren and his partner in basketball back in the spring whenever we were in area nine together. That was before I broke the tip of my right ring finger and twisted my ankle in a Saturday pickup game and had to retire from contact sports for fear it would knock me out of work. Back then I had earned the nickname "Kareem" and "The Tower of

Power." I sense he thinks he has met his match. Though I am an old man by ambulance standards, I still have the memory of how to swing a bat, and though my pitches lack his blazing speed, I am crafty with a whiffle ball, changing velocity, getting lots of movement, throwing the ball in and out, keeping him off balance.

As he winds and throws, I crouch and then step into the pitch, ripping it deep but foul, just to the left of the evergreen that serves as the left-field foul pole.

"You exploded on that one," he says.

The next pitch whizzes at my knees, and I narrowly avoid being hit.

On the two to one count, I step in again, catching the ball squarely over the middle-belt high, and drive it deep to center over the cement blocks and into the weeds. Home run.

"I'm not used to playing someone who knows how to swing a bat," he says. "Clemens is rocked."

"Conigliaro goes deep," I say. "The Sox take a one-nothing lead. Frank Malzone to the plate." I am the 1965 Boston Red Sox. He is the 1995 All-Star team.

In the bottom of the fourth, he rips the first pitch off former twenty-game winner Bill Monbouquette right at my head. I duck then turn to see it skip into the weeds for a Mo Vaughn double. I am stunned that he hit my submarine snaking curve. I fire a fastball at his head that bounces off his shoulder. I glare at him. I throw the big hammer swooping curve. He clocks it over the centerfield fence. This is followed by three blistering singles, then a towering blast over the trees in left. I come back out of the overgrowth to see him smiling. "Instant replay," he says, looking to the horizon and tossing the bat down like Barry Bonds.

"I quit," I say.

"Giving up already?"

"Yeah, my arm is killing me. I don't have any more throws left."

Before he can protest or call me a wimp, the radio calls our number and we are sent for a back pain.

❖

We start a new game in area nine that afternoon. I lead off with a single, but our number is called again and we're sent for a woman unresponsive on Whitney Street.

"I had runners on first and second and was ahead one nothing, wasn't I?" I say to Darren as he hits on the lights and sirens.

"Dream on," he says.

The game resumes in the parking lot of Hartford Business College. I go down quickly. The game is scoreless for two innings when he catches hold of my sinker and lines it by my head. I pelt him with the next pitch. He homers. He homers again. Soon it is five nothing. He hits his third homer of the inning. "Keep walking," he taunts as I plod after the ball that is still rolling away from me. When I turn back, he does his Barry Bonds slow-motion replay. I bean him twice in a row. My arm is really throbbing now, killing me.

I am saved by a call for a motor vehicle accident.

"If you were smart, you wouldn't beat me so badly," I say. "I don't think I'm going to play anymore."

"Girly-man," he says.

"I used to be good at this game."

"You want me to give you four outs and I'll pitch underhand?"

"Fuck you."

It is nearly dark when we resume play in a vacant lot off the Sisson Avenue ramp of I-84. We start the game from scratch. It is scoreless when I come up in the bottom of the third. After two singles to the pitcher's right, he hangs me a curve. It looks as big as a grapefruit. I am off balance, but manage to keep my hands back. I drive it high and deep. It drops on the far side of the crack line in the asphalt that we have declared to be the fence.

"You ripped that one," he says.

I glare at him.

He goes down in order, then we get a call for a man down on Broad Street, which turns out to be a drunk. I try to bring him around with ammonia inhalants, but he is too out of it. His pressure is okay, but he is tachycardiac. I give him an IV and check his blood sugar, which is fine. He smells of cheap wine, has snot coming out of his nose, and has flatulence all the way to the hospital.

It is now dark. We sit in the ambulance, waiting to be called in. "Well, you're ahead," he says. "We'll have to finish the game another day."

I eye him closely. "You were just toying with me," I say.

"You capitalized on my mistake. You hit it good."

"You hung it up there for me."

"You think so?"

"I know so."

He laughs. "It was a good game. We'll play again next week?"

"We'll see."

❖

That night on the news, I catch a glimpse of our ambulance at the accident scene. You can see the taped strike zone on the side.

Trauma Regs

On October 1, 1995, the new state trauma regulations go into effect. The regulations call for patients to be taken to designated hospitals that can best care for their injuries based on a triage algorithm. The idea is to get critically injured patients to operating rooms where skilled surgeons can save their lives.

The regulations took ten years to develop into law. When I went to the state health department in 1991, they were on the back burner. Because of my experience in EMS, I took an active role in reviving the regulations and making EMS a priority in the department. We formed a trauma committee, whose job it was to produce a draft of the regulations acceptable to the various warring factions in EMS that would meet the need. We chose Dr. Lenworth Jacobs of Hartford Hospital to chair the committee. A nationally renowned surgeon and a gracious, diplomatic man, he had the political skills necessary to bring disparate elements together.

There were many battles to be fought both within and without the EMS community. Emergency department physicians were worried surgeons would usurp their authority; small hospitals were worried big hospitals would take all their patients; volunteer EMS groups were worried new burdens would be placed on them. Dr. Jacobs, with help from Dr. Morgan, kept the focus on the patient. Dr. Jacobs reminded people that a trauma system was inevitable and that better it be developed by those who worked on the front lines than imposed later by bureaucrats. Dr. Morgan gave impassioned speeches about people dying needlessly that rang true to those who worked in the system.

I had thought at first that all you had to do was say "Let's do it," and it would get done, but government is a slow process. There were countless meetings, setbacks, and delays along the way. One of the hurdles we had to overcome was the resistance of some of the members of the Commission on Hospitals and Medical Care (the Commission) to the way we proposed to designate hospitals. Under our plan, in order to be designated as a trauma facility, a hospital first had to be verified by the American College of Surgeons, an organization that sets the standards for trauma facilities. The College verifies hospitals based on a hospital's showing it has met certain criteria such as patient volume, staffing, quality-assurance programs, etc., over a fourteen-month period. Existing law gave the OEMS the right to categorize hospitals based on treatment capability. The Cost Commission's Statutes gave them authority for approving new services. The Commission's argument was that they should get to approve trauma hospitals because they are new services. OEMS's argument was that we should get to approve them because we were designating them based on what they had already done. We had several meetings with Commission members over a period of many months. As new commissioners came and went, we had to make the same presentation again. In the end, I used my Weicker card to settle the issue. Ironically, before the regulations went into effect, the Commission itself was targeted for elimination.

I wasn't involved in the day-to-day handling of developing the regulations. That task was assigned to Marie Wilson of the OEMS staff, who worked diligently with Dr. Jacobs, Dr. Phillip Stent, the state's medical director, and others to craft the final package. I wanted them to be finished before I left the department, but it did not happen. Despite being pressed to the front burner, it still took another four years and many setbacks to come about, but it was worth the wait.

Now if a patient is critically injured, the ambulance crew is trained to bypass closer hospitals for trauma centers. Or depending on the proximity of the hospitals, the smaller hospital will immediately transfer the patient by helicopter to a Level I or Level II center, which has the experience to handle major trauma. Everyone injured in the state will have data on their injury and care input into the system, which will be a gold mine in terms of research information that can be used to improve treatments and for preventive measures.

❖

It is a nice feeling to see something in which I played a role reach the street. But the legacy I hoped to leave from my years at the health department is being threatened in other ways. I had the support of Governor Weicker and Commissioner Addiss in pushing for change in the EMS system. Today, there are both a new governor and a new commissioner in town. When I came to the health department in 1991, OEMS was located figuratively and literally in the basement of the health department. The then acting director of OEMS, Paul Connelly, reported to the bureau chief for regulation, who reported to the deputy for administration, who reported to the commissioner. While the bureau chief was a proficient administrator, he had no particular interest in EMS, which was consequently a low priority for the department. After I had been there a year, we moved the office out from under regulation and gave it independent reporting authority to the commissioner, created a statewide advisory committee, and launched a national search for a permanent director to fill the position that had been open for three years. I remember the day OEMS broke free, how happy everyone was to be liberated. All except Paul Connelly, who said to me, "Who is going to protect us when you're gone?"

In July, the new governor named the bureau chief commissioner of the health department. One of his first acts was to put OEMS back under the bureau of regulation. He eliminated Paul's job as deputy director, has been slow to refill vacant positions, and has floated a plan to entirely dismantle the office. He offered Michael Kleiner, the man we selected as the new OEMS director, a raise if he would accept a three-year temporary position to complete the overhaul of the EMS regulations. Kleiner, a savvy former director of paramedics in San Francisco with ten years of street experience and experience as a labor negotiator for his union, turned him down. Eliminating the office will require a change in law—the key will be to prevent the language from being tucked into a bill during a midnight session.

I occasionally run into people I dealt with, and they express dismay at what is happening. A few have said they miss me. But I don't miss it, and I know that I am not irreplaceable. Mike Kleiner can hold his own, and if he loses, he will have fought a good fight for the people in the street. I am confident of that. And I do know that my power base came from the fact that people knew the commissioner and the governor stood behind me. Without them, I couldn't have done anything.

❖

I am at Hartford Hospital when the intercom announces Life-Star is landing on the roof with a Room 1 trauma. Minutes later, they come through the doors with the patient c-spined to a board, two lines of fluid running, the patient intubated. The flight nurse delivers a crisp report as the patient is transferred over to the trauma table, where the gowned team descends on him. Ten minutes later, he is whisked out to the operating room, where a surgeon will save the man's life.

We get a call for a pedestrian struck. We race down Washington Street, past the health department. I look up at the large window on the third floor where I had my office. I used to sit with my feet up on my big desk and, looking out the window with binoculars, watch Life-Star land on the roof at Hartford or watch the ambulances whiz by. I am glad to be down below now on the street.

Celebrities

We go to Hartford Hospital to take a seven-year-old with a deformed spine and lung problems to Newington Children's Hospital. He is on his side, watching TV. The nurse introduces him to Glenn and me.

"This here's a professional basketball player," Glenn tells the boy, gesturing to me.

The boy holds up his hand for me to shake, which I do. "How are you?" I say.

"Good, sir," he says in a tired voice.

"He's a good kid," the nurse says.

"Newington's a good place," I say. "I used to live there for a while myself."

"Did you hear that?" the nurse says.

He nods.

It is not entirely true. I spent three days there after having a knee operation when I was ten. My roommate had been born with his organs outside his body and lived upside down in a bed that he was connected to through a steel pole in his head. In the hallway, there were all sorts of strange disabled kids with no feet and other weird things. The place gave me the willies big time, and I was glad to get out, though now I see what a wonderful place it is for kids.

When we get to Newington, we have to wheel our little friend into the waiting/playroom while they prepare his paperwork. They have giant stuffed animals, and Glenn and I get a kick out of playing with them and the kid. There is a hundred-gallon fish tank that he is watching. I get a five-foot-tall Tony the Tiger doll and stick his face on the other side of the tank. The fish scatter. The boy giggles.

Upstairs, we help him to his room. His nurse comes in and makes him smile by calling him the Big B.

In the hallway, a boy in a wheelchair with twenty balloons attached to the back is looking at me. "Are you a paramedic?" he says.

"Yes, I am," I say. I go over and shake his hand. "How are you today?"

"Good," he says. "You go to car wrecks and save people's lives?"

"We try."

"I'm going to be a paramedic someday."

"You'll be a good one, too," I say.

Some other kids come by and gather around us like we are celebrities. We shake their hands and joke with them. They look up at us like we are heroes. The nurses stand back, smiling.

Off Duty

It's my day off. I sit around the house. I've cleaned. I've eaten. I've worked out. I've written. I've watched TV. I've read. I'm anxious. I'm bored. I want to be at work. I want to be doing calls.

THANKSGIVING

Changing Seasons

It is the last day of our rotation again, a cold overcast day. Glenn is back at work after being out sick yesterday. He doesn't look well and says he'd just as soon not drive today, which is not at all like him. Our morning is quiet, so he sleeps in the back for an hour or so but doesn't feel much perkier. Our first call is for a person passed out at the bank on North Main. Welfare checks were distributed yesterday so the line at the bank is long. The guard tells us the woman is okay and doesn't want to go to the hospital. She is putting her money into her pocketbook as we approach. She is a young woman, five months pregnant, with a baby in a stroller. She looks pale and sweaty. I ask her to come sit in one of the bank chairs so I can examine her. Her skin is cool and clammy. Her pressure is 90/60. Her pulse is 76. Everything else checks out okay. She isn't in any pain. She was just tired. I ask when she last ate and she says yesterday. I tell her we'd be happy to take her into the hospital to get checked out. She signs a refusal and says she'll go to the community health center after she gets home. She says she'll take a bus. A friend who is with her says she'll watch out for her. "Make sure she gets something to eat," I say.

Driving back to sign on-line in the downtown area, I tell Glenn I was surprised that the woman was so insistent on not going and on later taking a bus. "Are we jaded in our view because all we deal with are those who abuse the system?" I ask. "Or is there a larger world of people out there like her who don't take advantage?"

"She's the exception. They're mostly all dirtballs." He launches into a critique of the welfare system. "They ought to just end it. Sure you've got to help those who can't work, but most of them can work. Put them to work cleaning the streets. I mean, look at the litter in this part of town."

"They're starting to clamp down," I say. "They're going to impose a time limit on how long you can be on welfare."

"Until it's no days, it'll be too long," he says.

❖

We do an accidental sleeping-pill overdose and a Cancer Center round trip, then are quiet for the entire afternoon, sitting down by the train station, under the highway overpass. Another crew comes by to talk for a bit. Brian Brown and Dave DiFlumeri. They haven't done anything all day either. Dave is precepting Brian and they are just waiting for Vinny Cezus of Hartford Hospital to ride with them to cut Brian loose.

"Did you do that call at City Place?" Brian asks.

"No that was Harper. Cerebral hemorrhage. Thirty-four-year-old lady. They tried to nasally tube her, but her septum was deviated. Her jaws were locked up. Pupils pinpoint."

They shake their heads.

"Happens just like that," Dave says.

We talk for a while about not much, then they head off to get something to eat.

"One of these days they're going to call you up and have you precept," Glenn says. "How long have you been on your own now?"

"Eight months. I think I'd be okay at it. I'm close enough to it to know what the preceptee needs, but I haven't done enough real bad ones yet. I don't have a nasal tube, and I could use some more regular tubes. It should be second nature before I precept someone."

Glenn is going to be starting medic school in January. I say maybe I'll precept him when he gets out. "We've done enough calls already, I could check you off quick. Done that. Done that. Yup, done that."

"That'd be good," he says.

I sleep in the back this time, and Glenn conks out in the front. We keep the engine running because we've got the heat on. Both radios are dead quiet.

I hear a knock on the front window and suddenly worry if maybe our radios went out and the company has come down and found us both asleep, but it is a man asking Glenn directions. Sorry to wake you up, he says.

After that Glenn can't sleep. He is singing along to the country music, and I can tell he is bored. I get up and get in the driver's seat. Jerk woke me up, he says. I gave him bad directions. Didn't mean to, he says, just wasn't awake.

Down the street by the railroad bridge I see a tall panhandler walking with a man in an overcoat. The man takes some change out of his pocket and gives it to the panhandler, then hurries off toward the fenced-in parking lot. The panhandler sees me looking at him. He comes over and gestures for me to roll down the window.

"Busy today?" he says.

"No, slow."

"That's good."

"Not really," I say. "We're sort of bored. Day goes by too slow."

"Oh, I get it," he says. "It's like the undertaker. You got to have business to get paid." He laughs.

"Sort of," I say.

"Well, let me ask you something," he says, suddenly becoming serious. "I'm a homeless man just out of the shelter, and I'm trying to round up some money to get a room at the YMCA. It's First Thursday tonight, and the cops don't take well to my kind being on the street with all the suburban folk in town, so I just want to get a warm room, and get out of the way. Could you help me out some?"

"I don't know," I say. "Payday isn't until tomorrow."

"I'm not talking dollars here, I'm just talking change."

"How much is a room?"

"Sixteen dollars and sixty cents," he says without hesitating a second.

I don't know if he's bullshitting, but it sounds good.

"How much you got?" Glenn says.

"Thirteen dollars and seventy-five cents."

I am surprised to see Glenn reach into his pocket and pull out a quarter. I reach into mine and give him a Susan B. Anthony silver dollar I got in change from the Charter Food that morning when I was buying my grape juice, pecan spin, and newspaper. "How do you like this quarter?" I say.

"Why, it's a Susan B. Anthony dollar. I'm no fool. I thank the both of you. Have a good day now. I hope it isn't too slow for you."

"Just so we're not picking you up," I say.

"I can go along with it," he says. "Good afternoon now." He starts walking up the hill toward Garden Street.

"You gave him a buck?" Glenn says.

"Well, I couldn't believe you were giving him money."

"Yeah, but I was going to say, 'Here's a quarter; now get fucking lost.' "

"You notice which way he's headed?"

"Yeah, the Y is back that way."

"What the hell. He had a good answer about the rent."

"Let's go drive around. I'm bored sitting here."

We spin around the downtown, looking as we always do for beautiful women, but the streets are nearly deserted. Those leaving work, all wearing coats, hurry toward their cars. No one is sitting in the windows of the Union Street bars.

A Heart History

We're covering downtown this morning when we are sent on a one up to Windsor for a possible cardiac arrest. It is a long drive, so I get in the fast lane and press the accelerator all the way to the floor. We're halfway up there when we get an update; it looks like it will just be a presumption. We should cut down to a five: lights and sirens until we are in the vicinity, then a quiet approach.

It is a nice house on a cul-de-sac, the kind of neighborhood I grew up in myself, safe for kids to play in the streets, yards to mow for five bucks. Two cops and a Windsor EMS volunteer are standing outside. "She's got rigor mortis with dependent lividity," the EMT tells us. "A heart history."

We enter the house. A large man wearing only his pants sits at the kitchen table talking with an officer. He looks at us. His eyes are bleary. "Hello," he says, choking on his words. "Come right in, gentlemen."

A cop points us down the hall. "Last bedroom on the right."

We walk down the hall. There are two beds. One is unmade; a sheet is pulled over the body in the other bed. I pull the sheet back. A woman sleeps on her side, her head on the pillow, her arms tucked in as if she were holding the sheet up to her neck to keep her snugly warm. She is cold; her face is mottled blue. Her arms are stiff and stiffened into position. She is long gone. I listen to her heart with the stethoscope but hear no sound. I apply the monitor and run a six-second strip of flat line. I detach the monitor and unstick the electrodes, which I put in my pocket.

I pull the sheet back up and tuck it up to her neck. Glenn pulls the sheet the rest of the way over her head.

We go back to the kitchen. The man stands as we enter. "I am sorry for your loss," I say. He nods as we shake hands.

"I need to ask a few questions."

"By all means," he says. He fumbles to pull the chair out for me. "I apologize for the state of the house. I had just given our dog an egg carton to play with. I'd turned the TV on and gone in to wake up Jennie so she could watch Kathie Lee and Regis as she does every morning." He starts to cry and moves a fist to his mouth.

"How long were you married?"

"Forty-one years."

"That's a long time. Kids?"

"Seven. Two are no longer with us."

"Grandkids."

He smiles. "Their pictures are up there." He points to the refrigerator. "The officers were looking at them."

"Great," I say. "I just need to get a few things for my report." I ask for her full name. He gives it to me and also tells me her maiden name in case I need it. I get her medical history.

"She had a weak heart," he says. "And seizures. She was pregnant with twins and had toxemia."

"Did the twins survive?"

He smiles. "They are both big strapping boys today."

I nod.

I get the list of medications then ask when he last saw her alive.

"Ten o'clock last night," he says. "I got her in bed and wished her good night." He fights back more tears.

"Well," I say, "thank you. The officers will take care of things from here."

He nods.

We look at each other, then I say, "Forty-one years. It sounds like you had a good life together."

"We did," he says.

I stand and he thanks us again and shakes both of our hands.

I walk out to the ambulance. I stop for a moment in the yard and, though the street is quiet, I picture kids playing, a Good Humor truck, a mother ringing a dinner bell. The neighborhood seems as large as the world. It is a good place.

Thanksgiving

The city is quiet. We do a call for an elderly man with asthma who feels better after a breathing treatment. We get called for a possible seizure on Broad Street, where we find an Audi parked at curbside, engine running, and a well-dressed man with a cellular phone in hand standing over a homeless man, who we've transported often before for drunkenness and seizures. The man with the phone tells us he saw the man fall to the grass and begin seizing. Though he has stopped seizing, he says the man should be seen at the hospital. We tell him we know the man and thank him for calling. The homeless man, who is coming out of his postictal state, refuses to go to the hospital with us. He says he hasn't taken his Dilantin, his antiseizure medicine, for two days. We tell him he's going to end up seizing again and we'll end up taking him. We say why don't you just come to Hartford Hospital with us. It is cold out, and they'll have something warm for you to eat. He says he doesn't care. He's not going. We can't take him against his will. An hour later another crew responds for a seizure, and they have to give him Valium to break it. He ends up at Hartford.

At eleven-thirty we go to Stop and Shop and buy a pumpkin pie and an apple pie, which we bring back to the office in West Hartford, where Laura Howe, the dispatcher, is preparing a feast for the road crews who will be rotated in for a Thanksgiving meal during the course of the day. We eat turkey, corn, mashed potatoes with gravy, stuffing, fresh fruit, cookies, rolls, and pie. Later when we are back in the city, we throw a football around.

Around five, we respond to a cut foot on Blue Hills Avenue. A twenty-six-year-old woman has dropped a pair of scissors on her foot, causing a small puncture wound. You can see Mount Sinai from her front door. She limps out to the ambulance, refusing to be assisted. I drive her down one block and across the street to the emergency entrance, where she limps in through the doors. They put her in the waiting room.

While Glenn is writing his report, Windsor ambulance radios ahead that they are bringing in a code. I meet them as they pull in the driveway and help them unload. Joe Stephano is the medic, and he has the patient tubed and being paced. A bag of saline is running through an IV in her jugular vein. I take over the CPR as we wheel her into the emergency department, where Joe gives his report. His other crew members, Fred and Susie Averill, both work for us. Susie says she knew it was just Joe and Fred on duty, so when the call came over the scanner as a cardiac arrest, she left her family at the dinner table to help them out. The woman is declared. Joe shocked her five times, gave her six rounds of meds, and paced her, but her time had come. They'd transported her two weeks earlier for a stroke.

I go home at seven, having done only four calls. Michelle has a plate of turkey, sweet potatoes, mashed potatoes and gravy, peas, and rolls from her mother's waiting for me when I get home. I heat it up in the microwave and wash it down with a cold beer.

Meanwhile, back in the city things start to heat up. As the holiday stress mounts, ambulances fly about the city—assaults, asthmas, chest pains. At eleven a man who had been barred from seeing his family the day before accompanies them to Thanksgiving dinner at a friend's apartment. He and his wife begin to fight. He pulls out a gun and pumps bullet after bullet into her body.

When Shirley Lessard and John Burrell arrive in 875, they declare the mother at the scene. Then they are directed to the car, where they discover the children. A two-year-old girl, shot in the head, is not breathing and has no pulse. The five-year-old boy has agonal respirations. He has been shot through the right hand, through the head, and out through the left hand, as he tried to block out the horrible noise. Shirley has two young kids at home. They race to the hospital, lights and crying sirens.

Respect

Sometimes I think it is all about respect. Wars have been started over loss of face. Millions killed. Today in the ghettos people shoot each other just because someone disses them or they just don't like the way someone looks at them.

I asked before when it is that a smiling child becomes a sullen youth. I think now it may be in the passage from the hope we are all born with to the despair in understanding that there are two worlds, one held up and the other put down. When the child sees, time and again, the lack of respect for him and his world—whether it comes from the outside or inside his own community—it can't help but sink in and poison.

Glenn and I are sent on a call for a pediatric with abdominal pain in the north end. The mother and the child, a roly-poly nine-year-old in a Michigan football jacket, meet us at the door, all set to go.

"Where's the sick one?" I ask, already knowing it is the kid.

"He is," she says. "He got stomach cramps at school and the nurse said he had a temperature of ninety-seven point eight."

"You have your state card?" I ask.

"I'm not on state," she says, a touch of anger in her voice at my presumption. "I don't got insurance. Does that mean you won't take me?"

"No," I say. "Just if you have state, you're supposed to call your HMO and get permission to take an ambulance. It's a new policy. If they don't think it's serious, they'll have you take a cab instead. It costs two hundred dollars to take an ambulance." I know the price won't make her bat an eye. She has no intention of paying it. She called the ambulance to save herself a five-dollar cab ride. The bill will go uncollected like so many others.

"He's got cramps," she says.

"What's he been eating? A lot of junk?"

"No."

"You've got to serve him vegetables," I say.

"Oh, he gets his vegetables. I cook him greens twice a day. I make sure he eats his vegetables."

While I am talking to her, I notice the boy looking intently from me to his mom and back to me. There is some worry in his eyes, and I think he senses that I have power over him and his mom and that I don't approve of them. He sticks close to her.

I ease my hard stance. "Okay, ma'am," I say, "which hospital would you like us to take you to?"

"Saint Francis," she says.

"Okay."

Walking to the ambulance, I sense even Glenn has picked up on it. He helps the woman into the back and calls the boy, "Little tiger." He is good to them as we ride in.

Lift Me Up

I arrive at work twenty minutes early every day. The morning supervisors, Chris Chausse and Christian Schmeck, give me the ambulance keys and a set of radios, and I go check out the rig. Other medics and EMTs sit in the office waiting for their ambulances to come in off the road or finishing their paperwork from the night's calls. A new medic unstraps his bullet-proof vest and says to his partner, "I can't stand a medic who says it's my way or the highway. I'm a medic, too, and they ought to take into consideration that I may have a valid point. I hold him personally responsible for a man's death. Remember that call we did that night? He wouldn't listen to me."

It is commonplace for EMTs to criticize others. Every morning I hear people putting down those who aren't there. I have done it myself over the years—it is hard to avoid—but I try not to engage in it. I believe that people criticize others because this is a tough job and they are unsure of their own skills and the only way to reassure themselves is to sit with others and put someone else down. It means that they are better than those people, and by criticizing them and not being challenged, then they are unchallengeable. I have heard EMTs putting others down and then I have worked with the talkers and not been impressed with their skills. I have found that whenever I put someone down, it turns around and whacks me on the butt. If I say I can't believe so-and-so missed an IV on that person, then sure enough, I blow my next IV. If I make fun of a nursing-home nurse, damn if I don't do something to make an ER nurse make fun of me. I try to keep my thoughts to myself now. If a partner of mine screws up, I try to let him know in a noncritical way. If I screw up, I talk about it and how I can avoid it the next time.

❖

We get called to an MVA by a basic crew that needs a medic for a patient pinned in a car having chest pain at the intersection of Sigourney and Asylum. Two cars are locked together facing in the same direction. The basic crew sends me to the second car. The passengers are a Hispanic woman who is crying out excitedly and her husband who is holding his chest. I lean in the window and check them out. One of the EMTs is in the backseat and gives me a report. The windshield is starred in two places. Neither of the passengers lost consciousness. The EMT has put cervical collars on both of them. Both their vital signs are stable. The man has had open-heart surgery and is having pain. I ask him to point to where it hurts. I press on the right side of his chest and he screams. He tells me it hurts more when he breathes. I am convinced it is a muscle-skeletal problem, not cardiac. The woman says her butt hurts.

As soon as the fire department arrives and pries the cars apart, I take out the man on a longboard, get him in the back of the ambulance, and start working him up. Glenn has already helped load the patient in the second ambulance, then helps the basic crew with the woman before joining me to drive to Hartford on an easy two. I give my report and my patient is put in Room 2. When I am writing my report in the EMT room, I hear over the intercom, "We have a second Room One." When I walk by, I see the room is crowded and wonder what Life-Star brought in. Then I see one of the basic EMTs walking out of the trauma room and hear that both of the patients they brought in were put in Room 1. It turns out the lady in the second car, whom I talked to but I never even looked at, had a flail chest, where three or more of her ribs were broken, causing her chest to sink when it should rise. I am upset with the basic for not triaging me properly, but I am more upset with myself for not checking each of the patients. It is my responsibility. I walk out to the ambulance, feeling worthless. Glenn tells me the basic crew didn't notice the flail chest until they were almost to the hospital. Maybe I wouldn't have noticed it either. She wasn't in evident distress at the time and her vital signs were stable. But I should have assessed her thoroughly, and if I'd done that—if I'd done my job—I would have noticed it.

When I see Rick Ortyl he asks me how it's going, and I say, I'm not being a very good paramedic, and tell him the story. He tells me a similar one that happened to him, not that it makes me feel any better. It is not that I killed anybody. They all got to the hospital and got the care they needed in a timely fashion. It's just that the potential for damage was there. I didn't do my job well.

❖

We get called to a nursing home for an unresponsive patient. The nurse says he is normally alert but confused. He has a long medical history. He is breathing okay, but has rales in the bases of his lungs. He has a fever. His blood pressure is high, and his pulse is around 100. On the monitor, he is in atrial fibrillation. He doesn't respond to my commands but seems to have equal grip strength. I can't figure out what is going on with him. It could be a transient ischemic attack (TIA), heart failure, or the onset of sepsis. I put him on oxygen, put in an IV line, and take him to the hospital. His condition is not clear-cut enough to give him any medications. He's just an old guy who is not with it anymore. I give my report at the hospital and they put him in a room, where eventually a doctor will see him. I go out on another call and never find out what was wrong.

❖

I do ALS all day, but all just basic—put them on the monitor, give them oxygen and an IV. Maybe a nitro for chest pain, or a breathing treatment for asthma or chronic obstructive pulmonary disease (COPD). I am feeling like a robot.

Right before we get off duty we do an MVA where we are the first ambulance in. The car in the middle of the road has the passenger side of the windshield punched out in the shape of a head. Two young men lie on the side of the road under blankets. I check them both out. They are both alert, though one has a nasty cut on his forehead. We call for a second ambulance. I take the guy who pushed out the windshield. On the three-minute trip to Saint Francis, I have time only to throw in an IV and get the man's name and birth date. I do not call for the trauma room because the patient is stable, but I ask for a doctor to look at him, given the mechanism of injury. The doctor checks him out briefly at triage, is unimpressed with the injury and my description of the windshield, and sends him to the main ER in back.

I am depressed when I get home. I recap my day to Michelle and tell her about missing the flail chest—how I feel I am not thorough enough and how I feel like I don't know as much as I should. All I seem to do is put the patient on oxygen, give them an IV, and put them on the monitor. She says I know more than I think I do. I say I have a hard time even remembering the names of the bones in the body, which is basic EMT material.

"What's this?" she asks, touching my knee.

"The knee," I say. "The patella."

"What pulse is this?" She touches the inside of my ankle.

"The posterior tibial."

"What's this?" She touches the side of my ribs.

"The costal margin."

"How about this?" She touches the side of my hip.

"The pelvis."

"What's the bone called?"

"I don't know. The sacrum?"

She starts laughing.

"The greater trochanter," I say.

She is laughing so hard I am afraid she will fall off the bed. "You're killing me," she says. "You're so funny."

"The ilium, the ischium."

"Stop it," she says. "You're making me laugh too hard."

She thinks I'm kidding.

❖

On Wednesday it is a nice day, bright and clear but cool enough to wear a windbreaker. Our first call is for a fall in West Hartford. We see a man sitting on the side of the road leaning against the legs of a police officer. A woman stands by him. "I was driving down the street when I saw him fall," the officer says. "He went down on his face."

The man's face is dirty with a few abrasions and a bloody nose. He looks disoriented.

"He has Alzheimer's," the woman says. "He was walking to church."

I check him out. He knows his name and where he is. He says he wasn't knocked out. "I've got to get to church," he says.

"Will he fall if you move your legs?" I ask the officer.

"He's unsteady," the officer says.

"He doesn't have good balance," his wife says.

We help him up, and he is able to stand, though he does sway some. We have a discussion about whether he should go to the hospital or not. The officer, who saw him fall, tells the wife he really should be checked out. She says he falls all the time, and that they end up waiting at the hospital for ten hours only to be told he's okay, and they go home. She doesn't want to take him. He does best at home. The officer says his nose looks swollen. I touch it but it does not cause undue pain. I tell the woman I understand what the officer is saying and that we always urge the patient be checked out, but I also understand what she is saying. It is her choice, and she can best judge how he seems to her. If she wants to take him home, we will help her since it is just down the street, and if she changes her mind, we will be happy to come back. "I want to keep him at home," she says. "This is where he belongs."

"Okay," I say. "I understand."

We help him into her car, where we first clean his face with sterile water and four by fours, then follow in the ambulance. With the officer, we help him out of the car and into the house. She wants him to sit in his lounge chair. The officer, who has been to the house before, directs us down the hallway toward the back den. We get the man settled in his armchair. "Thank you very much," the wife says. "Thank you for your understanding."

"Sure," Glenn says. "Don't hesitate to call us. We're just three numbers away."

"I will," she says. "Thank you again."

❖

That afternoon, we are sent to Park and Broad for a drunk. A cop is on scene, standing next to a man lying against the building. The man doesn't want to get up. When Glenn holds an ammonia inhalant to his nose, he takes a swing at us.

"Take it easy, take it easy," I say.

"Get that thing out of my face. Fuck you, bastards. Leave me alone."

"You have to come with us or the officer here will take you to jail."

"Fuck off."

We get him up. Glenn calls to see if he is banned from ADRC. They say they'll take him, but before they'll admit him we have to take him to Saint Francis for a Dilantin check. He doesn't want to go to Saint Francis. "I've been taking my Dilantin." He pulls his prescription out of his pocket and shows me. "I've been taking it. I don't want them taking no blood from me."

"It's come with us or go to jail," Glenn says, grabbing his arm.

He swings his arm loose. "Fuck off."

The officer goes to get his cruiser, which is parked across the street.

"Last chance," I say. "He's coming back to arrest you. Come on, we'll take you to Saint Francis."

"I don't want to go there."

"They'll check your blood, and then it's on to ADRC, where they have a clean bed waiting for you, hot food, too."

I keep talking to him in a low, steady voice. The cop has his car at the curb now and is getting out. The patient starts stepping up into the back.

"We're all set," I say to the cop.

"You want me to follow you?"

"No, we'll be all set."

I get the man in the back and keep him calm.

Glenn is hobnobbing with the cop. The back door is closed, and the man's alcoholic breath is starting to overwhelm me. Finally, Glenn gets in the front to drive.

He has the country music on just low enough to hear.

"Good music," the man says.

"You like that?"

"Country!"

"Turn it up," I say to Glenn.

"What?"

"Turn it up. The man likes it."

Glenn cranks it.

"Yeah!" the patient says. He starts playing air guitar.

It is a song by Alan Jackson.

"Living that honky-tonk dream!" the man sings along off-key.

"Yeah!" I say.

❖

We do BS all the rest of the day and all the next, but I am in a good mood. I get to speak Spanish with a little girl with a fever whose mom took her to a community health center. The PA at the health center gives us the history and says the little girl needs to be seen at the Hartford pediatric clinic to rule out pneumonia. She says the woman took her little girl to another hospital and they told her she wasn't sick enough to be seen. The PA has arranged for the child to be seen at Hartford. The PA compliments me on being able to speak Spanish, though I know that a Spanish woman has been laughing at me for the broken phrases I have been using. No doubt I have been saying something like do I hurt when you breathe. At Hartford I take the girl and her mother through triage, then back to the pediatric clinic, where I help her register. I say good-bye, and the little girl waves at me.

Out in the parking lot I stop off at one of the cars to say hi to the crew. The paramedic, who is newly cut loose, is upset about a call she did that went badly. They got called for a possible suicide attempt—a man allegedly drank some insecticide. They tried to get him to go to the hospital, but he denied he drank it and said he wouldn't go to the hospital. That was his right. A half hour later they were called back to the same address where the man was having a seizure and in flash pulmonary edema. They rushed him to the hospital, where he was now in critical condition. Several people—including a doctor—had been critical of them for getting a refusal on their first visit. I couldn't have kidnapped him, she says. I asked the cops on scene to commit him, but they wouldn't do it. What more could I have done?

I tell her not to worry too much about it and not to let the second-guessing bother her. No one who wasn't there can judge her. I tell her about the carbon monoxide call I did, and say if I had to do that again, I would come as close to kidnapping the man as I could, but there is only so much you can do. I say, in retrospect, both she and I could have called medical control, told them our situations, and made them share responsibility. I tell her the fact that the call is bothering her is good; the outcome was bad, so it should bother her. She wouldn't be any kind of a paramedic if it didn't. It is not an easy job. You are not going to succeed every time. All you can do is your best and learn from each call. She thanks me for what I say, but my words are not particularly original—I am just saying what others have said to me, what she herself will say to another paramedic down the line.

It is about time for us to get off, so they give us a BLS transfer—a man with hip pain going back to the Jefferson House in Newington from the

ER. We get the man settled into his nursing-home bed, and Glenn asks if he is comfortable. The man says if we could pull him up a little more, that'd be great. "Thank you, you're nice fellas," he says.

We wheel our empty stretcher through the hall, take the elevator down, and go past the fish tank out the main door to our awaiting ambulance, which will take us back to the office, where we will turn in our paperwork, hand over the keys to the next crew, and head home. We are both in good moods. I think that one of the nice things about this job is that you get so many chances to be nice to people—not that you always are, but when you are, which hopefully is often, it makes you feel good. There is more to the job than just giving people IVs and medical care. Sometimes I forget that. And as much as I like throwing in an IV or even better, sinking a tube, I like being nice to people. Lifting them up lifts me up.

Shoot-out on Amity Street

I come out of the Farmington Avenue office to find Glenn and two guys from another crew watching two police cars whiz past.

"You just missed a car chase," Glenn says.

"Huh?"

They tell me a gold Cadillac just raced past with a caravan of cars in pursuit.

A moment later we hear the click of the HPD portable and the call for 453. "Four-five-three, respond to Park and Amity. A shooting. On a one."

Four-five-three is over at Saint Francis, but Shawn is precepting a medic, so they have been getting funneled many of the good calls. I am not even disappointed.

"Change that," the radio crackles. "Four-five-one, you're closer. Park and Amity."

"Yes!" Glenn says.

We jump in 451 and hit the lights and sirens. I strap in.

Three minutes later, we're out. I grab the blue bag and duck under the police tape. I have never seen more police cars. There must be fifteen or twenty. I see a crew from the news already on scene. "Where's the shot guy?" I ask.

"Over by the car," a cop says.

In a small parking lot off the street there is a separate taped area, where I see a gold car, its windows shot out. One cop is standing with his hands in his pockets. I see a body slumped on the ground a few feet from the open driver's door.

I duck under the tape and kneel by the man. He is pale but breathing. I see blood in his hair. He is handcuffed. His pulse is rapid. I look for bullet wounds. "Where's he shot?" I ask the cop. There is no bullet wound in his head, just blood in his hair.

"Let him fuckin' die," the cop says. "He tried to run an officer over."

I notice a bullet wound through his hand, and a finger shot off. There is another wound in his wrist. I check his legs and see his femur is shattered. The leg is like jelly.

"Uncuff him," I say.

"No, I don't got the keys," the officer says. "You guys got any alcohol wipes? I got some blood on my finger."

"Uncuff him."

Glenn has the stretcher there now with the board and a cervical collar.

I am cutting his clothes off with my trauma shears looking for other wounds.

A captain comes over and pointing his finger at me says, "This man is going to the hospital cuffed. He assaulted officers and has tried to flee. He's going cuffed. End of story."

Glenn says, "Look at his leg, He's not going anywhere like that."

I let him argue with the cop. I get an oxygen mask on full and put the collar on his neck.

Another officer appears with the keys. We get the man on the board and we race in low position, under the tape, past the police cars and TV crews, and lift him quickly into the back of the ambulance. "Drive!" I say to Glenn.

He drives and gives the radio patch to the hospital while I work on the patient. There are no other wounds, but his pressure is only 90, and he is tachycardic. I tape head rolls to better secure his c-spine. I spike a bag of saline, strap a tourniquet on his left arm, and rifle in a sixteen. I get the flash, connect the line and it runs fast. I hook the monitor up. Sinus tachycardia. I put a tourniquet on the right arm, spike another bag of saline, and pop in another sixteen. I get the flash and hook up the line. The line runs. We're out at Saint Francis. Another crew helps us unload. "Two lines, good job," I hear someone say.

We burst into the trauma room, where the trauma team is waiting. I give the report. We switch him onto the table, and they take over. His pressure is up, but he is still tachycardic. I got almost a full liter into him in a few short minutes.

We later hear the story. It appears the man was observed doing drugs in his car when approached by an officer. He sped off, partially dragging the officer. He then led cops on a ten-mile police chase on and off the highway before he was cornered on Amity Street. He sped toward the police barricade, then at the last second swerved sharply to the right into the parking lot. The cops riddled his car with bullets. Over twenty shots were fired. A lot of jokes are made about their marksmanship and whether they should have shot or not, but I don't know. If a car were coming right at me sixty miles an hour and I had a gun in my hand drawn and ready to fire, I think I'd pull the trigger, too. As far as not wanting to uncuff the guy, if I was a cop, I'd probably want to keep him cuffed, too. But I'm not a cop. I'm a paramedic. I have to do my job. We got him uncuffed. Got him boarded, got him to the hospital fast, and I hit both of my lines on the fly.

Shots of Glenn and me are on the news at noon, six, and eleven, and again the next morning and evening as they do follow-up stories.

"You look good," people say.

I feel it.

HEARTBEAT

Heartbeat

In this last year in the city, I have seen many disturbing things that make me worry about the future of the city and grieve for its children. I sometimes think the circumstances of life in the city are so brutal, any energy that might go to loving has to go to living just so a person can get by. But as discouraging as the child abuse, the rampant drugs, the poverty, and random gunfire can be, there are times when I see things that give me a reason—no matter how small—to believe again. People are strong and love is hard to kill even in the darkest corners of the city.

❖

It is night. They send us to Mark Twain Drive, an older housing project off Albany Avenue, for a priority-one chest pain.

We go to several buildings looking for the right address. When we find it, the door is locked. As we call the police department on our radio to check the number, I hear a banging on the window to the right of the door. An old woman lying on a hospital bed pushes a cane through the bars on the window. Her keys dangle on the end.

I take the keys and unlock the outside door, then unlock the door to her apartment. She is a huge woman, an invalid with all her worldly needs within her reach. There is a portable toilet next to her bed. On the table to her left is a small refrigerator, small TV, phone, and coffee cans filled with water and washcloths. I approach her and take her pulse as I ask what is wrong. She says she has a pain in her chest that goes into her throat and makes it hard for her to breathe. Her pulse is slow and slightly irregular. Her breath is a little short, but her lungs are clear. Her arms are too big to take a blood pressure. The pills by her bedside indicate she has asthma, angina, and diabetes.

"What hospital do you want to go to?"

"Can't you give me anything here?" she says. "To make this heartburn go away."

On the heart monitor, she is very bradycardic—a slow pulse, a rate of 48. She has a condition known as sinus arrhythmia, in which her heartbeat is affected by her respirations. When she gets anxious and breathes more quickly, her heart rate picks up. She calms and it slows in time with her breaths.

I tell her I am concerned about her description of the pressure in her chest. Elderly patients can often suffer heart attacks with minimal outward signs. They need to be taken to the emergency department and evaluated.

"You can't give me anything for my heartburn?" she says.

"You really should go to the hospital," I say.

She tells me she doesn't like hospitals and hasn't been for over a year.

The phone rings. It is her daughter. I ask her about her mother's condition.

"She ain't been right since last Christmas. One of her grandsons was killed. She's been having trouble all year, but she won't go. She won't see a doctor, and she won't leave where she's at. We all losing patience." She sounds disgusted with her.

After I hang up, I say to the woman, "I know this home is very special to you. Your family wants you to go, I want you to go. We're all concerned about you. It's important you see the doctor."

She tears up. She is wringing her hands. She looks about the clutter of her room—at a rocking chair, at a picture of her family on the wall, a colorful shawl on her bed. I will learn later she has lived there for forty years after migrating north from South Carolina.

I put my hand on her arm. "Take your time," I say. "We don't need to go lights and sirens. We'll just take a nice slow ride to see the doctor and hopefully have you back here soon, but feeling better."

"My dear home," she says, dabbing at her eyes.

"I know."

She sobs quietly.

We wheel her toward the ambulance. A young boy, maybe fourteen, comes across the yard out of the darkness. "Grandmother," he says.

She looks up, surprised to see him. "Robert. You come to see me?"

"You okay?"

"You shouldn't be out," she says quickly.

"Mama said you were sick."

"You shouldn't be out. The streets aren't safe for young boys like you."

"I just came to say good-bye."

Her face softens. "You a good child. Give me a hug."

He bends over her and they embrace.

They hold each other.

She releases him. "You go home now," she says. Her eyes are wet. "Get yourself home."

He stands back. He holds his wool knit cap in his hands.

"You promise me you go right home."

"Yes, Grandmother," he says.

We bend our knees, grasp the bottom railings of the stretcher, then straighten our legs and lift her into the back of the ambulance. She waves good-bye to her grandson. My partner closes the door. I put a tourniquet on her arm and draw blood and put in an IV. I talk softly with her in the dimly lit back. We drive through the darkness. The green line on the heart monitor beats slowly as she breathes.

End of the Year

They put Christmas decorations up on Main Street. We have our first snowfall. I have been in the city almost a year now. Each shift I grow more confident. Some days are slow, others they bust us all day long. In between the runny noses and the drunks, and in between the nurses calling us ambulance drivers and having to carry luggage, plants, and get-well balloons for patients on heart monitors, I have some decent moments.

❖

I respond to a woman not feeling well in the city. She meets us at the curb, gets in the back, and says her heart is racing and her chest hurts. There is a look in her eyes that tells me this is not BS. I put her on the monitor. She is cranking at 220 beats a minute. I'm going to take care of you, I say. I throw in a line and push adenosine. The rhythm breaks. She goes down to 112. The pain in her chest is gone. "You should be in the hospital," she says, batting her eyes at me. "The way you make me feel better."

❖

They have assigned me for the day out in Bloomfield, working as the medic with the volunteers. We get a call for a difficulty breathing and arrive to find a man sitting out on the porch in his bathrobe. Even though it is near freezing out, his struggle for air has driven him out of the house. His pressure is high. I pump the cuff up to 260 and it is beating at that level. His lungs sound like a washing machine. Pink froth comes from his mouth. His head looks like it is about to explode. His veins are bulging out of his neck. It is dark on the porch. There are two cars in the narrow driveway, blocking our route to the ambulance. He looks like he can't take a step. Normally in Bloomfield, there is a crew of three to assist the medic, but tonight, because it is just before crew change, I only have Annie Worshoufsky. She has been an EMT a long time and knows this is a dire situation—the man is in pulmonary edema. We manage to get him out to the ambulance. We have 100 percent oxygen going through a nonrebreather. I shout at her to get my nitro and Lasix out of the biotech. I throw a tourniquet on his arm. He has only a tiny, spidery vein on his arm. I am not supposed to give him a nitro until I can get a line, but he needs it, and I need to get the line. "Give him one," I say to Annie, and she pops the tiny white pill under his tongue as I jab his arm. "Yes!" I get a flashback but can only advance the catheter a little way before it meets resistance. "Saline lock," I say, and she has it for me. "Eighty of Lasix," I say. "Put it in a ten cc syringe." To the patient, "Hang on, sir."

I screw in the lock and take the syringe of Lasix. I stick its needle through the rubber lock and pull back. Blood flows back through the catheter into the syringe. I know I'm in the vein, and slowly now I push the Lasix in. The nitro will dilate the man's veins, causing fluid to pool in his legs, easing the load on his heart. The Lasix will diaphorese him and let water escape into his kidneys and out through his ureter. "Give him another nitro," I say, as I check his pressure. Still over two hundred.

But now he is breathing easier. "How are you doing?"

He breathes a few deep breaths then says, "Better."

A moment later he looks at me and says, "I thought I was going to die."

I glance at Annie. She makes a face at me that says, "Yeah, me, too." I give her a look back: "No kidding."

His pressure comes down to the 170s. His lungs are clear except for some wheezing. The sheets are soaked through with his urine. "Don't worry about it," I say to him. "It happens a lot when we give Lasix. At least you can breathe. That's the main thing."

By the time we get to the hospital he is a new man and says he is ready to go home. I give my report to a doctor, who is moonlighting there, and he looks at me skeptically when I describe the state we found him in. He is unimpressed—he sees no signs of pulmonary edema. He listens to the man's lungs and says, "I'm concerned about his wheezes."

"I guess you had to be there," I say.

Back in the ambulance, Annie and I slap high fives. "We kicked butt on that one," she says.

"No shit," I say. "Good call. You were great."

"So were you," she says. "We knew what we had to do, and we did it."

"Amen," I say.

❖

Back working in the city, I am dispatched to a possible cardiac arrest. A moment later, Daniel Tauber, who is in the city in his fly car, comes on the air and says he's going to back us up. I think Daniel secretly loves to get to cardiac-arrest scenes and get the tube before the medic does. "Let's have him shocked, tubed, IVed, meded up, and out of there before Daniel gets there," I say to my partner. I am nervous about Daniel's coming. The call is in a bank off Main Street. We go through the door, and I see the man sitting in a chair, head on his chest. We are told he has been there for twenty minutes while his son conducted business with a bank officer. He is gray and as still as death. I grab him by the collar and whirl him down onto the floor. He is not breathing. I rip off his shirt, apply the monitor. Idioventricular. I go to the head, insert the laryngo-scope, see the chords, slide the tube in, pump air in, lung sounds solid. I secure the tube, then strap a tourniquet on the arm. He doesn't have much for veins, but I feel a slight sponginess in the forearm. I bang a twenty in, get the flash, just as Daniel walks in the door. "Line's in," I say.

"What do we have, gentlemen?" Daniel says.

I give him the report, and he joins in, passing me the drugs, then helping us get the patient on a board and out to the ambulance. He comes with me for the ride to the hospital. "You're shaking," he says to me as I'm doing compressions and he's ventilating. Normally I ventilate, and whoever comes with me does the compressions, but he is the chief paramedic and has earned the right to sit, while I pump up and down.

"I haven't eaten anything yet today. Been on the go. I shake when I don't eat." I will not tell him that I am shaking because he makes me nervous, that I do not want to fail in front of him.

"He could probably use another line. Mind if I do an EJ?" he asks.

"Go right ahead."

He pops a fourteen in the large external jugular vein that runs alongside the man's neck. "A little more fluid can't hurt. I haven't done one for a while. I was hoping to get the tube."

"Beat you to it, I'm afraid."

"You did a good job."

"Thanks."

I keep pumping away on his chest, pausing only to slam more epi and atropine in the line. The man is not going to make it, and while our talk may be light, we give our best and never stop trying. The effort is as much for his family and for those who will lie on this same ambulance stretcher in the future—for society—as for his departed soul. It is the assurance that people will get the best effort, and that is a comforting thing for all of us.

❖

But as always in this work, there are those calls that keep you humble. I respond to Newington for a woman not feeling well. She is lying on her bed, having a hard time breathing. Her husband says she's been sick for a couple of weeks, coughing up yellow phlegm. I am thinking pneumonia. Her skin is warm. I listen to her lungs. She has some wheezes. I give her a breathing treatment. Maybe she has bad COPD. Her pressure is 138. Her pulse 132. The Newington volunteers arrive and we carry her down the stairs on a chair. In the back I put in a line and we take off to the hospital. Her pulse is now 140. Her pressure 128 by palpation. I listen again to her lungs and they are filling with fluid. Though she has no history of heart or lung problems, I am thinking heart failure now. I give her some Lasix, start another treatment, and give her some baby aspirin on the outside chance she is having an MI. She has no chest pain, but she just can't seem to get a breath. Her pulse goes up to 150 with no ectopy. She starts to feel clammy. Nothing I am doing is working. Her pressure is falling. When we hit the ED doors, her heart is going at 157 on the monitor and she is ice cold. They rush her into Room 14. I give my report and the doctor calls for a chest X ray. When I am done writing my report, I stop by the room and see them doing CPR on her. They revive her. She is in third-degree heart block. She codes again. When I come back with another patient an hour later, she is dead. The doctor thinks it might have been a pulmonary embolus. She shows me the X rays, which I cannot decipher, and the twelve lead EKGs which show minor changes in leads I and III, possibly indicative of an embolus. I ask her what more I could have done. She says not much. I think I could have been quicker. An autopsy later shows a massive MI. I could have given nitro, not that it would have helped. And besides, by the time her lungs started filling up with fluid, her pressure was starting to crash. They said her arteries were closed shut. Still, it was not a call to boast about. Her family called for help and I couldn't provide it. She was alive when we were there and she didn't make it.

❖

Every few months I get together for lunch with old Weicker friends. They get me to tell my stories, and we have some good laughs. I tell them about the three-hundred-pound guy with the stomachache who ate the kielbasa that had been sitting out on his dresser for three days in one-hundred-degree heat. I tell them about the woman who claimed her boyfriend had assaulted her, and when I went to touch the strangle marks on her neck, pink makeup came off on my gloves. "Tell that one about shocking the guy," my friend Rick says. "The one where his last words are 'You guys are killing me.' "

I tell it, although reluctantly.

❖

The talk of Weicker running for president has died down. A poll in Connecticut found only 17 percent of the state's voters thought he should run. The other day there was an item on the news about his supplementing his six-figure income as president of a health research firm by taking a sixty-thousand-dollar-a-year position as a member of the board of directors of US Tobacco, a Connecticut company whose main product is chewing tobacco. The pundits on a local Connecticut-politics TV show say this effectively shows he won't run for president because being a health advocate and taking tobacco money makes him look like a hypocrite. One of them says Weicker doesn't see anything wrong with it, and knowing Weicker I agree with the pundit's observation. But I don't see how anyone other than Weicker could see it differently. There is a price to everything, and the sixty-grand pocket change for attending a monthly meeting doesn't come for free. Tobacco and health care don't go together. Tobacco kills.

❖

I respond to a cardiac arrest. A fifty-year-old man has collapsed under a large table in his law office. He is lying on his side, his face cyanotic, blood dripping down the side of his mouth from biting his tongue. I turn him on his back. He is not breathing. I rip his shirt open and attach the defib pads to his chest. He's in v-fib. I shock him at 200 J. He's still in v-fib. I hit him at 300 J. He goes asystole, but ten seconds later is back in v-fib. I shock him the third time at 360 J. This time he stays flat line. My partner, Jim Devaney, pulls him out from under the table. I lie on my stomach and insert the laryngoscope blade. My muddy boots knock over a pile of typed reports on the floor. I search for the cords. Jim applies pressure on the throat, which drops the cords down into view. I pass the tube, then push an epi and an atropine down the tube, but get no change in rhythm. The fire department arrives and helps us get the guy out onto the stretcher. They do compressions as we wheel him through the office past his horrified coworkers. In the back of the ambulance I get an IV line and push more epi and atropine, while Jim manages the airway and a firefighter drives. I call Saint Francis. They have an ER tech out front to help us unload. In the cardiac room Dr. Reidecker checks lung sounds and orders another round of drugs. Because the man is only fifty, they work him a little longer, but there is no change, and she reluctantly calls him. She tells us we did a good job and thanks us.

We go out in the hallway and thank the firefighters. Then we head back to the ambulance to begin the cleanup. In the middle of the floor is a pack of Camels—the dead guy's smokes. They must have fallen out of his shirt pocket. I think about bringing them into the cardiac room and leaving them with the paperwork but wonder what his wife will think when she sees them and imagine them heightening her trauma and grief. I toss them in the trash where they belong.

❖

Life is short. You have to take care of yourself and the people you love. I need to be more careful myself. I don't always wear gloves when I do IVs. Sometimes I lay the bloody needle on the bench, not able to pivot and drop it in the sharps box during the heat of the call. "Sharp on the

"He just started shaking, then he stopped breathing and went blue. I called nine-one-one. Did I do all right? Is he going to live? Is he going to live?"

"Does he have a seizure history? Has he done this before?"

"Not like this."

"Has he ever had a seizure before?"

"In Colombia."

"Does he take medication?"

"He left it in Colombia."

"Who are you?" I ask the older woman who is crying and holding her hand to her mouth.

"The baby-sitter."

"What hospital does he go to?"

"None. They just got here."

"Where are the parents?"

"Out."

I listen to his lungs and, hearing some junk, fear he may have aspirated.

Just then he starts seizing again. It starts with his head and neck, then his arms, and then his whole body is shaking.

"What can I do for you?" Art says. "You want another car to help us?"

"No, just take our equipment down and set up the stretcher. We'll work him down there. I'll carry him."

He needs Valium to stop the seizure, and to get that he needs an IV. He doesn't look like he has any veins I can see in here and the light is too dim. Plus I have to call medical control for permission to give the Valium, which is locked down in the ambulance. "We'll work him down there."

I lift him in my arms. He is slippery and covered with vomit and urine. His body shakes forcefully, and he is turning blue despite the oxygen around his face. When someone seizes they frequently stop breathing. "Carry the tank," I say to the baby-sitter, "and walk with me."

"Can I go with you? Can I go with you?" his brother says, running half circles around me.

"Sure," I say, "but you have to come now."

"Okay, okay. Is he going to be all right?"

"Yeah," I say, worried that I might be lying. "You did well, but we have some more taking care of to do."

I walk carefully down the stairs.

Art has the stretcher set up and a bag of saline spiked. I set the kid down on the stretcher—he is still seizing—and toss Art my narcotics keys.

I strap a tourniquet around his arm, then reach up to turn the interior lights on high, while Art unlocks the narc box and takes out the sealed package of drugs.

I see no veins, only tanned skin. He is a fat kid. I feel with my fingers, searching for the softness of a vein below the surface. Nothing in the hand or the forearm. In the bend of the elbow, I think I feel something. I touch lightly, feeling for the springiness of a vein and not the tautness of a tendon. I think I feel one. I close my eyes and touch softly. Yes. It's there. I swipe the spot with an alcohol wipe, take out a twenty-gauge needle, and hold it over the skin. My hand is unwavering. I focus on what I am doing. I try to become one with the vein. I go in. Flashback. Sweet Jesus. Thank you, Lord. I watch the blood slowly flow back into the chamber. Now I have to advance the catheter. It is an easy spot to blow it. If I'm not in all the way I can shear the vein when I advance. I can burst through the other side or run up against a valve. Please. Oh please. Let me advance. I push forward with the tip of my finger. The catheter slides in smoothly over the needle, going in up to the hub. Perfect. "Line," I say to Art. He hands me the line and I plug it in. "Open it up. How's it running?"

"Like gangbusters," he says.

I grab the portable radio. "C-Med North Central four-five-one Alpha one requesting a patch to SF Hospital with a doctor."

"Med eight."

As I'm waiting to be connected, Jackie Lackey and Janice Mihalak, our relief, arrive. "You need anything?" Jackie asks.

"Yeah, someone to drive."

Janice gets in and starts us on a two.

"This is SF go ahead."

"SF, this is four-five-one Alpha one-nine-nine. We're on scene with a five-year-old in status epilepticus. History of seizures, but he has not been taking his medication. Vitals. We've got him on oxygen and an IV in place. We found him cyanotic and vomiting with question of aspiration. He's been going again now about five minutes. I'd like to give him one milligram of Valium."

"Have you done a glucose?"

"No, but I'm doing that now." I nod to Art to do a glucose off the needle.

"If he's over one hundred, give up to three milligrams."

"Okay up to three, I'll push it slow."

I break open the seal and take out the Valium, which comes in a pre-loaded two cubic centimeter syringe. I use a one cubic centimeter syringe to draw three milligrams out of the back of the syringe. My hands are now shaking. I have trouble sticking the needle into the hub on the line.

"Here goes," I say to Art.

I push one cubic centimeter, but the seizing continues. I push the second and third cubic centimeter, and he stops cold. His entire body relaxes.

"It worked," Art says. "How 'bout that?"

I let out my breath, then a moment later I say, "Art . . ."

"What?"

I'm staring at the kid's chest. "Art, get the ambu-bag out. He's not breathing."

"Where is it?"

"In the pedi box."

Valium is a respiratory depressant, and a paramedic has to be prepared to assist with ventilations if the breathing goes down too low. Art gives me the ambu-bag and I hold it sealed tight over the boy's nose and mouth. Art hooks it to the in-house oxygen and cranks it full. I squeeze the bag, and air rushing into the boy's lungs causes his chest to rise. The bag fills again, and as the chest settles I squeeze another breath into him.

He begins to pink up. His pulse SAT reads 100 percent.

At the hospital we wheel him in still bagging him, but he has begun to breathe again on his own. In the code room we transfer him to the hospital gurney, and I give my report to the doctors and nurses. "He was cyanotic when we found him, vomiting, question aspiration upper right lobe. Best we can tell, he seized for five or six minutes, was out for five, then started back up again. I gave him three of Valium, which knocked out his respiratory drive along with the seizing. Blood sugar was one-sixty, by the way. He's starting to breathe on his own now. Sketchy history. Just moved here from Colombia. Apparently has a seizure history, but not taking any meds now."

They keep bagging him. His pulse SAT is 100 percent. When he starts to seize again, they give him some more Valium, then intubate him.

I go out to the ambulance where Art is cleaning up.

We look at each other. Both of us are drenched with sweat. I also have vomit and urine on me.

"Good work," he says.

"Thanks, it went well. Sorry I was giving you two and three orders at the same time. You were great."

"That's all right, we got the job done. It went well."

"You know," I confess to Art, "when I walked in that room, I thought that kid was dead."

He laughs. "Me, too. He looked dead."

"I thought, oh, fuck, this kid is dead."

"He was blue."

"He was. But I felt his little heart beating and said thank you, God."

We laugh nervously grateful, relieved, exhausted.

The Meaning of Work

My friend Susan Swift was the best speechwriter Weicker ever had. She sometimes put into his speeches the Martin Luther King, Jr., quote about excellence: "If it falls your lot to be a street sweeper, sweep streets like Michelangelo painted pictures, like Shakespeare wrote poetry, like Beethoven composed music; sweep streets so well that all the host of Heaven and earth will have to pause and say, 'Here lived a great sweeper, who did his job well.' "

You have to be able to hold your head up. It is hard sometimes. I've worked some jobs where I wondered what the point was other than to bring in a paycheck. I felt my life was passing me by and that nothing I did really made any difference. Worse, I knew I wasn't working hard. I had no pride in what I did. I felt that way a good part of the time when I was working at the state health department. I had some good ideas, but not the energy or patience to apply my all to it. I was ashamed of myself. Some afternoons, I'd put my beeper on and go play golf. It seemed only the generous paycheck and the occasional chance to write a big speech for Weicker kept me on as long as they did.

One of my favorite jobs was being a cabdriver in Alexandria, Virginia. After Weicker won in 1982, I quit to write and see the world. Anchored for a while by a reunion with my college sweetheart, whom I had broken up with after living together for a year in Washington following graduation, I stayed in the area. The cab job was great. I arose at five-thirty and was in my cab by six. I lived ten miles south of Alexandria and usually got a call to take someone into the city, pocketing ten bucks just for driving in. The way cab driving worked was I paid thirty-four bucks a day to the cab owner and pocketed everything I took in. By noon, I had paid my car rent and gas for the day. Every hour I worked was more dough in my pocket. Sundays were free if I paid the other six days. I worked hard, and every night came home hot and tired with pockets full of bills and change. I met interesting people and had access to lives and areas that were denied the average person. One hour I was helping an old woman carry her groceries into her row house, where her old man sat at the table in his T-shirt drinking vodka. Her son scowled at them both before heading out to the streets to hang with his gang on the corner. The next fare I was dropping off a man in a suit and briefcase at the White House gates.

But driving a cab didn't quite have the status of being a Senate aide, and my hours were long, and my girlfriend and I had problems, so soon I was on my way west, riding a bus to Iowa with only a sleeping bag, a knapsack, and a portable typewriter. When I was in college I had a writing teacher named James Alan McPherson, who as a young man wrote a book of short stories called *Hue and Cry*, which came out in 1969 and was greatly praised by Ralph Ellison. He later won the Pulitzer Prize for his second book of stories, *Elbow Room*. I spent a lot of time talking to him about life and writing. He told me writing was a noble way to live, and I felt that that was true, and his words stuck with me. He was out in Iowa now, so it was sort of a holy place for me, a journey I needed to make to find out about myself. I got a job working in a restaurant kitchen as a line cook, and I fancied myself like Sir Gareth in King Arthur, who works in the kitchens of Camelot for a year before becoming a knight.

Iowa City was a place where being a writer gave you a special status, which was nice for a while but could make you forget about the world at large and being a member of it. I have always liked new experiences and places. After a couple of years in Iowa I moved up to Saint Paul with my new girlfriend, Barbara, and her fourteen-year-old son, Jason, and we lived there together while I worked in factories and on assembly lines. I wanted to be like Joe Magarac—the man of steel—the greatest worker ever who one day saved his plant by stepping into the furnace and melting himself down to the finest quality steel. When I was working the line at a meat-packing plant, my job was to tear racks of barbecued-cooked beef ribs off a tree—a huge two-tiered cage that hung on rollers from the ceiling. Each layer held fifty hooks with two racks of beef ribs on each hook. I'd pull them out by the hooks, tear the ribs off the hooks, and throw them onto a table, where my partner, Nacho Soto, cut them in two with a huge knife. A woman then dipped the ribs in more sauce and dropped them into the plastic bags that five other workers moving in a circle would open, then close, and drop on the line for heat sealing and labeling by other workers before grabbing another long plastic bag. The ribs continued down the line, getting sealed, boxed, weighed, stacked, and carted out to the waiting trucks. The women complained that Nacho and I, who wore yellow raincoats and were covered in barbecue sauce, worked too fast. "*Que dicen ellas?*" Nacho would say to me in Spanish. "What are they saying?" I would tell him they said we were the best workers ever and when we died they would put us into the meat and sell us. He would laugh. "*En la carne con nosotros,*" I would say. "Into the meat for us."

On the way home, I would be afraid to go into the liquor store because I had so much barbecue sauce on me—in my hair and on my jeans and boots—they would think I murdered someone. On payday I used to get a twelve-pack of Grain Belt beer for $2.99, and at home, tired and beat, Barbara and I would drink and listen to music and dance till exhausted. Then we'd go to bed and exhaust ourselves some more. Even though I was making four dollars an hour, I felt like I had worth.

Still, time was pressing in on me and I didn't know where I—or we—were going. Weicker was coming up for election again soon, and I thought it might be my last chance to get on board with him. So I left Saint Paul and I went back to work for him, writing speeches and statements and sharing an office with Susan that was right on the corner of Constitution Avenue and C Street. Our window looked out on the capitol building. We ate lunch together every day and had good conversations. We helped each other with our writing. Sometimes we made fun of our boss, as all underlings do, but we admired him deeply and loved our jobs. When I went up to work on the campaign, Barbara moved east and we lived in an apartment in Springfield, though I didn't see her much with all the time I spent on the campaign. Losing was tough. It was unexpected, and it filled me with guilt. If only I had worked harder, I alone might have been able to turn things around. It was only five thousand votes out of a million cast. Something I could have done better would have made a difference.

Having your ass kicked gives you perspective when you get back on top. When Weicker won the governorship, I knew dog days would come again, so I enjoyed the victory for what it was and lorded it over no one. Today doing 911 calls—lugging my gear and stretcher—sometimes in and out of buildings where I used to preside in meetings doesn't bother me. I am no less who I was then, maybe I am even more so. I like to think that at thirty-seven, having earned my scars in life, work, and love, I can still stand as straight as my tired back will let me. I've screwed up before and will again, but on most days I think I'm doing okay.

❖

Around six every night it gets very busy. We clear the hospital and are the only ambulance available in the city, and the dispatcher says to us, "You are covering the world."

I think I may not be a senator, or the right-fielder for the Red Sox, or a rich man, but here I am covering the world. And no matter who gets sick, whether a poor man in the projects or the governor in his mansion, when they call for help, I will come through the door. A grandfather feels a twinge in his heart, a young man hits the brakes hard to avoid another car, a toddler climbs out on the window ledge. But thankfully, tonight, the twinge passes, the cars do not strike, the toddler crawls back inside and finds the warm arms of his mother.

The dispatcher tells us to come on in for the crew change. Shawn Kinkade, Victoria DeNino, and Adam Waltman are in. Ransford Smith is next in line after us. Alan Goodman, Annette O'Callahan, Joe Stephano, and Shirley Lessard are already on the road. At the base, I hand my narc keys over to Adam Fleit, who will take 451. The changing of the watch.

As I look around at my coworkers winding down after a long day or readying for the night, I think of all the medics I have known—the ones here and others across the state. The Tom Harpers, John Pelazzas, Chris Huppes, Jose Matises, Butch Fetzers, and others—they are not names well known to the public, but they are every bit as worthy of respect as the mayor, the schoolteacher, the policeman, the hometown sports hero, or the U.S. senator marching in the Main Street parade. You may never need them, but they are there looking out for you, in every city and town.

"Have a safe night," I say to Adam.

"Thanks. See you in the morning," he says.

As I drive home, my headlights illuminating the road, I think about my day. I took an expectant mother, whose water had already broken, to the hospital. In my arms I carried a man dying of cancer down two flights of narrow stairs to our waiting stretcher. I gave a man in his forties two nitro to relieve the pressure in his chest, gave a breathing treatment to a woman with asthma, and checked out a four-year-old's cut elbow while joking with his multiple brothers and sisters, ages three, five, six, eight, nine, and ten. Where was number seven? I asked. They giggled and said there was none. Come out, come out, wherever you are, I said. And they all laughed.

When I get home I park and walk into my building and down the long hall to my apartment. Behind the door I can smell chicken cooking. The room is warm. I set my briefcase on the table and say hello to Michelle, who is in the bedroom sitting at the desk studying physiology for her PA class. I ask her about her day—she did well on the test that she had been worried about—and she asks me about mine. I had a full day, I say, and not a bad one. I get a beer and put on the stereo. The Grateful Dead plays a slow country song called "Brown-Eyed Woman" that has a wonderful line in it about the bottle being dusty, but the liquor being clean.

I sit down on the couch and take my boots off. I enjoy my beer.